Catching Up | or
Leading the Way

American Education in the Age of Globalization

SUSTAINABLE
FORESTRY
INITIATIVE

Certified Fiber Sourcing
www.sfiprogram.org

ASCD cares about Planet Earth.
This book has been printed on environmentally friendly paper.

Yong Zhao

Catching Up | or
Leading the Way

| American Education in the Age of Globalization

∧SCD

Alexandria, Virginia USA

1703 N. Beauregard St. • Alexandria, VA 22311-1714 USA
Phone: 800-933-2723 or 703-578-9600 • Fax: 703-575-5400
Web site: www.ascd.org • E-mail: member@ascd.org
Author guidelines: www.ascd.org/write

Gene R. Carter, *Executive Director;* Nancy Modrak, *Publisher;* Scott Willis, *Director, Book Acquisitions & Development;* Genny Ostertag, *Acquisitions Editor;* Julie Houtz, *Director, Book Editing & Production;* Darcie Russell, *Senior Associate Editor;* Catherine Guyer, *Senior Graphic Designer;* Mike Kalyan, *Production Manager;* Barton Matheson Willse & Worthington, *Typesetter;* Carmen Yuhas, *Production Specialist*

Printed in the United States of America. Cover art copyright © 2009 by ASCD. ASCD publications present a variety of viewpoints. The views expressed or implied in this book should not be interpreted as official positions of the Association.

All Web links in this book are correct as of the publication date below but may have become inactive or otherwise modified since that time. If you notice a deactivated or changed link, please e-mail books@ascd.org with the words "Link Update" in the subject line. In your message, please specify the Web link, the book title, and the page number on which the link appears.

ASCD Member Book, No. FY10-1 (Sept. 2009, PSI+). ASCD Member Books mail to Premium (P), Select (S), and Institutional Plus (I+) members on this schedule: Jan., PSI+; Feb., P; Apr., PSI+; May, P; July, PSI+; Aug., P; Sept., PSI+; Nov., PSI+; Dec., P. Select membership was formerly known as Comprehensive membership.

PAPERBACK ISBN: 978-1-4166-0873-8   ASCD product #109076
Also available as an e-book (see Books in Print for the ISBNs).

Quantity discounts for the paperback edition only: 10–49 copies, 10%; 50+ copies, 15%; for 1,000 or more copies, call 800-933-2723, ext. 5634, or 703-575-5634. For desk copies: member@ascd.org.

Library of Congress Cataloging-in-Publication Data

Zhao, Yong.
    Catching up or leading the way : American education in the age of globalization / Yong Zhao.
        p. cm.
    Includes bibliographical references and index.
    ISBN 978-1-4166-0873-8 (pbk. : alk. paper)
    1. Education—Economic aspects—United States.   2. Education and globalization—United States.   3. Educational leadership—United States.   I. Title.
    LC66.Z47 2009
    370.973—dc22
                                                                2009020290

20 19 18 17 16 15 14 13 12 11 10 09   1 2 3 4 5 6 7 8 9 10 11 12

Catching Up | or 🐟
Leading the Way
American Education in the Age of Globalization

Preface vi

Acknowledgments xiii

1. Recent Education Reform in the United States 1

2. From the Missile Gap to the Learning Gap:
   Myth, Fear, and the Evolution of Accountability. 19

3. Why America Hasn't Lost Yet:
   Strengths of American Education. 41

4. Why China Isn't a Threat Yet: The Costs of High Scores 64

5. The Challenges, Part I: Globalization 98

6. The Challenges, Part II: Technology 114

7. What Knowledge Is of Most Worth
   in the Global and Digital Economy? 133

8. Global Competence and Digital Competence:
   The New Universal Knowledge and Skills. 160

9. Catching Up or Keeping the Lead:
   The Future of American Education 181

Afterword 199

References 203

Index 222

About the Author. 229

Preface

This book is about education in America but it began as a book about education in China. My original intention was to write about the mammoth challenges China faces in education to curb America's surging enthusiasm for China's education practices that seem to be an object of admiration, a model of excellence, or a source of competitive students who will threaten America's future. I was going to write about China's efforts to decentralize curriculum and textbooks, diversify assessment and testing, and encourage local autonomy and innovations in order to cultivate creativity and well-rounded talents. I was also going to write about China's repeated failures and unwavering desire to undo the damages of testing and standardization. But while I was going through the reform policies, scholarly writings, and online discussion forums and blogs about education in China, I realized that what China wants is what America is eager to throw away—an education that respects individual talents, supports divergent thinking, tolerates deviation, and encourages creativity; a system in which the government does not dictate what students learn or how teachers teach; and culture that does not rank or judge the success of a school, a teacher, or a child based on only test scores in a few subjects determined by the government.

Having grown up in China, experienced the Chinese education system as both a student and teacher, and closely studied its history and recent reforms as a researcher, I understand the reasons behind its reforms. China is determined to transform from a labor-intensive, low-level manufacturing economy into an innovation-driven knowledge society. An innovation-driven society is driven by innovative people. Innovative people cannot come from schools that force students to memorize correct answers on standardized tests or reward students who excel at regurgitating dictated spoon-fed knowledge. Thus China decided to change its "test-oriented education" into "talent-oriented education." To engineer this change, China made a conscious, global search for models—education systems that are good at producing innovative talents. As a country with the most Nobel laureates, most original patents, most scientific discoveries in the 20th century, and largest economy in the world, the United States of America seems a reasonable candidate.

In the meantime, the U.S. has been trying hard to implement what China has been trying to be rid of. An increasing number of states and the federal government have begun to dictate what students should learn, when they should learn it, and how their learning is measured through state-mandated curriculum standards, high school exit exams, and the No Child Left Behind Act (NCLB). There are calls for even more centralization and standardization through national standards and national testing, as well as through rewarding or measuring schools and teachers based on test scores.

I find this trend in American education perplexing. If China, a developing country aspiring to move into an innovative society, has been working to emulate U.S. education, why does America want to abandon it? Furthermore, why does America want to adopt practices that China and many other countries have been so eager to give up? But most vexing is why Americans, who hold individual rights and liberty in the highest regard, would allow the government to dictate what their children should learn, when they should learn it, and how they are evaluated?

What really pushed me to abandon my original writing plan is what I've witnessed over the last few years: broad damage inflicted by NCLB as well as the growing enthusiasm for more standardization and centralization. Frankly, when NCLB was passed, I did not expect it to have much impact on what goes on in American schools, given my experience with past reform movements. Apparently, I was wrong.

I was proven wrong by my son about five years ago. One day at breakfast he told me that he had figured out how to get a better score for his writing on the MEAP, the standardized testing Michigan uses to satisfy NCLB requirements. I knew he had always been a good writer for his age but he did not receive a great score on the MEAP that year. I actually did not care but he seemed concerned and had been working on an improvement strategy. My heart sank as he was explaining to me how he would improve his score. The essence of his strategy was to stop being creative and imaginative. Instead he would follow the scoring rubric, which was analyzed and taught by his teacher. Indeed his score improved the next round. Because of this experience and many other reasons, we decided that it was best to move him to a school that was not governed by NCLB. So he left public education in 10th grade.

I've also been proven wrong about my assumption that NCLB was just another reform movement by the many teachers and school leaders I've met in the last few years. Since 2004, I have given about 200 presentations to groups of teachers and education leaders on the topic of how schools must work to cultivate a diversity of talents, global competence, and digital competencies to cope with a world that has been significantly altered by globalization and technology. My audiences have been diverse and have included local school boards, legislators, community leaders, business leaders, as well as teachers, principals, superintendents, and technology specialists. The occasions have ranged from school opening days, professional development events, and national and international conferences. I've been invited to speak by teachers unions, local schools, state and national education professional organizations, and universities. I would like to think my audiences liked what I said because the number of requests for my presentation has been on the rise over the years. But almost every time I finish my talk, I am asked, "We agree with you, but what about AYP (Adequate Yearly Progress)?"

Then came more systematically gathered evidence that proved me wrong. Several studies discovered that NCLB caused a large proportion of schools to teach to the test and to reduce instructional time for subjects not required by NCLB. It has also been found that in order to raise test scores in NCLB-required areas, many teachers changed their instructional focus and pedagogical style. Some states, schools, and teachers have even been found to cheat on behalf of their students in order to meet the NCLB requirements.

The outcomes of NCLB were exactly what I had feared but refused to acknowledge. Based on my understanding of test-driven education systems such as those in China, Singapore, and South Korea, I anticipated that NCLB would perhaps raise test scores in the required subject areas but the nonrequired subjects would suffer and so would educators' morale and conduct. And that schools would eventually turn into test preparation institutions as the public learns to accept test scores as the only indication of performance for students, teachers, and schools.

The damages of NCLB are certainly disturbing, but what is even more fearsome is its spirit because while the law may be changed, its spirit seems to have a life of its own and keeps growing bigger and bigger. Although many have criticized the specifics of NCLB—whether the mandates are sufficiently funded, how AYP should be calculated, or whether it is realistic to implement the mandates—very few have challenged its spirit. Talks about national standards, international benchmarking, and more accountability are gaining momentum.

The spirit of NCLB is a chain of reasoning that goes like the following: American education is in crisis. This crisis is proven by two "achievement gaps": one international and the other domestic. The international gap is indicated by American students' consistently poor performances in international tests. The domestic achievement gap is the gap in test scores and other achievement measures such as high school graduation rates between inner-city minority students and their suburban peers. The crisis is assumed to have resulted from teachers and school leaders who are unwilling or unable to hold high expectations of their students and deliver high-quality instruction because they have become complacent or lazy. The solution is to hold these educators accountable for producing measurable outcomes with a variety of incentives and punishments including publishing school performances, allowing school choice, reorganizing low-performing schools, and possibly using performance-based teacher pay.

Standardization and centralization of curriculum and assessment are essential ingredients of this solution for an obvious reason. Unless all schools in a state or the whole nation is held to teach the same curriculum and all students are assessed using the same tests, it is impossible to compare what and how much students are taught or to distinguish good schools and teachers from poor ones. For this and other reasons, such as the moral argument that all students deserve and are able to study the same rigorous curriculum, standards have become one of the most enthusiastically embraced concepts in recent U.S. education reform efforts.

Although there are many problems with the well-intentioned spirit of NCLB, the most serious consequence is that it leads to homogenization of talents. While the intention is to ensure every child receives a good education, the problem is that NCLB practically defines good education as being able to show good scores in a limited number of subjects. Thus as schools conform to the standardized curriculum and attempt to provide "good education" so defined, children are deprived of opportunities to develop talents in other areas. In addition, those children who do not perform well on the required tests at the required time are discriminated against because they are considered less able and "at risk." Theoretically, different schools can teach more than what is mandated. In reality schools must ensure that they do well in areas that affect their reputation and standing, which means the subjects that are counted in standardized testing. It is also theoretically possible to develop standards for a broad range of subjects and activities and require all schools teach the same curriculum nationally or statewide, like what China used to do. But even in the case of China, only subjects that count in the high-stakes College Entrance Exam receive serious attention. In the U.S., such an effort is not even possible. The Clinton administration supported the development of national standards for nine subjects, but most of them failed to be accepted because of disagreement over what should be included in each subject.

As a result of adopting national standards, schools will produce a homogenous group of individuals with the same abilities, skills, and knowledge. Such a result will be disastrous to America and Americans because as globalization and technology continue to change the world,

America needs a citizenry of creative individuals with a wide range of talents to sustain its tradition of innovation. Americans need talents and abilities that are not available at a lower price elsewhere on earth. American education, despite its many problems, has at least the basics that support the production of a more diverse pool of talents. However, these basics are being discarded by NCLB and similarly spirited reform efforts.

The spirit of NCLB also denies the real cause of education inequality—poverty, funding gaps, and psychological damages caused by racial discrimination—by placing all responsibilities on schools and teachers. While schools can definitely do a lot to help children overcome certain difficulties, their influence has limits.

In a way, the reforms that aim to save America are actually putting America in danger. NCLB is sending American education into deeper crisis because it is likely to lead increasing distrust of educators, disregard of students' individual interests, destruction of local autonomy and capacity for innovation, and disrespect for human values.

Although NCLB and its damages were the impetus for this book, I did not write this book to criticize NCLB. Rather, I focused this book on the real challenges America faces and how to address them. It also discusses how recent reforms have served to distract our attention from the real crisis and have the potential to destroy what America already has to be prepared for the future world. The book begins with a discussion about the current reform efforts in the United States and why they are misguided, followed by a historical account of how the current reforms came into being. I then offer an abbreviated version of the book I was going to write about education in China to show the danger of centralization, standardization, and testing. The primary purpose of this book is to change the discourse about education, to move away from focusing on the past and move toward focusing on the future. Thus I devoted two chapters discussing what the future world might be like as a result of globalization and technological changes. These changes demand us to rethink what knowledge is of value in the future. The knowledge, skills, attitudes, and perspectives that will be valuable are discussed in the subsequent chapters. The final chapter makes some specific suggestions for policy makers, school leaders, and education practitioners.

Although I did not get to complete my book about education in China, I am content with my decision. Doing research and writing this book has been an immensely rewarding experience. I have been living in the United States for more than a decade. I have been a student, a professor, and a parent of two students in American education. I have also conducted research in many schools and interacted with policy makers, educators, parents, and business leaders. So in many ways, I am an "insider" of American education. But I have been fortunate to have been invited to work with educators in over a dozen countries in recent years and spend about one third of my time outside the U.S. each year to remain an "outsider." This book provided me the opportunity to integrate both my insider and outsider experiences and perspectives.

American education is at a crossroads. There are two paths in front of us: one in which we destroy our strengths in order to "catch up" with others in test scores and one in which we build on our strengths so we can keep the lead in innovation and creativity. It is my hope that this book can help change the discourse about education in the United States and convince some of the readers that "leading the way" is a better idea.

January 30, 2009

Acknowledgments

I am grateful to the many people who contributed to the book in different ways. Professor Keith Campbell of St. Mary's College is perhaps the one person who has had the most significant influence on my understanding of American education and culture. His intimate knowledge, insightful observation, and passionate criticism gave me a life-changing orientation to American public education. For that I am forever indebted to Keith. The book was inspired by an education reform conference of the Asian Pacific Economic Cooperation (APEC) initiated by the U.S Department of Education, the Chinese Ministry of Education, and the Chilean Ministry of Education in 2004. I must thank Dr. Susan Sclafani, then counselor to U.S. Secretary of Education Rod Paige, Vice Minister Zhang Xinsheng of the Chinese Ministry of Education, Dr. Alan Ginsburg and Ms. Adriana de Kanter of the U.S. Department of Education for involving me in organizing the research aspect of the conference. I am also indebted to the Hong Kong-based Sunwah Education Foundation and the William and Flora Hewlett Foundation for their financial sponsorship of the conference.

During the writing of this book, I benefited tremendously from conversations with Dennis Phillips of Stanford University, Vivien Stewart of the Asia Society, Gilbert Choy of the Sunwah Education Group, Fernando Reimers of Harvard University, Briand Caldwell of

University of Melbourne in Australia, Alma Harris of Warwick University in England, and Paul Conway of University College Cork in Ireland. Dr. Jing Lei of Syracuse University read the first draft of the book and provided invaluable feedback.

My colleagues at Michigan State University have been a source of great support and inspiration. Tom Bird and Ken Frank have been great listeners and devils' advocates almost weekly. I thank them for their wisdom and encouragement. I also thank Bill Schmidt for the many exciting conversations about standards and curriculum as well as education in China and America. Jere Brophy, Jack Schwille, Dick Prawat, and Bob Floden have all helped me shape my ideas. Barbara Markle has provided many opportunities for me to present my ideas to legislators and K–12 educators, which led to refinement of some of the ideas included in the book. Ken Dirkin frequently supplied useful resources and acted as an inspiring sounding board. My assistant Lisa Payne ably managed my schedule to allow me time to write.

My thanks also go to Chun Lai, Ruhui Ni, Jiawen Wang, Wei Qiu, and Naiyi Xie for their assistance with the references and proofreading the manuscript.

I must thank Sunwah Education Foundation in Hong Kong and Chairman Dr. Jonathan Choi for the vision and financial support that established the U.S.-China Center for Research on Educational Excellence. The Center provided me the opportunities to study education in China and the United States in depth. I must also thank the U.K.-based iNet and its parent organization, the Specialist Schools and Academies Trust (SSAT), for enabling me to interact with educators around the globe and giving me the opportunity to focus on global citizenship. I would also like to thank SSAT and Phi Delta Kappa (PDK) for allowing me to use some text from publications I wrote for them, namely *Preparing Global Citizens* (SSAT, 2008) and *Education in the Flat World* (PDK *Edge*, 2007).

I am grateful for the professional guidance I received from the capable staff at ASCD, especially Genny Ostertag, acquisitions editor, and Darcie Russell, my project manager.

This book could not have been completed without the support of my family. They did not only give me the time and encouragement, but also served as readers and sources of ideas. My wife, Xi Chen, was the first reader of each chapter and gave very candid yet encouraging comments. My son, Yechen, and my daughter, Athena, were also drafted to hear about the book many times. They provided stories and references, some of which are included in the book.

As usual, I end with a disclaimer. While many people have contributed in various ways to this book, all errors are mine and the views do not necessarily reflect those of the supporting organizations.

1

Recent Education Reform in the United States

I have never let my schooling interfere with my education.

—Mark Twain

The direction in which education starts a man will determine his future life.

—Plato

January 7, 2008, was an unusually nice day for Chicago. On this day, President George W. Bush brought a present to Chicago's Horace Greeley Elementary School. He came to announce that the school had been named a federal Blue Ribbon School, 1 of 12 in Illinois and 239 nationwide. With Secretary of Education Margaret Spellings by his side, Bush emphasized that this Blue Ribbon honor was not the same as those that might have been given at an earlier time, during what he termed a "kind of a feel-good era." Instead, he said, "it's a Blue Ribbon School because it's excelling. It's meeting standards" (Bush, 2008). And the evidence was Greeley's improved performance on tests: a gain of more than 36 percentage points since 2002 on the Illinois State Achievement Tests, to 83.3 percent of students meeting or exceeding state standards. Math scores had increased even more dramatically—up almost 52 percentage points to 90.2 in 2007 from 38.3 percent in 2002. Bush called Greeley "a center of excellence" and praised the school principal as a person who understood that "we have got to set high standards for our children and work with the teachers to achieve those standards" (Bush, 2008).

On the eve of the sixth anniversary of the day he signed the No Child Left Behind Act (NCLB), Bush used the occasion to call for the reauthorization of the law. Greeley was selected as the site for a reason: it exemplified the kind of results NCLB intended—improved scores on standardized tests for minority students. It proved, at least in his mind, that NCLB was working well. With a significant Hispanic population and new immigrants among its students, Greeley "is a school that is exceeding expectations because of high standards and using the accountability system as a tool to make sure that no child is left behind" (Bush, 2008).

The Greeley event highlighted the defining characteristics of education reform efforts in the United States during the early years of the 21st century: (1) excellence equals good test scores in math and reading, and (2) standards- and test-based accountability is the tool to achieve such excellence.

Test Scores as Indicators of Quality

No Child Left Behind has undoubtedly been the most significant component of recent education reform efforts in the United States. Although it intends to ensure that every child receives a good education so no child is left behind, its definition of good education is good scores on standardized tests in reading and math. The law requires that all children be given state assessments in reading and math in grades 3 through 8. If a child fails the test, she is judged not to have received a good education from the school. If the school does not make Adequate Yearly Progress (AYP) on student test scores, the school is considered not providing a good education to its students and is labeled "in need of improvement." The school then faces serious sanctions—from allowing its students to move to other schools to being restructured. Schools that produce good scores are considered good education providers. Those that see significant increases in test scores, such as Greeley, are rewarded and honored.

Although the current version of NCLB does not focus on high schools, it requires reading and math to be tested at least once from grades 10 to 12, and testing in science was proposed by the Bush administration. In addition, 22 states have enacted burgeoning high school reforms requiring students to pass a state exit exam to receive their high school diploma. In 2006, 65 percent of the nation's high school students and 76 percent of its minority high school students were enrolled in school in these 22 states.

Math, reading, and perhaps science have become the most valued content of education. Students who perform poorly on a state math or reading test are considered at risk, no matter how well they do in other areas. Schools, too, are judged by their students' performance on math and reading tests, regardless of what other educational opportunities they provide. As Bush said during his visit to Greeley, his philosophy started with a "refusal to accept school systems that do not teach every child how to read and write and add and subtract" (Bush, 2008).

The virtually exclusive emphasis on math, reading, and science is also evidenced by the American Competitiveness Initiative (ACI) Bush proposed in his 2006 State of the Union address:

> [W]e need to encourage children to take more math and science, and to make sure those courses are rigorous enough to compete with other nations. We've made a good start in the early grades with the No Child Left Behind Act, which is raising standards and lifting test scores across our country. Tonight I propose to train 70,000 high school teachers to lead advanced-placement courses in math and science, bring 30,000 math and science professionals to teach in classrooms, and give early help to students who struggle with math, so they have a better chance at good, high-wage jobs. If we ensure that America's children succeed in life, they will ensure that America succeeds in the world.

The high school reforms in many states show the same tendency. Many states have increased the number of required courses in math,

English, and science. And in most states, the high school exit exams are primarily in those three subjects.

The almost exclusive emphasis on math, reading, and science is also clearly evidenced by funding appropriations. For example, NCLB's Reading First program has received more than $5 billion since 2002. No other subjects have received the same attention. A U.S. Department of Education initiative titled *Strengthening Education: Meeting the Challenge of a Changing World* was released in February 2006, following Bush's State of the Union address. The document lists Bush's education agenda for 2006. It states, "The American Competitiveness Initiative [ACI] commits $5.9 billion in FY 2007, and more than $136 billion over 10 years, to increase investments in research and development, and strengthen education and workforce training" (U.S. Department of Education, 2006). Programs on Bush's 2006 education agenda fall into four categories:

• The FY 2007 commitment to education is $380 million, which emphasizes math instruction from the earliest grade levels and ensures that high schools offer more challenging coursework.

• The High School Reform Initiative will bring high standards and accountability to high schools by aligning their academic goals and performance with the No Child Left Behind Act.

• Additional Current Math and Science Initiatives: The Department of Education's FY 2007 overall request for math and science initiatives, including funding for ACI, is a 51.3 percent increase over the 2006 amount.

• The National Language Security Initiative will address our shortage of people who speak languages critical to our national security and global competitiveness by encouraging earlier and stronger coursework in critical need foreign languages from kindergarten through postsecondary education; increasing proficiency among all speakers; and providing incentives for government service and teaching critical need foreign languages (U.S. Department of Education, 2006).

Foreign language education is the only other subject mentioned besides reading, math, and science, but it is the last item, and no specific dollar amount or actions are specified. And the mere $114 million for the National Language Security Initiative actually requested by Bush for FY 2007 was to be shared across the departments of Education, State, and Defense, and the Office of the Director of National Intelligence. As a result, the Department of Education requested $57 million, almost a rounding error compared with the amount devoted to Reading First.

Standards and Accountability

> *Accountability is an exercise in hope. When we raise academic standards, children raise their academic sights. When children are regularly tested, teachers know where and how to improve. When scores are known to parents, parents are empowered to push for change. When accountability for our schools is real, the results for our children are real.*
>
> —George W. Bush
> (U.S. Department of Education, 2002)

This quote in a PowerPoint presentation used by the U.S. Department of Education to explain NCLB best explains the logic of the reform and underscores the central role of accountability, standards, and testing in the reform efforts. No Child Left Behind required that all states develop rigorous curriculum standards in math and reading following its passage, and in science by 2005. Today all 50 states have developed such standards and grade-level expectations. These standards must be reviewed and approved by the U.S. Department of Education.

To ensure implementation of these standards, tests must be developed. Every state has developed standardized tests according to these standards. Some states even prescribed textbooks to go with these standards, requiring publishing companies and authors to include and cover certain topics in depth.

No Child Left Behind has also mandated an extensive accountability system involving the state and the local education agency (LEA). Specific responsibilities are assigned to the various agencies involved in education, and punitive consequences are explicitly spelled out if the agency fails to fulfill its responsibilities. States and schools have developed elaborate systems to collect, analyze, and report data required by NCLB to show Adequate Yearly Progress. To further hold schools accountable, data on student performance must be published in local papers, and a school report card, with information about school performance as judged by NCLB requirements, must be provided to parents.

Closing the Achievement Gap: Goals of Recent Reform Efforts

The massive reform efforts in the United States have been intended to close two types of so-called achievement gaps in order to deliver a better future for America and all Americans. The first is the gap inside the United States and among the different subgroups of the population; the second is the gap between the United States and other countries. In the NCLB proposal released by President Bush on July 3, 2001, the Executive Summary begins with mention of these two gaps:

> As America enters the 21st Century full of hope and promise, too many of our neediest students are being left behind.
>
> Today, nearly 70 percent of inner city fourth graders are unable to read at a basic level on national reading tests. Our high school seniors trail students in Cyprus and South Africa on international math tests. (Bush, 2001, p. 1)

The phrase "achievement gap" is often used to refer to the performance gap between minority students, particularly African American and Hispanic students, and their white peers, and similar disparities between students from low-income and well-off families in a number of areas: standardized test scores, grades, dropout rates, and college completion rates. For example, results of the 2003 National

Assessment of Educational Progress (NAEP) show that 39 percent of white students scored at the proficient level or higher in 4th grade reading, but only 12 percent of black students and 14 percent of Hispanic students did so (National Center for Education Statistics, 2003b). The gap in math was even larger, with 42 percent of white 4th graders scoring at the proficient level or above and just 10 percent of black students and 15 percent of Hispanic students achieving the same result. Thirty-eight percent of 4th graders who were eligible for free and reduced lunch scored below basic in math, whereas only 12 percent of those who were not eligible scored at the same level (National Center for Education Statistics, 2003c).

Similar gaps exist in the dropout rate and the graduation rate. In 2006, the dropout rate for white, African American, and Hispanic youth was 5.8 percent, 10.7 percent, and 22.1 percent, respectively (National Center for Education Statistics, 2008). A study on high school graduation rates (Swanson, 2008) shows similar disparities: in 2003–04, high school graduation rates were 76.2 percent for whites, 57.8 percent for Hispanics, and 53.4 percent for blacks. The report found that in the nation's 50 largest urban areas, where most low-income and minority students reside,

> [o]nly about one-half (52 percent) of students in the principal school systems of the 50 largest cities complete high school with a diploma. That rate is well below the national graduation rate of 70 percent, and even falls short of the average for urban districts across the country (60 percent). Only six of these 50 principal districts reach or exceed the national average. In the most extreme cases (Baltimore, Cleveland, Detroit, and Indianapolis), fewer than 35 percent of students graduate with a diploma. (Swanson, 2008, p. 8)

Although closing the achievement gap between subgroups of students within the United States has certainly been a strong motivator for the recent reforms, closing the gaps between the United States and other countries has perhaps been an even stronger force because it concerns the well-being and future of the U.S. economy and involves a majority of Americans, including more powerful Americans—the middle class and big businesses. The sense of an economic threat from other countries has long been associated with the sense that the American education system is much inferior to those of its foreign competitors.

The achievement gap between U.S. students and foreign students is often illustrated by citing test scores on international comparative tests such as the Trends in Mathematics and Science Study (TIMSS), the Programme for International Student Assessment (PISA), and the Progress in International Reading Literacy Study (PIRLS). In all these tests, the United States has not fared well. Results of the 1995 TIMSS show that U.S. students outperformed students in only 2 of 21 countries in math and finished significantly below students in 14 countries; U.S. students were significantly below students in 11 of 21 countries in science and were significantly ahead of students in only 2 countries. On the advanced math test, of the 15 countries participating, the United States was outscored by 11 countries. The PISA results were no better; American 15-year-olds ranked 24th among students in 40 countries that participated in the 2003 study (Committee on Prospering in the Global Economy of the 21st Century [National Academies], 2006). In terms of reading and literacy, 4th graders' performance on PIRLS in 2006 gave the United States a midpoint rank—18th out of 40 countries. The disappointing news is that between 2001 and 2006, U.S. students' reading ability as measured by PIRLS did not show any measurable improvement, despite all the efforts of NCLB to improve reading (Baer, Baldi, Ayotte, & Green, 2007).

The gap is also identified in terms of the number of students pursuing degrees in math, science, engineering, and technology. In October 2005, the National Academies released a report titled *Rising Above the Gathering Storm: Energizing and Employing America for a Brighter Economic Future*, written by a panel of 20 prominent individuals with diverse backgrounds. This report was the result of a study requested by Congress to assess America's ability to compete and prosper in the 21st century. The panel presented the following information:

• In South Korea, 38% of all undergraduates receive their degrees in natural science or engineering. In France, the figure is 47%, in China, 50%, and in Singapore, 67%. In the United States, the corresponding figure is 15%.

• Some 34% of doctoral degrees in natural sciences (including the physical, biological, earth, ocean, and atmospheric sciences) and 56% of engineering PhDs in the United States are awarded to foreign-born students.

• In the U.S. science and technology workforce in 2000, 38% of PhDs were foreign-born.

• Estimates of the number of engineers, computer scientists, and information technology students who obtain 2-, 3-, or 4-year degrees vary. One estimate is that in 2004, China graduated about 350,000 engineers, computer scientists, and information technologists with 4-year degrees, while the United States graduated about 140,000. China also graduated about 290,000 with 3-year degrees in these same fields, while the United States graduated about 85,000 with 2- or 3-year degrees. Over the past 3 years alone, both China and India have doubled their production of 3- and 4-year degrees in these fields, while the U.S. production of engineers is stagnant and the rate of production of computer scientists and information technologists doubled (Committee on Prospering in the Global Economy of the 21st Century [National Academies], 2006, p. 16).

To some, these kinds of gaps spell clear danger to the future of the United States. *New York Times* columnist Thomas Friedman has been quoted as saying, "When I was growing up, my parents told me, 'Finish your dinner. People in China and India are starving. I tell my daughters, 'Finish your homework. People in India and China are starving for your job'" (Pink, 2005b). The world's best-known writer on globalization, Friedman has often used this vivid and simple image to warn Americans that the Chinese and the Indians may take away their children's jobs.

Some have gone even further, likening the superior academic performance of other nations to the situation surrounding the launch of *Sputnik*, the first artificial satellite, which was once viewed as the symbol of the Soviet Union's superiority in military technology and a potent threat to the security of the United States. In 2007, Robert Compton, a venture capitalist, produced a documentary film to show how Indian and Chinese students are outdoing their American counterparts in education. The film, *Two Million Minutes: A Global*

Examination, compares the lives of six students in China, India, and the United States through their final year of high school. The point of the comparison is clear, at least according to the filmmaker: American students are squandering their precious two million minutes—the estimated time that students spend in high school—playing video games and partying, while their peers in China and India spend more hours studying math and science, with a strong motivation to enter the best colleges because they all aspire to become top scientists and engineers. The filmmaker compares the situation to the context surrounding *Sputnik*:

> Just as the Soviets' launch of a tiny satellite ignited a space race and impelled America to improve its science education, many experts feel the United States has reached its next "Sputnik moment." The goal of this film is to help answer the question: Are we doing enough with the time we have to ensure the best future for all? (Compton, 2008)

Sputnik has been used quite frequently to invoke a sense of urgency among Americans by many who share Thomas Friedman's "they are eating our lunch" belief. A report jointly issued by "fifteen of [the] country's most prominent business organizations" in 2005 uses *Sputnik* as the primary rhetorical device to express their "deep concern about the United States' ability to sustain its scientific and technological superiority through this decade and beyond" (Business Roundtable, 2005, p. 1). The report, *Tapping America's Potential: The Education for Innovation Initiative*, begins as follows:

> Almost 50 years ago, the Soviet Union shocked Americans by launching Sputnik, the first Earth orbit satellite. The U.S. response was immediate and dramatic. Less than a year later, President Eisenhower signed into law the National Defense Education Act, a major part of the effort to restore America's scientific pre-eminence.

The signing organizations "feel strongly that the United States must respond to this challenge as energetically as we did to the Soviet Union's launching of Sputnik in the 1950s" (Business Roundtable, 2005, p. 2). The U.S. Department of Education expressed similar thoughts in

2006 in a report titled *Answering the Challenge of a Changing World: Strengthening Education for the 21st Century*:

> This global challenge requires bold action and leadership. America has done it before. Following the Soviet Union's 1957 launch of Sputnik, the world's first satellite, Congress passed and President Eisenhower signed into law the *National Defense Education Act of 1958*. . . . Today, America faces not a streaking satellite but a rapidly changing global workforce. (p. 4)

The concerns seem to be well justified. The rise of China and India as the world's new economic powers is an undeniable fact. An average of double-digit growth in gross domestic product (GDP) over two decades propelled China ahead of the United Kingdom, making it the fourth-largest economy in the world, after the United States, Japan, and Germany in 2006. And India has become the epicenter of the high-tech boom. Multinational information technology companies have rushed to set up research and development centers in India. India's economy is set for a growth spurt. It clocked an 8.4 percent rate of growth in GDP for the fiscal year 2005–06, surpassing the advance estimate of 8.1 percent and the previous year's growth rate of 7.5 percent. But more unsettling to the United States is the future.

China and India may have found the secret to turning their combined two billion citizens into highly competitive workers: education in science, math, and engineering. Statistically, even a small fraction of them can kick the United States out of the playground. To make matters worse, associated with the rise of China, India, and other developing countries is the sense that education in the United States has become obsolete or broken.

"America's high schools are obsolete," said Bill Gates, then chairman of Microsoft, at a 2005 conference of governors and chief education officers from all 50 states. Not only are American high schools "broken, flawed, and underfunded," according to Gates, but "even when they're working exactly as designed, [they] cannot teach our kids what they need to know today," because "it's the wrong tool for the times" (Gates, 2005). At the same conference, Margaret Spellings, then newly appointed as secretary of education in the Bush administration, reinforced the assessment and reiterated the call for reform of America's high schools.

Others have pronounced the whole education system, not just high schools, to be "broken." For example, the Ed in '08 campaign (now Strong American Schools), supported by two of the wealthiest charitable organizations—the Bill and Melinda Gates Foundation and the Eli and Edythe Broad Foundation—has compiled a list of disturbing figures:

• 1.2 million students drop out of high school every year: A student drops out of high school every 26 seconds. That's 1.2 million per year—or 6,000 a day.

• 1/4 of high school students don't graduate on time: More than a quarter of high school freshmen fail to graduate from high school on time.

• 3 in 10 college freshmen repeat high school classes: Although 80 percent of 10th graders plan to earn a college degree, 3 in 10 college freshmen have to repeat high school courses and nearly half fail to graduate.

• 70% of 8th graders can't read at grade level: Seventy percent of 8th graders can't read at their grade level—and most will never catch up.

• Math teachers lack math-related degrees: More than a third of middle and high school math classes are taught by someone who lacks even a college minor in a math-related field.

• States set low standards: 25 million students attend school in states that have set proficiency standards for 4th grade reading below even the most basic level.

• U.S. ranks 19th in graduation rate: America's high school graduation rate ranks 19th in the world. (Forty years ago, we were first.) (Strong American Schools, 2008, p. 1)

Questioning the Achievement Gaps

The statistics are compelling. Indeed, significant gaps separate minority and majority students, the poor and the rich, and the United States and many developed and developing countries in the world. But are these truly important gaps? That is, will these gaps really decide the future of American children? Are there more important gaps to close? Can the reform efforts truly close the gaps, and if so, at what costs?

We need some criteria to make the judgment. Education is supposed to prepare future citizens—that is, to equip them with the necessary skills, knowledge, attitudes, and perspectives to live a prosperous and happy life as well as to perform responsibilities required of them as citizens of a society. School performance, however it is measured, is considered an early predictor of students' future success and an indicator of the quality of the education they receive. Thus an undisputable criterion would be whether the achievement gaps can predict future success and be used as indicators of the quality of education a particular school provides, which is the underlying assumption of the current reform efforts.

The Gaps Between Majority and Minority Students

We need to look at the gaps separately, beginning with the gaps in dropout and graduation rates between the minority groups, particularly Hispanics and African Americans, and the white majority. These gaps almost certainly put the minorities at a disadvantage for securing high-income jobs in the future. Plenty of evidence shows the close association between amount of education and future earnings. According to a study by the U.S. Census Bureau, average earnings (in 1999 dollars) were $18,900 for high school dropouts, $25,000 for high school graduates, $45,400 for college graduates, and $99,300 for those with professional degrees such as MD, JD, or DDS (Day & Newburger, 2002). Clearly, if students drop out of school early, their chance of obtaining a high-income position in the future is slim.

The gaps in test scores can have the same damaging effect on minority groups because test scores are closely associated with education experiences and access to college. Most colleges in the United States still use grades and scores on standardized tests such as the SAT and the ACT as primary criteria in the admission process.

However, these gaps in dropout rates, graduation rates, and test scores are the results of a set of complex issues that the recent reform efforts have failed to address. David Berliner, a well-respected education researcher at Arizona State University, wrote in 2006:

I do not believe that NCLB is needed to tell us precisely where those failing schools are located, and who inhabits them. We have had that information for over a half century. For me, NCLB is merely delaying the day when our country acknowledges that a common characteristic is associated with the great majority of schools that are most in need of improvement. It is this common characteristic of our failing schools that I write about, for by ignoring it, we severely limit our thinking about school reform. (p. 950)

That common characteristic is poverty. In this essay, Berliner brings in abundant data to show clearly that poverty significantly affects school performance and is responsible for the gaps between the poor, urban, minority students and their middle-class, suburban, white peers.

Berliner also provides compelling evidence to show the negative effects of impoverished neighborhoods on the achievement of youth living in them, as well as the negative effects of severe medical problems experienced by poor youth. In addition, strong evidence shows that even a small reduction in family poverty significantly improves school behavior and performance of students. The United States has the highest rate of child poverty among developed nations, a condition that has persisted for decades, without clear signs of disappearing in the near future. In fact, Berliner suggests that the situation may have become worse, due to the recent increase in income gaps in the United States.

Additionally, schools in impoverished communities often have fewer resources than their more affluent counterparts. Teacher shortages and lack of parental involvement, extracurricular activities, technology resources, and funds for libraries are persistent problems facing these schools. Thus the so-called achievement gaps are a result of the resource gaps, a problem that cannot be solved by simply holding the schools and teachers more accountable and giving the children more tests.

Another explanation of the gaps lies with the tests themselves. Test bias is a well-acknowledged phenomenon in the education measurement business. Many researchers have shown how IQ tests are biased against minorities because the tests use language and situations that are more familiar to white, middle-class students. However, psychologist Robert Sternberg discovered another type of bias that is perhaps more important in explaining the achievement gaps.

Sternberg proposed that success requires a broad range of abilities, but schools often focus on only one and ignore others. Conventional tests do the same. Following his "triarchic theory," Sternberg and his colleagues at Yale developed the Sternberg Triarchic Abilities Test. The test measures not only conventional abilities—memory and analytical abilities—but also two other types deemed important by Sternberg: creative abilities and practical abilities.

The test was used to select participants for a summer camp program at Yale and was given to high school students nationwide. The participants were then put into five groups: high analytical, high creative, high practical, high in all three abilities, low in all three abilities. The results were surprising:

> The high-analytical group looked pretty much like a standard high-ability group: mostly white, middle-class and attending strong schools. But the high-creative and high-practical groups were much more diverse in terms of ethnic, socioeconomic and educational background. In other words, we found we had selected more minority students not through any program of affirmative action but through a program of recognizing and valuing abilities that schools typically neglect, both in their instruction and in their assessments. (Sternberg, 1998)

Similar results were replicated in other studies. These results suggest that gaps between certain minority groups and their white peers are outcomes of the tests, which neglect to assess other abilities that are as important but not as valued. Furthermore, Sternberg and his colleagues also found that when instruction matches the ability, students learn better. In this sense, conventional instruction provided in schools can be said to alienate minority students, further widening the gaps.

Another psychologist, A. Wade Boykin of Howard University, suggests that there is a fundamental conflict between certain aspects of African American culture and the implicit culture of most American schools (Neisser et al., 1996). This conflict may result in African American students being judged problematic and incompetent by teachers who hold a different view and in the students feeling they are being imposed upon culturally. Boykin has argued that "the successful education of African American children will require an approach that is less concerned with talent sorting and assessment, more concerned with talent development" (Neisser et al., 1996, p. 95).

In summary, the gaps between minority students and their majority peers are important, but they have not really been addressed by the recent reform efforts. In fact, the reform efforts may have further disadvantaged minority students by forcing them into a narrow set of subjects and testing them in only one type of ability. The results may demonstrate to them how incompetent they are, which can further exacerbate their already devastating lack of self-esteem and aspiration. These gaps should be addressed through policies aimed at reducing poverty, recognition of a broad range of talents and abilities in assessment and college admissions criteria, and reconsideration of the value of different talents and knowledge.

The Gaps Between the United States and Other Countries

The gaps in performance on international tests between U.S. students and their counterparts in other countries are a completely different story. The connection made between students' performance on these tests and their or their nations' future economic well-being is at best speculative. In fact, an empirical study that examines the relationship between countries' performance on international tests and other indicators of the countries' well-being shows either a negative correlation or no correlation between the two. In this study, Keith Baker, a retired officer of the U.S. Department of Education, looked at the relationship between the results of the First International Mathematics Study (FIMS) and the 11 participating countries' success in terms of national wealth (GDP), rate of growth, individual productivity, quality of life, livability, democracy, and creativity 40 years later. These indicators, according to Baker, should be what really matters to a nation. FIMS was administered in 1964 on 13-year-olds in 11 Western, developed countries. The United States finished second to last. Today, some 40 years later, the students who took the test would be in their 50s and would have been the primary workforce over the last 30 years. If FIMS measured something that matters, that something should have predicted a country's condition to some degree. But Baker found either no correlation or a negative correlation. For those who are especially worried about the United States losing its economic competitive edge because of lower scores of U.S. students, Baker (2007) writes, "In short, the higher a nation's test score 40 years ago, the worse its economic performance" (p. 102). In conclusion, Baker argues:

> In the face of such evidence, we can do more than reject the widely held hypothesis that high test scores lead to national success in the future. We can also hypothesize that high test scores are damaging to nations. That the U.S. comes out on top in national success in 74% of the comparisons with higher-scoring nations is statistically significant ($p < .0001$, binomial test). (p. 103)

Baker is not the only one who has pointed out the lack of connection between test scores and nations' successes. I discuss other similar efforts later in the book.

Baker's conclusion goes against the recent reform and popular rhetoric that says American education is in crisis, and unless quickly and forcefully resolved, the crisis will lead to the decline of the United States as a nation and Americans as individuals. If test scores are not such reliable indicators of the quality of education or good predictors of a nation's or an individual's success, how did the United States come to accept the general notion that its public education system is broken and to support the reform efforts to put more standards and tests in schools? After all, NCLB was a bipartisan effort and overwhelmingly supported by both parties in Congress. The push for more math, science, and reading as well as more accountability has enjoyed support from the broad business sector and the public. How was the public convinced that American education needs such fixes if the fixes do not really solve the problem?

More important, if low test scores are not a problem, does that mean American education is not in crisis? Does it mean that schools should continue the way they were before NCLB and Americans should hope that they will be just fine? Definitely not. Our world is going through a dramatic transformation brought about by economic globalization and technological advances. It is a fact that the United States is facing stiff competition from countries such as China and India. It is also a fact that the United States has been losing jobs to other countries. American schools are undoubtedly not adequately equipped to prepare future citizens to live successfully in the new world. But the solution is not more math, science, and reading; more testing; and more accountability as prescribed by NCLB. In fact, NCLB could lead America into deeper crisis.

What we need is a paradigm shift in thinking about education, both what we should teach and how we should deliver it. What does the new paradigm look like, and how can schools and educators work to realize it?

I address these questions in the remainder of the book. I start with a historical analysis of how the perception of American education in crisis became so widespread and how recent education reform efforts evolved as a response.

2

From the Missile Gap to the Learning Gap:
Myth, Fear, and the Evolution of Accountability

Every year, if not every day, we have to wager our salvation upon some prophecy based upon imperfect knowledge.
—Oliver Wendell Holmes Jr., U.S. jurist

The most destructive element in the human mind is fear. Fear creates aggressiveness.
—Dorothy Thompson, U.S. journalist

The warning that American education is broken is not new. Neither are the proposed fixes. A look at history helps us understand how American education has become increasingly authoritarian and how the public and even educators surrendered their rights to governments to decide what counts as good education.

The "Missile Gap"

On October 4, 1957, the former Soviet Union caught the world's attention and threw the American public into a panic with a device about the size of a beach ball. It successfully launched *Sputnik I*, the world's first artificial satellite. On November 3, the Soviets launched *Sputnik II*, this time carrying a heavier payload, including Laika, the world's first dog to travel in space.

The *Sputnik* launches startled Americans, who were both astounded by the technical superiority of their archrival and fearful of the military implications of the technology. The belief that a huge "missile gap" existed between the Soviet Union and the United States quickly became shorthand for the imminent crisis facing the United States.

"A crisis is a terrible thing to waste," Stanford economist Paul Romer once said. And this crisis was not wasted. John F. Kennedy made good use of the crisis in both his reelection campaign for the U.S. Senate and later his bid for the presidency. Shortly after the *Sputnik* launch, the Massachusetts senator declared that "the nation was losing the satellite-missile race with the Soviet Union" because the United States was "behind, possibly as much as several years, in . . . the development, perfection, and stockpiling of intermediate-range ballistic missiles and long-range ballistic missiles." Kennedy accused the Eisenhower administration of "putting fiscal security ahead of national security" and warned that "the [missile] gap [would] begin in 1960." If the Eisenhower policies continued, there would be "great danger within the next few years" (Preble, 2003).

Kennedy's speeches on the missile gap figured prominently in the midterm election of 1958. His most forceful speech on this topic, delivered on the floor of the Senate on August 14, 1958, was widely distributed to leaders of the Democratic Party and other officials at the request of the Democratic National Committee as a way to help prepare Democratic candidates for subjects that would figure in political debates across the nation (Preble, 2003). Kennedy defeated his opponent, Boston lawyer Vincent J. Celeste, by a wide margin and was reelected to a second term in the U.S. Senate in 1958.

The missile gap was further used in Kennedy's presidential campaign in 1960. In September and October of that year, Kennedy faced his Republican opponent, Richard Nixon, in the first televised presidential debates in U.S. history. The superiority of the Soviet Union economically and militarily was one of Kennedy's effective weapons against the Eisenhower-Nixon administration in these debates. He alleged that the Soviet Union had "made a breakthrough in missiles, and by '61-2-3 they will be outnumbering us in missiles. I'm not as confident as he [Nixon] is that we will be the strongest military power by 1963." Kennedy attacked Nixon for putting color television ahead of national security, referring to Nixon's earlier comment to Soviet leader Nikita Khrushchev that, although the Soviet Union might be ahead in the development of rocket thrust, the United States was more advanced in the development of color television (Helgerson, 1996).

On November 8, 1960, Kennedy defeated Nixon and became the youngest man and the first Catholic to be elected U.S. president. The missile gap argument helped tremendously. As Robert McNamara, secretary of defense during the Kennedy and Johnson administrations, later recalled in an interview with CNN,

> a major element of the election campaign that President Kennedy had just won was the charge by the Democrats, including President Kennedy, that Eisenhower had left a missile gap; that the Soviets had been permitted, by inaction on the part of the U.S., to build up a superior nuclear missile force. (McNamara, 1998)

But the "missile gap," as it turned out, did not exist. Again, McNamara on CNN:

> So clearly my first responsibility as Secretary of Defense was to determine the degree of the gap and initiate action to close it. So my deputy Ros[well] Gilpatric and I immediately began to work on that, on January 21st, 1961. And it took us about three weeks to determine [that] yes, there was a gap. But the gap was in our favor. It was a totally erroneous charge that Eisenhower had allowed the Soviets to develop a missile force superior to the U.S.

The missile gap was a myth, a misperception that was easily sold to the American public at that time. Whether Kennedy promoted it intentionally remains a matter of historical debate. People still disagree as to whether he was given the wrong information or he selectively picked and chose the information that would advance his career (Helgerson, 1996; McNamara, 1998; Preble, 2003).

Fear as a Political Strategy

Myths can be dangerous. Often they are based on inaccurate information and misinterpretations. As such, they lead to misinformed actions, which can result in unimaginable and disastrous consequences. It is difficult to imagine today what the world would be like had the "missile gap" myth not been invented. Could the Cold War have ended earlier? Could we have avoided the Cuban missile crisis? Would John F. Kennedy still be alive had he not won the presidency? History cannot be rewritten, but it should teach us something.

Fear is a basic animal emotion experienced by all human beings. It has tremendous adaptive value, helping us to avoid threats and alerting us to danger and the need to react under stressful conditions—thereby helping us to survive (Marks, 1987). On the other hand, as the "missile gap" myth illustrates, fear can also be manipulated and used to drive public policy. Adolf Hitler is one of the most striking examples of the effective use of fear as a strategy to mobilize the public. As early as 1919, he clearly invoked the "danger" posed by the Jewish people to justify his call for the "irrevocable removal" of Jews from German life (Hitler, 1919); and later, he used the same strategy to justify actions that led to World War II. But fear has been used to drive public policies in almost every society. As history professor Joanna Bourke (2006) writes in *Fear: A Cultural History*, "Public policy and private lives have become fear-bound; fear has become the emotion through which public life is administered" (p. x).

NDEA: The Beginning of Federal Government Involvement in K–12 Education

Fear of the implications of Soviet technological and military prowess was widespread in the United States after the *Sputnik* launch and the repeated media and political discussions that followed. Public fear enabled American politicians to achieve many things that had not been possible before, including providing federal assistance to public education, an area of power that, because it is not mentioned in the U.S. Constitution, was reserved for state and local governments.

The *Sputnik* launch led directly to the National Defense Education Act (NDEA). Passed in 1958, NDEA was the first piece of comprehensive federal education in the United States to provide aid to education at all levels, public and private. "To help ensure that highly trained individuals would be available to help America compete with the Soviet Union in scientific and technical fields, the NDEA included support for loans to college students, the improvement of science, mathematics, and foreign language instruction in elementary and secondary schools, graduate fellowships, foreign language and area studies, and vocational-technical training" (U.S. Department of Education, 2008a).

The significance of NDEA cannot be overstated. It marked the beginning of an increasing involvement of the federal government in education. In the ensuing decades, the federal government passed more legislation concerning education, including the Vocational Education Act of 1963, the Higher Education Act of 1963, the Elementary and Secondary Education Act of 1964, and, of course, the No Child Left Behind Act of 2002. The NDEA transformed the American education landscape. Funds provided by NDEA stimulated innovations; expanded the talent pools in science, technology, engineering, mathematics, and foreign languages; and resulted in new curriculums. Although it included programs for both K–12 and postsecondary education, its influence has been much bigger in higher education than in K–12.

The passage of NDEA is a telling example of the usefulness of a crisis, real or imagined. Before the launch of *Sputnik*, several attempts had been made to establish a federal program to provide monetary aid to public education, but all ended in failure. Legislators were reluctant to have the federal government play a role in education. But *Sputnik* changed everything. It was Stewart E. McClure, the chief clerk of the Senate Committee on Labor, Education, and Public Welfare from 1955 to 1969 and from 1971 to 1973, who masterfully connected the launch of *Sputnik* to education and brought the idea to Senator Lister Hill of Alabama. Years later, during an interview, McClure proudly recounted his role:

> I think if there was one thing I ever did in my work on the Hill, my work for my whole career, it was to focus Lister Hill's attention on the opportunity which *Sputnik*, this Russian satellite, gave all of us who were

struggling, and had been for decades, to establish a federal program of monetary aid to public education, and private, too, in some instances. And I'm really very proud of that. Of course, someone else could have come along with the same idea, and probably did a week later, but I was first. (Stewart E. McClure, p. 112)

McClure acted on his idea quickly. He "cooked up a memorandum" and gave it to his friend John Campbell, executive assistant to Senator Hill, who was traveling in Europe "when the damn satellite was shot up, so the impact on him must have been even stronger than it was here" (p. 112). Apparently the memo had the desired effect, "because within ten minutes after he was in the office, the staff had a call, 'Come on over here. Got your memorandum, St'rt, let's see what we can do.' It worked. And he then set us to business" (p. 113).

Also very clever was the title of the bill, which explicitly makes education an issue of national security. "I invented that God-awful title: the National Defense Education Act," says McClure. "If there are any words less compatible, really, intellectually, in terms of what is the purpose of education—it's not to defend the country; it's to defend the mind and develop the human spirit, not to build cannons and battleships. It was a horrible title, but it worked. It worked. How could you attack it?" (p. 118).

No doubt, this was a masterpiece of politics. McClure and Senator Hill both saw the opportunity *Sputnik* presented and took advantage of it to push their agenda. McClure was very proud of having been able to

> grab this opportunity which would never come again, when the public was all upset and people were fretting in the streets about "oh, my God, we're behind," and all that stuff. So it was, as the Latins used to say, *carpe diem*, "seize the day," and we did, and we did. . . . And then we had a bill, and then we had a law, and then we had a program, and then we began teaching people science and math and languages all over the country. It was a grand achievement, I think. (p. 117)

NDEA was passed because of the perceived connection between education and efforts to counter the Soviets. Such a connection suddenly elevated the status of education and justified the federal government's involvement. This connection dissolved all previous resistance because the American public was so fearful that they accepted the idea that putting money—federal money—into education would help them fight the Soviets.

Although NDEA, with its billions of federal dollars for research and education, undoubtedly helped to boost scientific and technological advancement in the United States, there is no hard evidence that its investment in the nation's K–12 schools was responsible for maintaining the nation's superiority in science and technology, let alone winning the Cold War. Considering that the United States launched its first artificial satellite in 1958, put the first American in space in 1961, and landed on the moon in 1969, it would be difficult to suggest that NDEA improved the education system so fast and so effectively.

Sputnik was not the only thing that convinced Americans that their education system was in crisis. There were many ill-informed helpers. To support the idea that the Soviets' technological superiority over Americans was due to their better education system, evidence was sought and found. Education researcher Gerald Bracey (2006a) describes one of those ill-informed helpers:

> In red letters against a black background, *Life* magazine's cover of March 24, 1958, shouted "Crisis in Education." A stern-looking Alexei Kutzkov in Moscow and an easy-smiling Stephen Lapekas in Chicago, both high school juniors, stared out at the reader. Pictures showed Kutzkov conducting complicated experiments in physics and chemistry and reading aloud from *Sister Carrie* in his English class. Lapekas was seen walking home with his girlfriend, dancing in rehearsal for a musical and retreating from a geometry problem on the blackboard. "Stephen amused his classmates with wisecracks about his ineptitude," read the text.
>
> One leaves the *Life* article convinced that without massive and immediate school reform, the Russians will bury us. (Lapekas became a Navy pilot, then a commercial pilot for TWA; I am told Kutzkov works for the Russian equivalent of the FAA. The article so devastated Lapekas that he will not talk about it even today.)

By now, we all know what happened to the nation that supposedly offered its citizens a superior education. The Soviet Union no longer exists!

A Nation at Risk:
The Threat from Japan, Korea, and Germany

"Those who fail to learn the lessons of history are doomed to repeat them," said the philosopher George Santayana, and history keeps repeating itself for American education.

On April 26, 1983, the National Commission on Excellence in Education submitted a report to U.S. Secretary of Education T. H. Bell and "the American People." The title of this report reveals the commission's view on the quality of American education: *A Nation at Risk: The Imperative for Educational Reform.*

"Our Nation is at risk," begins the report, clearly intending to arouse fear, including fear of others (foreigners), because "[o]ur once unchallenged preeminence in commerce, industry, science, and technological innovation is being overtaken by competitors throughout the world" (National Commission on Excellence in Education, 1983, p. 1). Describing the rise of other countries as one source of the risk, the report says this:

> The risk is not only that the Japanese make automobiles more efficiently than Americans and have government subsidies for development and export. It is not just that the South Koreans recently built the world's most efficient steel mill, or that American machine tools, once the pride of the world, are being displaced by German products. It is also that these developments signify a redistribution of trained capability throughout the globe. (p. 1)

The other source of the risk, according to the commission, was the fact that the "educational foundations of our society are presently being eroded by a rising tide of mediocrity that threatens our very future as a Nation and a people." The commission asserted that the decline of quality in American education was so serious,

> [i]f an unfriendly foreign power had attempted to impose on America the mediocre educational performance that exists today, we might well have viewed it as an act of war. As it stands, we have allowed this to happen to ourselves. We have even squandered the gains in student achievement made in the wake of the *Sputnik* challenge. Moreover, we

have dismantled essential support systems which helped make those gains possible. We have, in effect, been committing an act of unthinking, unilateral educational disarmament. (p. 1)

To support the premise that America was at risk because of its poor education system, the commission listed some 13 "indicators of the risk," including American students' poor performances on international academic tests; the country's high rates of functional illiteracy; its declining test scores on the SAT and other standardized tests; and the increasing need for remediation courses in math, science, and English for college students and employees. In the context of rising demands for new skills in science and technology, the commission quotes Paul Hurd, an education consultant, for its conclusive assessment of America education: "We are raising a new generation of Americans that is scientifically and technologically illiterate" (p. 3).

To avert this risk, the commission made five main recommendations:

1. Five "new basics" of high school curriculum: four years of English; three years each of math, science, and social studies; and a semester of computer science. In addition, the commission recommended two years of foreign language for the college-bound.

2. Higher expectations for academic performance: rigorous and measurable standards and heightened admissions requirements at postsecondary institutions.

3. More time for learning: better use of the school day, lengthened school days, or a longer school year.

4. Better teachers and teaching: better preparation of teachers, and more recognition and reward for teaching as a profession.

5. Government intervention (leadership) and accountability: "hold educators and elected officials responsible for providing the leadership necessary to achieve these reforms"; have citizens "provide the fiscal support and stability" necessary to achieve the reforms; and let the federal government have "*the primary responsibility* to identify the national interest in education."

A Nation at Risk did not result in any immediate legislation for education at the federal level. In fact, the federal education budget was sharply cut in 1984. But this report, hailed by some as the most important education document in the 20th century, laid the foundation for changes in American education in the ensuing decades and thus is primarily responsible for pushing American education down the path of greater federal control in a number of ways.

First, the commission's damning portrait of American education continues and has been enriched by further international studies such as TIMSS and PISA, scholarly writings, and media reports of how other countries outperform the United States in education. The dominant image of American public education today is still an image of a system that is broken and obsolete. The nation remains at risk, according to many media stories published in 2003, on the 20th anniversary of the release of the report.

Second, the report (not necessarily with foresight and intention) helped make a smooth transition from the Cold War to the global economy as a rationale for viewing education as a national security issue. NDEA had made education a vital issue for confronting the Soviet Union, but that political entity disappeared in 1989. Thanks to *A Nation at Risk*, America did not need to look for new enemies to mobilize against. New enemies were already present, as evidenced by competition for global economic dominance from Japan, Germany, Korea, and, more recently, China and India. Thus Americans could not be complacent. The nation was still at risk.

Third, the report planted the seeds for how government could penetrate more deeply into education. Holding educators accountable and implementing centralized education standards were among the recommendations that have been picked up by both Democrats and Republicans at the federal and state levels as the primary mechanisms for regulating education.

Finally, the report paved the way for business people to become legitimate speakers on and advocates for education concerns. Because the report made education an economic issue, it was only right to make educators hear the voices of business and make sure that business needs were met. Eventually, the perception that schools were run inefficiently and should be held accountable also led some people to believe that business leaders would know how to run educational institutions better than educators. Over the past two decades since the release of the report, the number of business leaders taking the national stage to speak on education issues has steadily increased.

In hindsight, despite all the historical importance it has garnered, the report would have met a similar fate as numerous other such documents had it not had political value. In 1981, when the commission was put together, Ronald Reagan had just won his first presidential election, in part because of his tough stance against the Soviet Union and his promise to dismantle the federal Department of Education, which had been created by his opponent, President Jimmy Carter. Reagan was not even interested in the commission. In fact, he rejected the suggestion of his secretary of education, T. H. Bell, to form such a commission. Bell later decided to organize the commission on his own.

When the commission was organized, Reagan met with its members and gave them five "cardinal orders," which collectively show his interest in education:

> Bring God back into the classroom. Encourage tuition tax credits for families using private schools. Support vouchers. Leave the primary responsibility for education to parents. And please abolish that abomination, the Department of Education. (Holton, 2003, p. B13)

After the commissioners, who ignored Reagan's orders, finished their report, they met with the president again. But according to Gerald Holton (2003), a Harvard professor who served on the commission and drafted the report, it appeared that "the one important reader of the report had apparently not read it after all." Reagan "said that he was glad to have received it; indeed, he went on, the report was fully in accord with his own ideas on retrieving excellence in education: by bringing God back into the classroom, by tuition tax credits, by vouchers, and—he pointed at Secretary Bell—by abolishing the Department of Education." According to Holton,

> The report would have died there in the state dining room of the White House. But then something happened to change everything. The commissioners were looking at one another in dismay and astonishment, and in a stage whisper loud enough to be heard by reporters in back, one commissioner said simply, "We have been had."

For the reporters, that was like blood before sharks. A conflict between Reagan's words and what the commission's report might contain seemed the stuff of scandal, the favorite subject of most journalists.

The report immediately became a hot topic. Articles about it appeared on the front page of almost every major newspaper in the United States. And many reproduced the short report in its entirety.

No clever politician would waste such press coverage—certainly not Ronald Reagan, who faced reelection the next year. Although he remained popular among male voters, Reagan had difficulty winning over women because they were more concerned about family issues such as education than about the Cold War. "Reagan, seeing the favorable national response, skillfully associated himself with the report in broadcast-media appearances" (Holton, 2003). The political payoff was great for Reagan's reelection. During his campaign, Reagan gave a total of 51 speeches on the need for education reform, and as Secretary Bell writes in his memoir, the purpose was "to get the greatest possible mileage from the commission report" (1988, p. 149). According to Bell, Reagan masterfully "stole the issue from Walter Mondale—and it cost us nothing"; focusing on the need for education reform "obscured concerns about cuts in welfare, aid to dependent children, Medicaid, and other social programs" (p. 155). In the end, Reagan defeated Mondale and won reelection.

Apparently Gerald Holton was not happy that Reagan had used the report for his political gain but did not pay attention to education. Writing on the eve of the 20th anniversary of the release of *A Nation at Risk*, Holton (2003) said, "In short, Reagan used 'A Nation at Risk' as a Trojan horse to help win the election. We had been used." But Holton and his fellow commissioners should be happy; had the report not been of political value, it would have been buried long ago.

The report did more for the Republicans than simply return Reagan to the White House for a second term. As columnist Tamim Ansary (2007) writes,

By the end of the decade, Republicans had erased whatever advantage Democrats once enjoyed on education and other classic "women's issues." As Peter Schrag later noted in *The Nation*, Reagan-era conservatives, "with the help of business leaders like IBM chairman Lou Gerstner, managed to convert a whole range of liberally oriented children's issues . . . into a debate focused almost exclusively on education and tougher-standards school reform."

No Child Left Behind: The Arrival of the Dictator in Education

Today, a life-sized bronze statue of President George W. Bush stands outside Ohio's Hamilton High School to commemorate a historic day for the school and, indeed, the nation. The day was January 8, 2002, when President George W. Bush signed his landmark education law, No Child Left Behind, at the school. To show bipartisan support for the law, the signing ceremony was presided over by Representative George Miller, a Democrat from California; Senator Edward Kennedy, a Democrat from Massachusetts; Senator Judd Gregg, a Republican from Vermont; and Representative John Boehner, a Republican from Ohio who chaired the House Committee on Education and the Workforce at that time. Hamilton was in Boehner's home district. At the ceremony, Bush (2002) made the following proclamation, to reportedly deafening applause: "And today begins a new era, a new time in public education in our country. As of this hour, America's schools will be on a new path of reform, and a new path of results."

Having been selected out of 90,000 high schools nationwide contending for this honor, Hamilton High was understandably proud, so proud that the community erected a glittering statue of the president signing the law outside the school's entrance. But that pride would soon be dampened when Hamilton High was branded a failing school in August 2004, just two years later, under the provisions of Bush's law.

The case of Hamilton High, a school in an award-winning district, was not unique. Nationwide, "thousands of schools—even those rated highly in their own states—fall short of the standards of No Child Left Behind," according to a story in the *Chicago Tribune* (Rado, 2004).

The "failing school" label is certainly not something to be proud of. Moreover, it carries serious consequences. According to the law, a school so labeled faces sanctions such as reorganization, losing students, or even closure. Worse yet, the label leads to the public perception that the school delivers a poor education, though many may not be well informed about the confusing formula used to determine whether a school meets the NCLB requirements.

The cornerstone of NCLB is accountability through standardized testing in math and reading. Although NCLB was the first legislation to truly bring the federal government as a regulator into American public education, it did not just happen. Its measures, principles, bipartisan support, and enthusiastic public reception created a perfect storm after two decades of cumulative efforts inspired by *A Nation at Risk*.

The Reagan White House did not do anything substantial in education following the public rhetoric on the campaign trail about *A Nation at Risk*, but Reagan did use his 1984 State of the Union address to claim credit for the report and promote standards and competition in education: "Just as more incentives are needed within our schools, greater competition is needed among our schools. Without standards and competition, there can be no champions, no records broken, no excellence in education or any other walk of life" (Reagan, 1984).

Secretary of Education Bell did much more to promote the idea of competition through the well-known and controversial "wall chart" he created in 1984. The chart ranked states by their educational attainment using ACT and SAT scores. The chart was retained for the next six years, but not without controversy. Many educators and state officials raised concerns and protested its limitations and misuses, but the media loved the idea (Vinovskis, 1999).

The media loved the idea because its consumers, the public, loved the idea. Public education is one of the largest investments Americans make, and it affects their future on many levels. They naturally want to know how well their schools perform. But the quality of education is an extremely complex phenomenon that cannot be easily demonstrated or understood. What the public is familiar with are test scores and grades. Despite the obvious flaws and limitations of using student test scores and grades to measure the quality of education

(Nichols & Berliner, 2007), the American public, short of other easy-to-understand measures, seems to have accepted the notion that test scores are accurate measures of the quality of their schools. In the *Second Annual Survey of the Public's Attitude Toward the Public Schools,* jointly conducted by PDK/Gallup in 1970, 75 percent of those interviewed approved the proposal to give national tests to students in their local schools so their educational achievement could be compared with that of students in other communities; only 16 percent opposed the idea (Gallup, 1970). (The same poll found that 66 percent of parents favored spanking.) In 1987, in the 19th PDK/Gallup survey, 70 percent of the respondents favored the proposal to report student test scores as education achievement so that state-by-state and school-by-school comparisons could be made (Gallup & Clark, 1987).

Being able to reduce the quality of education to some kind of score that allows comparison across different states appeals to the public in a simplistic fashion. It is misleading, but immensely popular.

The popularity of test scores among the public provided a ready tool for a group of governors who were concerned about educational issues in their states as the economic situation worsened in the United States and public ratings of schools declined in the 1980s. The group included Republicans Lamar Alexander of Tennessee and Thomas Kean of New Jersey; and Democrats Bill Clinton of Arkansas, Bob Graham of Florida, James Hunt of North Carolina, Richard Riley of South Carolina, and William Winter of Mississippi. They called for tougher school standards, better pay for teachers, and more state funds for K–12 education. But their education reform initiatives were not always enthusiastically embraced by state legislators. "To overcome the reluctance of state legislators to increase taxes to pay for these improvements, governors frequently had to mobilize the public on behalf of public school reforms" (Vinovskis, 1999, p. 7).

Fear was used again. By then, lower test scores had been accepted as a sure sign of a deteriorating education system, and a poor education system was seen as the cause of economic troubles. This view was expressed by Governor Lamar Alexander, chair of the National Governors Association (NGA), at the 1985 NGA meeting in Idaho:

Better schools mean better jobs. Unless states face these questions [about education], Americans won't keep our high standard of living. To meet stiff competition from workers in the rest of the world, we must educate ourselves and our children as we never have before. (National Governors Association, 1986, p. 2)

Good schools result from tougher standards, higher educational goals, and strong accountability measures, according to the governors. Richard Riley, the South Carolina governor who later became secretary of education in the Clinton administration, explained this logic in a 1988 speech endorsing the call for the establishment of state and regional educational goals by the Southern Regional Education Board—an influential organization of southern governors, legislators, and education officials:

Why are educational goals important? Simply put, the citizens of any state are not likely to achieve more in education than they and their leaders expect and aim for. . . . Significant educational improvements do not just happen. They are planned and pursued. (Riley, 1988, p. 63)

To hold educators accountable, to assess progress toward goals, and to measure to what degree students are meeting the standards, tests are needed. Thus

[t]he NGA was interested in using quantitative indices, but felt that the use of SAT and ACT scores in the wall chart was misleading and inaccurate. The NGA endorsed the expansion of NAEP to test and report student outcomes at the state level—thereby significantly contributing to the movement to collect and disseminate state-level comparative student achievement data in the 1990s. (Vinovskis, 1999, p. 19)

The governors' efforts eventually developed into a national movement. In 1989, George H. W. Bush, who had just been elected as president to succeed Reagan, held a landmark conference with the nation's governors in Charlottesville, Virginia. The summit was chaired by then governor Clinton. After many rounds of negotiations, President Bush and the nation's governors issued a joint statement on September 28. The statement stressed the importance of education for America's future in a competitive world:

Education has always been important, but never this important because the stakes have changed: Our competitors for opportunity are also working to educate their people. As they continue to improve, they make the future a moving target. We believe that the time has come, for the first time in U.S. history, to establish clear, national performance goals, goals that will make us internationally competitive. (Vinovskis, 1999, p. 38)

The key to better education, according to the joint statement, is goals, accountability, and assessment to monitor progress:

The President and the nation's Governors have agreed at this summit to:
- Establish a process for setting national education goals;
- Seek greater flexibility and enhanced accountability in the use of Federal resources to meet the goals, through both regulatory and legislative changes;
- Undertake a major state-by-state effort to restructure our education system; and
- Report annually on progress in achieving our goals. (Vinovskis, 1999, p. 39)

The Charlottesville summit of 1989 ushered in a new era in American education, an era of establishing national educational standards. In his 1990 State of the Union address, President Bush announced the National Education Goals for the year 2000; shortly thereafter, he and Congress established a National Education Goals Panel. Federal funds were allocated to support the development of national standards in several areas, and professional organizations such as the National Council of Teachers of Mathematics and the American Association for the Advancement of Science published standards in their respective areas.

By now the national standards movement had gained considerable public support. In 1992, Bill Clinton, a Democrat, won the presidential election. He did not differ much from his predecessor on educational issues and further injected the federal government into K–12 education. In 1994, Clinton signed into law the Goals 2000: Educate America Act. This legislation set national educational goals, to be achieved by the year 2000, in eight areas: school readiness; school completion; student achievement and citizenship; teacher preparation and professional development; mathematics and science; adult literacy and lifelong learning; safe, alcohol- and drug-free schools; and parental participation.

These were ambitious goals, and most of them were not achieved by 2000. For example, the legislation set out to improve the school-completion rate for all students and eliminate the gap in high school graduation rates between minority and nonminority students by 2000. But according to a report of the National Center for Education Statistics that tracks high school dropout rates in the nation, "while progress was made during the 1970s and 1980s in reducing high school dropout rates and increasing high school completion rates, these rates have remained comparatively stable during the 1990s" (National Center for Education Statistics, 2001).

With regard to what students should learn, the legislation set the following goal and objectives:

With regard to what students should learn, the legislation set the goal of all students leaving grades 4, 8, and 12 with demonstrated competency in English, math, science, foreign languages, civics and government, economics, art, history, and geography; and all schools preparing students to "use their minds well, so they may be prepared for responsible citizenship, further learning, and productive employment in our Nation's modern economy." The legislation set out specific objectives, including increased achievement "in every quartile," with distribution of minority students in each quartile more closely reflecting the student population as a whole; improvements in areas such as reasoning ability and problem solving; involvement in citizenship and community service activities; access to physical education and health education for all students; and increased knowledge of foreign languages and world cultures.

Most of these objectives were not accomplished. But this legislation further justified the role of the federal government in K–12 education through national education standards. The legislation created the National Education Standards and Improvement Council to certify national and state content and performance standards and opportunity-to-learn standards. State assessments and national standards for many subjects were developed (Mid-continent Research for Education and

Learning, 2008). The federal government's role in dictating what subjects are valued and should be taught in schools would remain weak if the government merely supported and sanctioned national standards; without measures to force their implementation, schools could still do whatever they liked. To enforce the standards, the public needed to be mobilized again.

In March 1996, IBM CEO Louis Gerstner and Governor Tommy Thompson of Wisconsin convened another education summit at IBM's executive conference center in Palisades, New York. Forty-one governors, most of them Republicans, and 44 executives of major businesses from virtually every state attended the summit. CEOs from IBM, AT&T, Bell South, Eastman Kodak, Procter & Gamble, and Boeing were on the planning committee. President Bill Clinton also dropped by. No student and only one or two teachers had been invited. Professional educators and their organizations were left out for the most part.

The governors and business executives reiterated their impatience with the abysmal state of American education, particularly "with the parents of school children who consistently believe that their children's schools are fine; it's all the other schools that have problems." They wanted all parents to know that "those who do the hiring know that only a few public schools are as good as parents think" (Lagowski, 1996, p. 383). The solution was standards and assessments, and the two needed to go hand in hand because "it is clear that simply setting goals is not enough," states the unanimously adopted Policy Statement of the Summit.

The summit participants pledged their commitment to do the following:

• Set clear academic standards . . . in core subject areas.

• Assist schools in accurately measuring student progress.

• Make changes to curriculum, teaching techniques, and technology uses based on the results.

• Assist schools in overcoming the barriers to using new technology.

• Hold schools and students accountable for demonstrating real improvement (Eakin, 1996).

The governors promised to develop and establish "internationally competitive academic standards, assessments to measure academic achievement, and accountability systems in their states" within the next two years. And the business executives vowed to "clearly communicate to students, parents, schools, and the community the types and levels of skills necessary to meet the workforce needs of the next century and implement hiring practices within one year that will require applicants to demonstrate achievement" and to consider "the quality of a state's academic standards and student achievement levels as a high-priority factor in determining business-location decisions" (Eakin, 1996).

Directly connecting employment and business opportunities with academic standards and student performance was certainly an effective strategy to mobilize the public to take standards and assessment more seriously. But it was not as effective as a national test. To bring even more force behind implementing standards, President Clinton called for a voluntary national test program in 1997. In his 1998 State of the Union address, Clinton announced that "[t]hanks to the actions of this Congress last year, we will soon have, for the very first time, a voluntary national test based on national standards in 4th grade reading and 8th grade math" (Clinton, 1998). The Republican-controlled Congress resisted and eventually killed the program.

As of 2009, there are no mandated national curriculum standards and national tests in the United States. Nevertheless, according to Michael J. Petrilli and Chester E. Finn Jr. of the conservative Fordham Foundation, "the federal government has pushed far too deeply into the routines and operations of the nation's public schools, now regulating everything from teacher credentials to the selection of reading programs" (Petrilli & Finn, 2006). Ironically, both of them are calling for national tests and national standards.

Even without national standards and national tests, there is little doubt that education in the United States has become authoritarian. Through NCLB, the federal government has been telling Americans that reading and math are the most valued subject areas and what schools should teach. Through various high school exit exams and state core curriculum programs, the state governments have decided that math, science, English, and possibly social studies are of most worth if Americans are to succeed in the global economy.

And schools have complied. According to a study by the Center on Education Policy issued in 2007, five years after the implementation of NCLB, about 62 percent of districts had increased instructional time for English or math, or both, in elementary schools, and more than 20 percent reported increasing time for these subjects in middle school. To accommodate this increased time in English and math, 44 percent of districts reported cutting time from one or more other subjects or activities (social studies, science, art and music, physical education, and lunch or recess) at the elementary level. The decreases were not trivial, adding up to a total of 145 minutes per week across all of these subjects, on average, or nearly 30 minutes per day, for an average reduction of 32 percent in the total instructional time devoted to these subjects since 2001–02 (McMurrer, 2007).

Teachers and students have complied as well. "Teachers and principals are poring over test results with unprecedented intensity. Struggling students are receiving extra lessons in reading and math, sometimes at the expense of class time in other subjects," reports another study by the Center on Education Policy (Rentner et al., 2006, p. 2).

In addition to NCLB, the burgeoning high school reforms have resulted in 22 states requiring students to pass a state exit exam to receive their high school diploma. In 2006, 65 percent of the nation's high school students and 76 percent of the nation's minority high school students were enrolled in school in these 22 states. These "exit exams are encouraging teachers to spend more class time on tested subjects" (Kober et al., 2006, p. 5). More than limiting what is taught and learned, state tests also constrain how teaching and learning are conducted. A study found that more than 30 percent of teachers nationwide report that they do not use computers when teaching writing because the state writing test is handwritten (Russell & Abrams, 2004). This situation is astonishing considering that computers are not only the tool of the trade for writing but also have been found to be especially beneficial when used to teach writing. It is even more unsettling when one considers that schools are supposed to prepare students for the future, which is increasingly powered by technology.

The Road to Educational Dictatorship

Clearly, American education has been moving toward authoritarianism, letting the government dictate what and how students should learn and what schools should teach. This movement has been fueled mostly through fear—fear of threats from the Soviets, the Germans, the Japanese, the Koreans, the Chinese, and the Indians. The public, as any animal under threat would, has sought and accepted the action of a protector—the government.

However, like the missile gap, the so-called learning gap is a myth. The fear has been founded on misinformation and misperceptions. The road to authoritarianism has been built on incorrect assumptions and politics. In Chapter 3, I show that what have been considered the weaknesses of American education are precisely its strengths and that many countries in the world are working hard to emulate it. I also explain how reform proponents and concerned business executives misjudged, like the politicians before them, what really matters for an education system and what really counts as educational excellence.

3

Why America Hasn't Lost Yet:
Strengths of American Education

To succeed and to prosper in the creative age, the United States and other nations and regions around the world will need to make the transition from industrial to creative societies by investing in their people, building up their creative capital, and remaining open, tolerant societies.

—Richard Florida (2005, p. 245)

Every individual matters. Every individual has a role to play. Every individual makes a difference.

—Jane Goodall

A quarter of a century has passed since the publication of *A Nation at Risk*. The United States remains a superpower, dominating the world as the most scientifically and technologically advanced nation. The United States ranked number one out of 131 countries on the 2007–08 Global Competitiveness Index, which measures "the ability of countries to provide high levels of prosperity to their citizens" (World Economic Forum, 2007). The core innovations that drove the global digital revolution were created in the United States; the leaders of the computer and Internet industries are from the United States. Moreover, nearly two-thirds of the 300,000 patents issued in 2002 went to Americans (Florida, 2005). In a report prepared for the U.S. secretary of defense and released in 2008, researchers at the RAND Corporation found that the United States continued to lead the world in science and technology, accounting for 40 percent of total world spending on research and development, receiving 38 percent of the patents for new technology inventions issued in the industrialized nations, employing 70 percent of the world's Nobel Prize winners, and serving as home to three-fourths of the world's top 40 universities (Galama & Hosek, 2008, pp. xv–xvi).

For the American people, the last 25 years have not been as disastrous as one would have concluded from the gloomy assessment of *A Nation at Risk*. Despite the waves of economic turmoil, outcries about job losses, outsourcing, and the 9/11 terrorist attack, per capita income for Americans rose from $9,494 ($18,266 in 2006 dollars) in 1983 to $26,352 in 2006 (U.S. Census Bureau, 2008). The annual average unemployment rate declined from 9.6 percent in 1983 to 4.6 percent in 2007, according to data from the Bureau of Labor Statistics (2008). In terms of education attainment, an area that should be most directly connected to *A Nation at Risk*, the U.S. Census Bureau reported the following:

> In 2003, over four-fifths (85 percent) of all adults 25 years or older reported they had completed at least high school; over one in four adults (27 percent) had attained at least a bachelor's degree; both measures are all-time highs. In 2003, the percentage of the adult population who had completed high school increased for the first time since 2000, when it was 84 percent. (Stoops, 2004, p. 1)

In 2003, the National Science Foundation reported a 40 percent increase in the number of college graduates between 1993 and 2003, and a 1 percent increase in the number of all college graduates holding science and engineering jobs during the same period, from 11 percent in 1993 to 12 percent in 2003 (Kannankutty, 2005).

How could "a nation at risk" and a "generation of Americans that is scientifically and technologically illiterate" accomplish this?

Did the report-induced reforms lift U.S. education out of mediocrity and save the nation from crisis?

Apparently not. Although the report received tremendous attention and ushered in an era of education reform, "its goals have not yet been realized," according to Diane Ravitch (2003), former U.S. assistant secretary of education and professor at New York University. Many would agree.

In April 2008, U.S. Secretary of Education Margaret Spellings unveiled a report to commemorate the 25th anniversary of *A Nation at Risk*. The report gives what I consider an official assessment of the implementation of the specific recommendations made in *A Nation at Risk*. According to the report, progress has been made in only two out of the five areas recommended for improvement, and the two areas are directly related to NCLB: standards and accountability, and leadership and financial resources. In the other areas, curriculum content, teacher quality, and time, progress has been slow and little. In terms of curriculum content, the report says "it is a national shame that nearly a third of our high school students still do not take the rigorous program of study recommended in 1983 for all students," and "[b]oth easy courses and this smorgasbord still remain, with diluted content now hiding behind inflated course names. The educational achievement of 17-year-old students has largely stagnated since then" (U.S. Department of Education, 2008b, pp. 3–4). Although the "time dedicated to academics during the school day in the United States has risen slightly since 1983, . . . we are spending fewer hours per week on academic subjects and have a shorter school year than many other industrialized countries" (p. 6). And in terms of teacher quality, "while most teachers have taken the steps necessary to meet their states' Highly Qualified Teacher definition, there is little evidence to conclude that this provision has led to notable increases in the requisite subject-matter knowledge of teachers or to increases in measures of individual teacher effectiveness" (p. 6).

Roy Romer, former governor of Colorado, is the chair and chief spokesperson of Strong American Schools, a nonprofit project responsible for running Ed in '08, a campaign aimed at pushing a national curriculum and standards, more accountability, and teacher merit pay.

In April 2008, Romer wrote the following in an op-ed piece in the *Denver Post*: "[W]hile 'A Nation at Risk' was successful in transforming the national dialogue over education, it fell short in transforming our nation's education policies. In the 25 years since its release, many of the problems first noted in the report have actually gotten worse." In the same month, Romer's organization released a report titled *A Stagnant Nation: Why American Students Are Still at Risk*, which includes a "Report Card on Selected Reforms Recommended by *A Nation at Risk*." The report card lists the following "selected reforms":

- Content:
  - Raise high school graduation requirements.
- Standards:
  - Grades should be indicators of actual learning.
  - System of nationwide tests that signal readiness for the next stage of learning.
- Time:
  - Significantly expand students' learning time.
- Teaching:
  - Make teaching salaries performance-based and market-sensitive.

The report card shows *F*s on the first Standards reform component (grades) and on the Time and Teaching reforms. It shows a *C* on the second Standards reform component (nationwide tests) and an *A* on Content (Ed in '08, 2008, p. 4). In the press release accompanying this report, Romer is quoted as saying the following:

> Our schools have been underperforming for 25 years. America is slipping farther and farther behind the rest of the world academically because we have been unable to enact meaningful reforms or substantially improve student learning in the last quarter century. (Strong American Schools, 2008)

The fallacy seems obvious here. If American education has been at risk for more than 25 years—some say 40 years—and continues to deteriorate, and if education is said to determine a nation's and its citizens' success, how can we explain the fact that America continues to be competitive? We can come up with a number of propositions. The first is that education is not related to a country's economic success. This proposition can be easily refuted because it has been generally established that the educational attainment of a country's citizens has a direct effect on its economic prosperity and other indicators of success. The second proposition is that American education has not been in crisis—at least not in the way the reformers have suggested. The crisis was manufactured (Berliner & Biddle, 1995) for political reasons, as discussed in Chapter 2. A large portion of the evidence used to support the "crisis" assessment has been intentionally selected or misinterpreted, or is the result of deep social and cultural issues outside the schools. Keith Baker's study of the relationship (or lack thereof) between performance on international tests and indicators of nations' success discussed in Chapter 1 suggests a third possibility. Because test scores do not predict a nation's success and the persistent poor performance of American students on international tests since the 1960s has not resulted in its demise, it is useful to consider what really helped the United States to maintain its global lead.

Thus far, most international studies have focused on the technical aspect of education but failed to understand the philosophical aspects. Guided by the firm belief that test scores equal quality of education and, by association, quality of students as citizens, what is being taught, and how it is taught in schools, researchers have focused on how certain subjects (especially math, science, and reading) are taught in the classroom. They have also focused on how high-performing countries organize the knowledge into standardized curriculum, how national standards and high-stakes tests encourage teachers and students to spend more time on these subjects, and what distinguishes teachers in high-performing countries from low-performing ones. Of course, if we look hard enough, we can find answers. As a result, researchers have found differences between high-performing countries and low-performing ones in curriculum arrangement, teacher knowledge and practices, standards, and testing. These factors may explain the differences in test scores, but they are only a small part of the educational experiences of a child. What really matters, or what really helped the United States maintain its lead, may lie somewhere else, such as in the overall philosophical approach to education, the aggregation of all activities outside and inside the school, and how teachers and students treat one another.

Talent Shows: Showcasing the Strengths of American Education

It was an exciting day for the children at Central Elementary School in Okemos, Michigan. They had two opportunities to show their talents to their parents, friends, siblings, and classmates—one in the afternoon and one in the evening. I was invited to attend the evening performance by my 5th grade daughter. For about an hour, my wife and I, together with about 100 other parents, watched, laughed, and applauded as the show went on in the school gym with a makeshift stage. The 3rd, 4th, and 5th graders displayed their talents: singing, dancing, karate, piano, violin, drum, fashion show—anything as long as it was "G-rated," according to my 9-year-old. The event was funny, amusing, mesmerizing, and pride-invoking for the adults, but dead serious for the children. The performances were of uneven quality, as one might expect. Some were pretty good, but most were not that great. Nonetheless, all the performers won enthusiastic applause from the audience.

This was not the first time I had attended such an event involving my children. This was, I am certain, not the only such school event happening all around the country on that day. But every time I attend an event like this, I cannot help but discuss with my wife the differences between education in China and the United States. Both my wife and I were born in China and went through the Chinese education system, although in different situations. I attended a very impoverished rural village school, whereas she attended a much better school in a large city. All the students in my school were children of peasants, and most of the students in her school were children of college professors. But surprisingly, our reflections on the talent show were almost identical.

What struck us most is the lack of standards in these talent shows. There was no selection process to decide who was qualified to enter the show. All students in the three grades were invited and could enter the show if they filled out a form. The short audition was simply to let the organizers know what each student was planning to do. There was no judge, no assessment of the performance during the show. No prize or award was given after the show, either. But all the performers took the show seriously, dressed in their best, and some even appeared nervous. No doubt they worked very hard to win over the audience and took great pride in their "talents." And they were all rewarded. Regardless of what and how they performed, they received loud applause for their effort.

In the lack of standards and evaluation we see one of the greatest values of American culture expressed in education: the value of individuals. Deeply ingrained in the American culture are the fundamental rights of the individual, respect for and celebration of individual differences. The United States of America was founded on the principle that all persons have equal rights and that government is responsible to, and derives its powers from, its individual citizens. The Declaration of Independence and the Bill of Rights make clear that the very foundation of government rests on the inalienable rights of the people and of each individual. Throughout U.S. history, we have seen a constant struggle to protect individuals against the tyranny of government and special interest groups. Although not perfect, the United States is perhaps one of the few countries in the world where individuals are so valued. To a much greater degree than others in the world, Americans have espoused the belief of Albert Einstein that "all that is valuable in human society depends upon the opportunity for development accorded to the individual."

The talent show was a demonstration of this belief, expressed through the vehicle of American education, which according to Thomas Jefferson should be "adapted to the years, to the capacity, and the condition of every one, and directed to their freedom and happiness" (Jefferson, 1904, p. 204). Accordingly, all children have the right to pursue freedom and happiness. All children should be accepted and be provided with equal opportunity to help realize their potential. Thus, the talent show held by a public school should allow each child who wishes to participate to do so.

The lack of standards and assessment may provoke some critics of American education to argue that these kinds of practices lead to a lack of rigor in education, and it may be precisely that attitude that has caused American students' low performance on international tests. But I argue that activities such as the talent show at Central Elementary School represent one of the greatest strengths of American education for a number of reasons.

First, the talent show is inclusive. It enables everyone, not only those who are endowed with superior talents or family wealth, to participate. More important, it recognizes a broad range of talents, not only those sanctioned or desired by certain groups. As a result, it preserves a pool of diverse talents for the country, and such diversity is precisely one of the factors that has kept America strong (a point I discuss later in this chapter). It also teaches the children, our future citizens, to respect others, to understand that people have different talents and that all talents are needed. Furthermore, it broadens children's perspectives. Through these talent shows, they may discover new talents in their classmates, new talents in themselves, and new areas that they may become interested in.

Second, the talent show encourages initiative and responsibility. The freedom to enter the show is also a responsibility for the students. They must take the initiative to enter and assume the responsibility to prepare for the show, to be there on time, and to deliver their best performance. As well, they must face the consequences of their choice and actions. For these young children, it does take courage to face a public audience of their parents, siblings, and friends. But when they are intrinsically motivated, they become courageous. Being able to take initiative and assume responsibility is critical for successful citizens in modern society.

Third, the activity sends a strong message to the community, the public, and the parents that our schools value different talents, that their children are all talented in different ways. This message is important for parents because they often look to schools for criteria to judge their children, to assess how their children are doing in school. Maintaining a broad definition of success in the community is key to maintaining a diversity of talents in a society.

Last, the activity helps all the children to be proud of their strengths rather than focusing on their weaknesses. Everyone is talented, but in different ways and in different areas. By now, more than 25 years after Howard Gardner's seminal book *Frames of Mind: The Theory of Multiple Intelligences* was first published in 1983, we generally accept the idea that there is more than one "intelligence" and each of us possesses a unique set of intelligences. As Gardner wrote in his introduction to the 10th edition of his 1983 book,

> In the heyday of the psychometric and behaviorist eras, it was generally believed that intelligence was a single entity that was inherited; and that human beings—initially a blank slate—could be trained to learn anything, provided that it was presented in an appropriate way. Nowadays an increasing number of researchers believe precisely the opposite; that there exists a multitude of intelligences, quite independent of each other; that each intelligence has its own strengths and constraints; that the mind is far from unencumbered at birth; and that it is unexpectedly difficult to teach things that go against early "naïve" theories or that challenge the natural lines of force within an intelligence and its matching domains. (Gardner, 1993, p. xxiii)

Gardner initially proposed that the "multiple intelligences" included seven different types: linguistic, logical-mathematical, musical, bodily-kinesthetic, spatial, interpersonal, and intrapersonal. But seven is only an arbitrary figure for the ranges of human intelligences, as Gardner himself acknowledges. Later, he added more types.

Gardner suggests that each individual manifests varying levels of these different intelligences. That is, we are "intelligent" in different domains, more intelligent in some areas than others. In other words, we are born to be good at something but poor at other things. As a result, each of us has a unique talent profile.

Of course, most of us are not polarized—that is, able to do something extremely well but unable to do other things at all. This lack of extreme is why the majority of the population, regardless of race or gender, can sing, dance, play chess, learn to speak different languages, perform basic mathematical operations, learn to read and write, paint, and swim, but few of us can sing as well as Luciano Pavarotti, dance as well as Margot Fonteyn, play chess as well as Garry Kasparov, speak as many languages as Harold Williams, master mathematics as well as Johann Carl Friedrich Gauss, write as well as William Shakespeare, paint as well as Leonardo da Vinci, and swim as well as Susie O'Neill, no matter how hard we try.

The difference in our predisposition to learn something at birth, or aptitude, may not be huge in the majority of the human race, but it does result in differences in the speed we require to learn new things and the ultimate level we can reach. As Jane Goodall says in her book *In the Shadow of Man*, "Some humans are mathematicians; others aren't." This at least partially explains why some people are better at learning foreign languages than others, some students can learn to read earlier than others, and some can excel in math courses while others can play better music.

Talent shows and similar activities are the venues where children can discover their own unique talents and maintain a positive self-image. Because schools—American schools included—primarily focus on academic talents and discriminate against other talents, talent shows and the like become extremely important in helping children appreciate what they have, instead of what they don't have. Being able to recognize one's strengths and be supported by others is critical for success in later life, as Jenifer Fox (2008) writes in her book *Your Child's Strengths: Discover Them, Develop Them, Use Them*.

Talent shows are just one example from American education, which has traditionally created a culture that respects individual differences, endorses individual interests, and supports a broad range of talents. Other examples include the numerous after-school extracurricular activities, such as various clubs, athletic activities, music and art programs, scouts, and field trips. In comparison, Asian countries such as China and Japan spend much less time on extracurricular activities (Stevenson & Stigler, 1992). Traditional research has tried to draw a connection between students' involvement in extracurricular activities and their academic performance, which could be important. Although the research on the effects of extracurricular activities on academic performance remains inconclusive (Hunt, 2005), what such activities cultivate in a person and a people is perhaps much more important. For individuals, extracurricular activities affirm the value of their existence, boost their self-esteem and sense of success, encourage them to pursue their own interests, and help justify and maintain their interests. For a nation, a broader definition of success and of what talents are valuable, beyond academic performance in a few subjects, preserves and cultivates a diversity of talent. Such diversity is essential for adapting to changing societies and economies.

Learning from Honeybees: Advantages of Diversity

Scientists have found that genetic diversity enhances a population's ability to adapt to a changing environment. That is, the more genetically diverse a group is, the more likely it can survive and adapt to environmental changes. Genetic diversity also enhances productivity—at least among honeybees. Heather Mattila and Tom Seeley, two researchers at Cornell University, found that the productivity of the genetically diverse honeybee colonies far exceeded that of the uniform colonies during swarming, an energy- and resource-depleting activity that stresses the entire honeybee population (Mattila & Seeley, 2007).

Although biologists understand that diversity is important for a healthy ecosystem, "it is true of an economic system as well . . . the competitive place won't just focus on industrial diversity, but perhaps even more importantly on human diversity," according to urban development and planning expert Donovan Rypkema (Florida, 2005, pp. 35–36). The importance of talent diversity for national development has been well demonstrated by Richard Florida from an economic perspective and Amy Chua from a historical perspective.

In his two books about the so-called creative class—*The Rise of the Creative Class* and *The Flight of the Creative Class*—University of Toronto professor Richard Florida documents the increasing importance of creativity for economic growth and suggests that tolerance is one of the three factors (the other two being technology and talent) that drive economic growth and innovation in today's society. He and his colleagues studied economic growth in different regions in the United States to find out "why some places are better than others at

generating, attracting, and holding on to these critical factors of production," and their answer is "their openness, diversity, and tolerance—or lack thereof" (Florida, 2005, p. 38).

Tolerance is the central theme of Yale law professor Amy Chua's
book *Day of Empire: How Hyperpowers Rise to Global Dominance—and
Why They Fall*. In the book, she explains why and how "hyperpowers"—
countries that once gained world dominance—achieved and lost such
powerful positions in history. A historical look at the rise and demise
of various historical hyperpowers—Persia, Rome, Tang China, the
Mongols, the Dutch, the British, and the United States—reveals a simple yet fascinating pattern: these hyperpowers were all extraordinarily
tolerant, inclusive, and pluralistic. This does not necessarily mean that
the ruling class of these world-dominating powers treated all people
in their societies equally, at least by today's standards; but they all
found ways to fit the newly added peoples, either through coloniza-
tion or migration, into the existing society. Thus, Chua argues, the
hyperpowers succeeded by harnessing the skills and energies of individuals from very different backgrounds and by attracting and exploit-
ing highly talented groups that were excluded in other societies. And
these powers (except for the United States—at least not yet) ultimately
lost their dominance and faded into history because they somehow
lost their tolerance.

How does talent diversity work in relationship to a country's
prosperity? First, different talents complement each other. Economic
productivity or any large-scale projects, such as wars, require a multi-
tude of talents. It is difficult to imagine a war involving just one type
of individual. You need some who are good at planning, some good at
commanding, some good at information gathering, some good at pre-
dicting the weather, some good at geography, and some good at the
actual fighting. You need some for food preparation, some for logis-
tics, some for making weapons, some for using the weapons, and
some for entertaining the troops. The complementary function of
diverse talents is confirmed by research. Richard Florida (2005, p. 7)
cites research by Gianmarco Ottaviano of the University of Bologna
and Giovanni Peri of the University of California at Davis to show
the connection between ethnic and cultural diversity and economic

growth in U.S. regions. The researchers found that "a more multicultural urban environment makes U.S.-born citizens more productive" because the immigrants have skills that complement those of the American people, and they provide valuable services that Americans would prefer not to do.

Second, talent diversity breeds innovation and encourages innovators. Different talents bring different and often fresh perspectives. Historically, major changes in science, technology, business models, and social sciences were often started by individuals who were on the margin of, new to, or even outside the mainstream of the field they later contributed to. Taking the information technology industry as an example, Bill Gates of Microsoft, Steve Jobs of Apple Computers, Larry Ellison of Oracle, and Michael Dell of Dell Inc. all were young college dropouts and revolutionaries of the IT industry in their own ways. They brought different and fresh perspectives and were not part of the establishment. In the IT industry, cultural and ethnic diversity seems to play a role as well. Google's cofounder Sergey Brin is a Russian immigrant; eBay's founder, Pierre M. Omidyar, is a French-born Iranian immigrant; and Yahoo's cofounder Jerry Yang is a Chinese immigrant from Taiwan.

Third, talent diversity prepares societies for change. Just as genetic diversity is critical for the viability of biological species, so is talent diversity for societies. When the natural environment changes and new diseases develop, genetic diversity makes it possible for species to adapt to these changes and avoid being wiped out. Human societies change, too. New technologies bring new industries and render old ones obsolete, thus displacing jobs. Competitors from foreign countries or regions force changes in industries when they gain advantage in terms of labor costs, access to markets, or natural resources. To cope with major changes, a society needs a diverse pool of talent to continually lead new development and work in the new industries.

In the last century, the U.S. economy has gone through significant transformations. One hundred years ago, in the early part of the 20th century, the structure of employment dramatically shifted from agriculture to industry. In the decades following World War II, the U.S. economy transformed again, this time from industry to services. In 1900, almost 38 percent of the U.S. workforce was employed in agriculture; the number dropped to 6 percent in 1960. Today, less than 1 percent of the U.S. workforce is in agriculture (Florida, 2005). Manufacturing, the largest component of the industrial or goods sector, employed 13.5 million people in 1947 and peaked in 1979 with 19.5 million employees, but has since dropped to 14.5 million; the share of manufacturing in total nonfarm employment declined from 33 percent to 11 percent (Bureau of Labor Statistics, 2008). In the meantime, the total number of employees in the service sector has increased dramatically. The service sector includes the following "supersectors" defined by the Bureau of Labor Statistics: trade, transportation, and utilities; information; financial activities; professional and business services; education and health services; leisure and hospitality; other services; and public administration. Since 1945, the total number of employees in the service sector has increased from 25 million to 109.3 million.

Major shifts in employment structure indicate dramatic changes in the need for different kinds of talent. To cope with these changes, a diverse pool of talent can adapt much more effectively than an impoverished one. For example, if everyone in the United States had been good only at manufacturing, it would have been very difficult for the country to quickly adapt to new industries such as information technology, which has grown significantly since the 1990s as the manufacturing industry has declined.

"Children Are Like Popcorn": Second Chances

"Children are like popcorn," Mrs. Lippe, my son's 1st grade teacher, told me at a parent-teacher conference. "They all pop, some sooner and some later," she added, "but in the end, they all pop." Mrs. Lippe's words are still fresh in my mind after almost 10 years. During those 10 years, I have met many teachers in different situations, including those who took my classes, attended my lectures, joined international study tours I led, and, of course, taught my two children. I found that Mrs. Lippe's view of children is shared by many of the teachers I have interacted with in the United States. The belief that every child can "pop," can learn, and can prosper is deeply ingrained in the mind of American teachers. As a result of this belief, American students are given many "second chances" instead of being judged and sorted into different groups based on their performance at a very early stage.

Different societies take different approaches to talent development. American sociologist Ralph Turner contrasted two different systems of social mobility through education in an essay published in *American Sociological Review.* In this essay, Turner (1960) compares secondary education in the United States and Britain and suggests that the American system is characterized by "contest mobility," whereas "sponsored mobility" is norm in the British system. According to Turner, in a system of contest mobility, everyone is assumed to be equal and participates in the same contest for upward social mobility. Achievement is attributed directly to the effort each contestant puts in. Those individuals who put in more effort are better rewarded as "the governing objective of contest mobility is to give elite status to those who earn it. . . . Under the contest system society at large establishes and interprets the criteria of elite status" (p. 858). Contest mobility systems tend not to make early decisions and judgments about an individual—the race is always going on and people should have many opportunities to participate. As a result, in contest mobility systems, individual talents, as diverse as they may be, are tolerated and preserved until much later, when specialization is called for.

In contrast, in systems of sponsored mobility, an individual's admission to the elite groups is sponsored by the existing elites, similar to the process of gaining access to exclusive social clubs that only admit new members sponsored by existing members. Sponsored mobility systems tend to identify potential members for each social group early, according to their perceived "qualifications" and "merit." Students in sponsored mobility systems are subject to path-defining examinations and tests early in their life and are sorted accordingly toward the forms of schooling and training that are deemed "appropriate" to their perceived talents and that will determine their subsequent educational and occupational careers. Consequently, in sponsored mobility systems, the talents that are valued and hence suitable for promoting to elite social groups are announced and encouraged early, whereas other talents are suppressed or sorted into less desirable social groups.

Correspondingly, contest mobility systems are likely to follow a decentralized education model, in which local control of schooling is encouraged. The local community, parents, educators, and students are allowed to make decisions about what is important to teach and learn. There is generally no high-stakes testing that follows a centralized curriculum or academic standards. In contrast, for a sponsored mobility system to function, it must have standardized tests, and the tests are used almost as the exclusive mechanism to sort students. These tests typically focus on the talents or knowledge deemed valuable by the elite groups.

The American education system is a quintessential example of the contest mobility model. It provides a more egalitarian platform for individuals to develop their talents and pursue their interests by delaying selection until after high school. In this system, students are not sorted early on into different tracks in school (which lead to different social groups after school) based on a few high-stakes tests. Students thus have ample opportunity to experiment with different activities and programs before graduating from high school.

As a result, this system gives "late bloomers" a chance to succeed. It is no secret that individuals develop at different paces, as Mrs. Lippe said. For genetic and environmental reasons, some individuals develop their talents earlier and faster than others. Even two individuals with the same level of giftedness can have two different developmental trajectories, according to psychologist Dean Simonton (2005), a distinguished professor at the University of California at Davis. An early selection approach would favor only the "early bloomers," but not everyone is a child prodigy. Instead, history has witnessed plenty of late bloomers in all fields of human activity. They are like the ugly duckling in Hans Christian Andersen's story. In his early life, the young swan was ugly, clumsy, and strange, judged based on the standards of ducks. He was too large, ate too much, and did not have the same beautiful feathers as his duck brothers. It was not until he was fully developed that he found out he was actually a swan, and a beautiful one.

In addition to providing opportunities to succeed, the contest mobility model provides a broad range of opportunities for individuals to explore their interests, because it doesn't sort them when they are young. The American system attempts to treat everyone equally and provides the same opportunities to all students. The students thus can try out different options and decide what they would like to pursue much later than students in some other countries. We all know that we are not really certain about what we want to do or what we are good at until we have experienced it; this is especially true when we are young. We know plenty of people who change their interests and their careers during their lifetime. Schools thus should be the place for us to experience and experiment with different options in life and decide what we want to pursue later. This opportunity is critical in helping individuals discover their true passion and fully develop their strengths.

Being able to work on things that we truly love not only makes it more enjoyable for us but also increases our productivity. When we are passionate about what we do, we are more likely to put in more effort and be more creative. It appears that the American education system has indeed produced a workforce that is more concerned about personal interest than external reward. A World Values Survey found that when asked to select the important aspects in a job, about 82 percent of Americans mentioned "a job that is interesting." In stark contrast, only 18 percent of Chinese mentioned this. More than 42 percent of Americans selected "Doing an important job" as their first choice when looking for a job, while only 23 percent of Chinese made the same choice (World Values Survey, 1999–2004).

Furthermore, the American education system has helped its graduates to develop a belief that their own efforts can make a difference in their life and in the world. It instills in them a "can-do" spirit regardless of their own backgrounds. It helps develop the American cultural ethos that is embedded in the American dream, portrayed by such writers as Horatio Alger. This has been confirmed by empirical research. For example, Deborah Abowitz (2005), a sociology professor of Bucknell University, conducted a study of American college students and found that they indeed believed in the American dream and the notion that with hard work anything is possible. She found that the students strongly supported the statement that "one can live well in America" and strongly disagreed that family background was the most important factor in determining social mobility.

An Imperfect System That Others Seek to Emulate

My comments on the strengths of the American education system can be and have been perceived by many as an unqualified endorsement, as if I were saying that American education is perfect. The truth is that I am very critical of American education. In no way do I think American education is perfect. It is riddled with serious problems, such as the vast inequalities between the rich and the poor; the outdated, irrelevant, and America-centric curriculum; the lack of qualified teachers; the disengagement of students; and the increasing faith in testing.

Moreover, the strengths I praise can also be viewed by some as weaknesses. The amount of time American children devote to talent shows, athletic activities, and other social interactions necessarily takes away time and attention that could be devoted to studying the core academic subjects, for example. The contest mobility model, although creating an environment in which individuals can explore their own interests, participate equally in the contest for as long as possible, and try out a broad range of subjects before specialization, can be viewed as a waste of time and resources. The "mile wide and inch deep" curriculum affords more flexibility for students and teachers to learn and teach, but it does allow the possibility that some teachers and schools may choose to do only the minimum, in which case the students suffer from low expectations and a lack of rigor.

Consequently, the strengths of American education are also at least partially responsible for the poor performance of U.S. students on international tests. They spend considerably less time on the tested subjects such as math, reading, and science than their peers in high-performing countries because they are engaged in other activities. And time on task is perhaps one of the best predicators of performance. In addition, not everyone in the United States views math, science, and reading as the most important thing in life, and as a result not everyone puts in as much effort on them. When compared with students in other countries where test scores in math, reading, and science matter so much to social mobility that almost everyone focuses on these subjects, it should be no surprise that U.S. students do not test as well. Put another way, suppose we have two groups of 10 individuals. In one group everyone studies math, and in the other each member studies something different. We should expect that the first group will perform better, on average, than the second group, on math tests. But the first group would do poorly when judged against measures of diversity or performances in areas other than math.

We thus face a choice of what we want: a diversity of talents, of individuals who are passionate, curious, self-confident, and risk taking; or a nation of excellent test takers, outstanding performers on math and reading tests.

The current education reformers in the United States seem to have made a choice, albeit a wrong one, in my opinion. The reformers have chosen test scores in a limited number of subject areas (the core academics) over diversity, individual interests, creativity, and the risk-taking spirit that has helped sustain a strong economy and society in the United States. In fairness, the reformers, the proponents of standards and standardization, accountability, and the core academics, do not really intend to destroy the strengths of American education. They reason that standards, accountability, and high-stakes testing will not lead to the loss of the traditional strengths of American education, that creativity and high academic achievement are not mutually exclusive, and that knowledge of math, reading, and science are the most important knowledge for the future.

I, too, would like to believe these arguments and would like to see excellent academic achievement, great test scores in math and science, and all our children "above average," like the children in Garrison Keillor's Lake Wobegon. And it seems theoretically possible. But unfortunately, the reality does not seem to support the belief. As mentioned in Chapter 1, NCLB has already led to a narrowing of curriculum, elimination or reduction of time devoted to other activities and subjects that are not directly related to improved test scores in math and reading, and teachers shifting their focus to teach to the test.

An even more illuminating way to understand the consequences of standards, high-stakes testing, and an exclusive focus on a narrow set of subjects is to examine other education systems that have a long history of implementing these strategies and are eager to abandon them. There are many such educational systems, including those in

China, South Korea, Singapore, and Japan. These countries, like the United States, have embarked on massive education reforms, but their reform efforts are moving in the opposite direction. These countries have been admired by Americans as models of excellence because of their impressive performance on international comparative tests in math, science, and reading. However, their reform efforts seem to be emulating American education: more local autonomy, more flexibility, more choice, less testing, less content, and less standardization. Let's examine these examples more closely.

China

In 1999, the highest governing bodies of China (the Central Committee of the Chinese Communist Party and the State Council) issued the *Decision to Further Educational Systemic Reform and Promote Quality-Oriented Education* (Zhonggong Zhongyang [Central Committee of the Chinese Communist Party] & Guowuyuan [State Council], 1999). The document establishes the fundamental goal of Chinese education as providing all children, the socialist successors, with quality education that promotes moral, academic, physical, and aesthetic excellence. It announces a series of significant changes in China's education system:

• Abolish the entrance examination for middle school. All elementary school students should enter middle school directly, without taking an exam.

• Encourage secondary and elementary schools to implement their own graduation examinations.

• Develop new approaches for evaluating and assessing schools, teachers, and students that are consistent with the spirit of "quality education."

• Forbid local governments from imposing admission rates on schools and using admission rates as measures of school quality. The public, parents, and students should be encouraged to contribute to the evaluation of schools.

• Reform college entrance exams and admissions. The subjects and content of college entrance exams should focus on assessing students' abilities and overall qualities. Qualified provincial governments are encouraged to implement a variety of experiments with the college admissions and exam systems. Grant colleges more autonomy in admissions decisions.

• Expand access to higher education. By 2010, the gross enrollment rate in higher education should reach 15 percent.

• Reform school curriculum and diversify textbooks.

In 2001, the Ministry of Education introduced a set of policies focusing on curriculum reform (Jiaoyubu [Ministry of Education], 2001). The most significant ones are the following: (1) develop new curriculum standards to replace the national syllabus, and restructure school curriculum to allow more flexibility at the school level and more choices for students; (2) allow any publisher to publish textbooks following the curriculum standards, which essentially ends the 50-year monopoly of the People's Education Press, formerly a branch of the ministry; and (3) grant local governments the freedom to choose textbooks.

The new curriculum aims to "equip students with patriotism, collectivism, a love for socialism, and the Chinese cultural traditions, as well as moral-ethic values, democratic spirit with Chinese characteristics" (Jiaoyubu, 2001). Furthermore, the new curriculum has as its goal fostering creativity, developing practical abilities, and cultivating scientific and humanistic spirit as well as environmental awareness. It is also intended to ensure that students develop physical and mental fitness, good aesthetic tastes, and healthy lifestyles.

South Korea

In 2001, South Korea, one of the consistent top performers in international comparative studies such as TIMSS, released a new national curriculum, the 7th National Curriculum (Ministry of Education and Human Resources Development, 2001). It aims to cultivate creative, autonomous, and self-driven individuals who will lead the era's developments in information, knowledge, and globalization through a number of strategies:

• Promote fundamental and basic education that fosters sound human beings and nurtures creativity.

• Help students build self-leading capacity so that they well meet the challenges of today's globalization and information development.

• Implement learner-oriented education that suits the students' capability, aptitude, and career development needs.

• Ensure expanded autonomy for the local community and schools in curriculum planning and operation.

Singapore

Since 1997, Singapore, another frequent high flyer in international comparative studies, has engaged in a major curriculum reform initiative. Titled *Thinking Schools, Learning Nation*, this initiative aims to develop all students into active learners with critical thinking skills and to develop a creative and critical thinking culture within schools. Its key strategies include the following:

• Explicitly teach critical and creative thinking skills.
• Reduce subject content.
• Revise assessment modes.
• Place greater emphasis on processes instead of on outcomes when appraising schools.

In 2005, the Ministry of Education in Singapore released another major policy document, *Nurturing Every Child: Flexibility and Diversity in Singapore Schools*, which called for a more varied curriculum, a focus on learning rather than teaching, and more autonomy for schools and teachers (Ministry of Education, 2005).

Japan

Since 2001, Japan has been working to implement its *Education Plan for the 21st Century*, which has three major objectives. The first is "enhancing emotional education," that is, cultivating students as emotionally well-rounded human beings. The second objective is "realizing a school system that helps children develop their individuality and gives them diverse choices" by moving toward a diverse, flexible educational system that encourages individuality and cultivates creativity. The third is "promoting a system in which the school's autonomy is respected" through decentralizing educational administration, enhancing local autonomy, and enabling independent self-management at the school level (Iwao, 2000).

Divergent Paths

Clearly our Asian counterparts have taken a very different—in fact, opposite—approach in their education reform efforts. While the United States is moving toward more standardization and centralization, the Asian countries are working hard to allow more flexibility and autonomy at the local level. While the United States is investing resources to ensure that all students take the same courses and pass the same tests, the Asian countries are advocating for more individualization and attending to emotions, creativity, and other skills. While the United States is raising the stakes on testing, the Asian countries are exerting great efforts to reduce the power and pressure of testing.

Why are the Asian countries, which some American reformers admire, eager to abandon their education tradition, which seems to have resulted in high test scores or academic excellence, and instead learn from America? The answer is simple: because they know very well the damage that results from standardization and high-stakes testing. In the next chapter, I use China as an example to show the wide range of negative consequences of excessive testing and standardization.

4

Why China Isn't a Threat Yet:
The Costs of High Scores

*Some labor with their minds, and some labor with their
strength. Those who labor with their minds govern others;
those who labor with their strength are governed by
others.*

— Mencius, Chinese philosopher

*I would suggest that all students be given an additional
hour of sleep. . . . Be sure to make nine hours of sleep a
rule. An order to this effect should be issued and enforced;
there should be no argument about it. Let young people
have enough sleep, and the teachers too.*

— Mao Tse-tung

On November 20, 2006, China's Premier Wen Jiabao invited six education leaders in higher and basic education to the State Council for a
special meeting that also included high-level government officials in
charge of education. "I have been pondering over a few questions for
quite a while now, and I want to ask for your advice today," Wen said,
opening the meeting in his usual straightforward and humble manner.
He then told of a visit with Qian Xuesen, a well-known rocket scientist

who had studied at MIT, received his Ph.D. from the California Institute of Technology, and served on the faculty there before returning to China in the 1950s and leading China's early space programs. "Last year when I visited Qian Xuesen, he told me that one of the important reasons that China has not fully developed is that not one university has been able to follow a model that can produce creative and innovative talents; none has its own unique innovations, and thus has not produced distinguished individuals." Wen continued, "In my understanding, Mr. Qian's 'distinguished individuals' are not ordinary talents, but truly distinguished masters. Our student population has been on the rise, and our universities are getting larger, but how to prepare more distinguished talents? This is a question that causes great anxiety in me." Wen spent the next three hours listening and talking with the participants (B. Li, 2006).

Premier Wen's Anxiety

Wen has plenty of reasons to be anxious and concerned over the shortage of creative and innovative talent. Despite China's astounding double-digit growth for more than two decades, its economy remains one that is labor intensive rather than knowledge intensive. The growth has been largely fueled by its vast and cheap labor instead of technology. In other words, as the "world's factory," China has been mostly making things invented or designed elsewhere (Shenkar, 2006). According to a report of the Chinese National Statistics Bureau, only about 2,000 Chinese companies owned the patent for the core technology used in the products they produced in 2005; that number represents less than 0.003 percent of all Chinese companies in that year (X. Zhao & Wu, 2005). As a result, although products worth billions of dollars are made *in* China, they are not made *by* China. For example, only the four wheels and one battery on the Hyundai automobile produced at the Hyundai plant in Beijing are made by China (Wen, 2008).

As such, cheap labor does not generate large profits. Bo Xilai, China's former minister of commerce, once told a group of French business leaders that in order for China to import one Airbus 380 aircraft, it needs to export 800 million shirts (Xinhua News Agency, 2005). Bo's comment illustrates the problems of China's labor-intensive and low-profit economy. An even more telling example is the toy industry in China, which exports about 70 percent of the world's toys. On average, China makes about half of a U.S. dollar for a toy with a $10 retail price in the United States or Europe (*Beijing Youth Newspaper*, 2003). Worse yet, a worker in China is paid 17 U.S. cents for the Bratz doll that sells for $16 or more in the U.S. retail market (Rushe, 2006).

An economy built on cheap labor is very volatile in a world where plenty of countries have a cheap workforce. Rising labor costs and increasing value of its currency have already threatened China's status as the "world's factory." Thousands of factories in the Pearl River Delta region have been closed since 2007. Located in south China, with easy access to Hong Kong and Taiwan, the region has been the gem of China's economic growth since the late 1980s, with more than 40 percent of China's total exported goods manufactured there (Sina.com, 2007). Despite tens of thousands of companies in the Pearl River Delta region, not one has invented a single product that has been adopted and used widely (Sina.com, 2007). With labor costs, the value of the RMB (China's currency), and the price of raw materials and energy all rising, these companies have no choice but to close or relocate. A similar trend is sweeping across the Yangtze River Delta, another region that has enjoyed impressive economic prosperity since the late 1980s.

China understands the importance of technology and innovations. It has adopted a so-called market for technology strategy, expecting that by opening its vast and lucrative market, it can somehow obtain technology from advanced countries (Shenkar, 2006). But after 20 years, it has realized that the strategy does not really work. Today, China has joined the World Trade Organization and opened its market, but it has not received the kind of technology transfer it expected. All major industries, from cars to aircraft, from computers to medicine, from railroads to mining, are dominated by foreign corporations that own the core technologies. China, despite its effort to insist that foreign companies transfer technology, remains low on the value chain.

Indigenous innovation is still a dream for China, according to Oded Shenkar (2006), a professor of management at Ohio State University and author of *The Chinese Century*, a book that by and large praises China's development and predicts that China will be a superpower of the 21st century. Shenkar uses the number of patent applications and granted patents to show how China has failed to "establish, so far, an effective indigenous network of technological innovation" (p. 69). Only 200 applications were filed by Chinese nationals in 1995, and 299 in 1997. According to Lu Yongxiang, president of China's Academy of Sciences and vice chairman of the Standing Committee of the National People's Congress, 99 percent of Chinese companies did not apply for a single patent between 1998 and 2003 (Sun, 2006).

The number dramatically increased in 2005, when China ranked third in patent applications, with an increase of 33 percent from the year before, according to statistics reported by the World Intellectual Property Organization (WIPO). However, only about 50 percent of the 170,000 patent applications submitted to China's State Intellectual Property Office in 2005 were from within China. In addition, the number of patent applications filed does not necessarily correspond to the number of patents granted. In 2005, only 21,519 patents originating in China were granted, while more than 134,000 originating in the United States were granted (WIPO, 2007).

The types of patents make a big difference, too. In 2001, more than 72 percent of the patents granted to foreigners by the Chinese patent office were in the category of invention, whereas only 5.43 percent granted to Chinese nationals fell in this category. Most of the patents granted to Chinese were in the other two categories: appearance and functional design (Shenkar, 2006). Thus patent applications do not necessarily reflect innovation, as Chen Naiwei, director of the Intellectual Property Research Center at Shanghai Jiaotong University, cautions. In an article by the Science and Development Network, a nonprofit organization based in the United Kingdom that tracks science development in developing countries, Chen is quoted as saying, "In order to encourage patent applications, many local governments have provided patent fees to enterprises and science institutes, resulting in the rapid growth in application number." Chen also confirmed earlier findings about the types of patent applications filed by Chinese: "Most patents filed in China are for new design appearance or new models, which do not require great technical innovation" (H. Jia, 2007).

Chinese leaders like Wen are aware of the danger of an economy dependent on cheap labor instead of technology. Just a few months before Wen's meeting, the Chinese president and Communist Party leader Hu Jintao called for the country to become a country of innovations in his speech at the National Science and Technology Conference. Hu expressed deep concerns about the nation's scientific and technological achievement: "Presently our nation's overall science and technology development remains significantly behind advanced nations in the world and cannot support our nation's social and economical development" (Hu, 2006). In the speech, Hu issued the challenge to build China into an "innovative nation," which later was written as a national goal in the report of the 17th Congress of the Chinese Communist Party in 2008.

Innovation comes from innovative people. "The key to scientific and technological innovations is talents," said Hu in his speech. "Excellent scientists and groups of science and technology talents are the decisive factor of a nation's science and technology advancement." But China has "a severe shortage of outstanding talents in science and technology," according to President Hu. Hence Premier Wen Jiabao's meeting with education leaders described at the beginning of the chapter.

Americans' Glorification of China's Education System

President Hu and Premier Wen's assessment of China's shortage of innovative talent highlights the gravest challenge facing China in its effort to become a truly modernized nation, a challenge often masked by its rapid economic development and statistics related to educational accomplishments, and a challenge many outside observers fail to notice. China's economic performance has been nothing but stunning. With two decades of double-digit growth, China has emerged as an economic giant, surpassing the United Kingdom and France to become the fourth-largest economy in the world measured by gross domestic product (GDP).

Equally stunning are China's educational accomplishments. China presently operates the world's largest formal education system, with a total student population of more than 300 million, an increase of 100 million since 1985 (Chinese Ministry of Education, 2007b). China has almost eliminated illiteracy among its 1.3 billion citizens (Asia Society, Business Roundtable, & Council of Chief State School Officers, 2005). By 2007, China had extended its nine-year compulsory education program to 99 percent of the age cohorts, an increase of 7.2 percent nationwide since 2003, and an increase of 21 percent in the western, less developed areas (Xinhua News Agency, 2008). In 1978, 400,000 out of 11 million who participated in the first college entrance exam after the Cultural Revolution (winter of 1977 and summer of 1978) were admitted to college, with an admissions ratio of 29 to 1. In 2007, about 9.5 million students took the college entrance exam and about 6 million of them were admitted to college, for an admissions rate of 1.9 to 1, which means nearly 60 percent of those who took the exam were admitted to higher education institutions. The number of undergraduate students increased to more than 17 million in 2006 from just over 1 million in 1980, and the number of graduate (master's and doctoral) students grew 50-fold, from 21,604 in 1980 to more than one million in 2006 (Chinese Ministry of Education, 2007a).

China's amazing accomplishments in education have not gone unnoticed by outside observers. For example, the Asia Society, a New York-based nonprofit organization that promotes understanding of Asia, recently published two reports praising China's education system and suggesting what the United States can learn from China. One report was coauthored with the Business Roundtable and the Council of Chief State School Officers. Titled *Education in China: Lessons for U.S. Educators*, it was the result of a study tour by a delegation of American K–12 education and business leaders who "met with Chinese students, teachers, principals, researchers, and senior government officials, including the Minister of Education" (Asia Society et al., 2005, p. 5). The second report, *Math and Science Education in a Global Age: What the U.S. Can Learn from China*, was based on a conference on math and science education in China and the United States organized by the Asia Society and bringing together high-level government officials and scholars from both China and the United States (Asia Society, 2006).

The Asia Society is, of course, not the only admirer of Chinese education. "Already, China has pulled way ahead of the U.S. and the rest of the world by one key measure," writes journalist John Schmid (2003) of the *Milwaukee Journal Sentinel*. "China graduates in excess of three times more engineers—electrical, industrial, bio-chemical, semiconductor, mechanical, even power generation—with bachelor's degrees than the U.S. university system." In this case, admiration also became a warning to the United States. The gap between the number of engineering graduates in China and in the United States later gained more credibility and significance in a report from the National Academies (National Academy of Sciences, National Academy of Engineering, Institute of Medicine, and the National Research Council). The press release for the report, *Rising Above the Gathering Storm* (Committee on Prospering in the Global Economy of the 21st Century [National Academies], 2006), gives actual numbers to show how China and India are already ahead of the United States in preparing engineers: "Last year more than 600,000 engineers graduated from institutions of higher education in China. In India the figure was 350,000. In America, it was about 70,000" (National Academies, 2005). These numbers were later proven to be grossly exaggerated due to a lack of understanding of how China defines "engineers," but "given this lofty pedigree [of the National Academies], the statistics then appeared in the *New York Times*, the *Boston Globe*, the *Chicago Tribune* and on many Web sites" to show that China's education system had surpassed that of the United States (Bracey, 2006b).

The glorification of China's education is not just a recent phenomenon. Many media stories, scholarly works, and personal observations praising Chinese education have come out over the years. Of the many works that promote the perception that China provides a better education to its children than the United States, Harold Stevenson and James Stigler's book *The Learning Gap: Why Our Schools Are Failing and What We Can Learn from Japanese and Chinese Education* is perhaps the most influential. The book was first published in 1992, and a second edition was published in 2006, which indicates that "after so many years, the book is still being read" (Stevenson & Stigler, 2006, p. 5). The authors used a combination of test scores and observations of the behaviors of teachers, parents, and students to show how Chinese and Japanese education is better than American education. In fairness, the authors did "warn the reader that our writing focuses more often on the positive aspects of Asian education and parenting than problems" (p. 9), and their discussion covers only elementary schools. However, the positive aspects are so overwhelming and the authors dismiss so many of the negative aspects of Asian education as "common stereotypes" or biases that it is not difficult to read the book as a complete endorsement of Chinese and Japanese education. Compared with Americans, Chinese and Japanese students have higher academic achievement in math and reading; they spend more time in school and on school subjects at home; their parents hold higher expectations of them; their teachers are better prepared and teach more effectively; and their social life and schools are better oriented to help them achieve academically (Stevenson & Stigler, 2006).

A more recent glorification came in a different format—the documentary film *Two Million Minutes*, described in Chapter 1. The film, which compares the lives of six high school seniors—two each from the United States, India, and China—shows that the American students spend much more time socializing and playing sports than the Chinese and Indian students, who spend more time on academics while also taking part in other activities such as music and sports. The implication is that the Indian and Chinese students are thus better prepared to compete in the global economy.

The Meaning of Good Education: Reconciling the Contradiction

Premier Wen Jiabao's concern over China's shortage of "distinguished talents" in science and technology is valid; so are the praise and glorification of China's education achievements. The two perspectives may appear to contradict each other, yet both are true reflections of Chinese education. In fact, the same contradiction exists in the U.S. education system, albeit in a different way. As discussed in Chapters 1 and 3, although American students' academic performance as measured by tests in certain subjects is worrisome, the United States remains strong in science, technology, and other economic activities, which suggests that American education has defied the "crisis label" and been able to produce the talent necessary to support the nation's economy. These seeming contradictions are mere reflections of our measures of the quality of education.

The common measure of the quality of a nation's education system has generally been associated with schooling: percentage of population having access to schools, school completion rates at different levels, years of schooling, quality of teachers and teaching, and students' performance on what schools teach and test (as indicated by grades and standardized test scores). Using these school-oriented measures, education in the United States can be said to be on the decline, problem ridden, and in crisis, whereas education in China can be said to be making great progress, on the rise, and worth emulating.

The other measure is the quality of the products of an education system. The quality of a person is difficult to describe in specific terms, but generally it is the total package of knowledge, ability, attitudes, perspectives, moral values, and ethical standards. It is what the person can do in real life instead of scores received or years spent in school. This measure is unfortunately not always quantifiable, but it is more important because it is more relevant to a person's well-being and what that person can contribute to society.

This measure takes a longer-term view than measuring what a student learns in school weekly, monthly, or annually. It looks at a country's economic development and what a person can actually do in real life and work. Judged on this measure, China's education seems to be consistent with Premier Wen's assessment. First, as noted earlier, knowledge and innovation coming from the indigenous talent pool— the products of the Chinese education system—contribute little to the Chinese economy. Second, despite the millions of college graduates, multinational companies in China are having a difficult time finding qualified candidates for their positions (Farrell & Grant, 2005). According to a recent survey of U.S.-owned enterprises conducted by the American Chamber of Commerce in Shanghai, 37 percent of the companies responding said that finding talent was their biggest operational problem. A separate study by the *McKinsey Quarterly* found that

44 percent of the executives at Chinese companies reported that insufficient talent was the biggest barrier to their global ambitions (Lane & Pollner, 2008). Third, a study by the global consulting firm McKinsey found that fewer than 10 percent of Chinese college graduates would be suitable for work in foreign companies (Farrell & Grant, 2005). Fourth, a large proportion of college graduates have not been able to find employment. According to statistics released by the Ministry of Education, the one-time placement rate for college graduates has been hovering around 70 percent since the year 2000. In 2007, China graduated about 4.1 million college students, and about 70 percent of them found employment, which means more than one million did not have a job when they graduated (Tian, 2008).

Ideally, the two measures of education quality should be consistent. That is, the quality of education measured by school-related factors, such as test scores, should consistently predict the performance of school graduates in society. But unfortunately, this is often not the case. As Daniel Goleman (1995) writes in his classic book *Emotional Intelligence: Why It Can Matter More Than IQ*, "One of psychology's open secrets is the relative inability of grades, IQ, or SAT scores, despite their popular mystique, to predict unerringly who will succeed in life. . . . At best, IQ contributes about 20 percent to the factors that determine life success, which leaves 80 percent to other forces" (p. 34). One of the reasons for this inconsistency lies in Albert Einstein's famous saying: "Not everything that can be counted counts, and not everything that counts can be counted." Another related reason is that what schools value and measure may not be what is important in real life. Worse yet, what is valued in schools may hurt what is valuable in real life, resulting in high performers in school but low performers in society. This is what has happened to education in China.

The Land of High-Stakes Testing

I would not be writing this book if I had been born one year later, because 1982, the year I graduated from high school, was the last year that mathematics was not required for admission to all college majors.

The Cultural Revolution had completely disrupted China's education system. Between 1977, the year when China resumed using national college entrance exams to select college students, and 1982, math was not counted toward the total score that was used as the sole criterion for college admission for foreign language majors. Foreign languages (primarily English and some Russian) were only partially counted for other majors. I was not good at math (although later in life I developed computer software on statistics, learned to do computer programming with complicated databases, and designed computer games). I was not particularly good at English, either, considering that I had only two years of English taught by a teacher who himself was only a high school graduate and barely knew English. But to avoid math, I chose to major in English language education, and luckily my scores in Chinese language, history, and geography were high enough for me to be admitted to the newly developed English Language Education major at Sichuan Institute of Foreign Languages in Chongqing, China. If I had been born a year later and had to take the exam in 1983, I am sure I would not have been able to get into college because I would have failed the entrance exam's math portion, on which I scored 3 points out of 100.

Education always performs two functions—to select and to educate. A nation's education system functions on behalf of society to decide what kind of talents, knowledge, and skills are useful and what kinds are not. It is intended to cultivate the ones that are valuable and suppress the ones that are deemed undesirable. High-stakes testing is one of the most effective ways to convey what a society values and to pressure all involved in education—parents, teachers, and, of course, students—to focus all their efforts on what is tested.

China has a long history of using tests to select government officials, the elite class. As early as AD 605, during the Sui dynasty (AD 581–618), the central government began to use a national exam system to select government officials. The system, the *keju*, also known as the Imperial Exam or Civil Exam, was further developed during the Tang dynasty (AD 618–907) and continued to be used by successive emperors until 1905, when it was officially abandoned by Emperor Guangxu of the Qing dynasty (1636–1912).

Hailed by some as China's fifth grand invention (after the compass, gun powder, paper, and movable type), the *keju* was an effective way for the emperors to identify and recruit talented individuals to join the ruling class from a broad pool—that is, the whole nation instead of just a small group of existing elites and their descendents. One of the greatest emperors of the most prosperous dynasty in Chinese history, Taizhong of the Tang dynasty, upon seeing the files of the individuals who had just been selected through the *keju*, exclaimed, "All great people under the sky are now working for me."

During its 1,300-year history, the *keju* was almost the only path of upward mobility in China. It was practically the only way for ordinary Chinese to join the elite. The implementation of the *keju* varied during different times, but in general, especially in recent dynasties, it was hierarchically organized. The system began with local exams, which selected candidates for more advanced exams, and ended with a few individuals participating in the final exam held in the capital and administered by the emperor himself. Different levels of government positions were assigned to those who passed different levels of the exams. Passing the exams was considered one of the most important accomplishments in a person's life. Indeed, the two happiest moments for an individual in China were said to be the wedding night and seeing one's name on the list of people who had passed the *keju*. It was the pursuit of a lifetime for many. With no age limit or limit on how many times one could try, historical records show that some persisted in taking the tests into their 70s. The most famous case took place in 1699, when an individual took the test at age 102 (S. Jia, 2006). Chinese literature has many stories—romantic, sad, happy, and bizarre—about individuals who studied for the *keju* or about their long journeys to the sites where the *keju* was held.

Although the *keju* itself was not an education system but a political system, because of its high stakes it determined what education was about in China for centuries. Virtually all education activities were about preparing for the *keju*. What was tested was what was being learned and taught.

The Confucian classics were the core content of the *keju* for most of the 1,300 years it was held. The exams by and large tested rote memorization of the classics or regurgitated interpretations of the classics. For example, one of the common formats was to remove certain words from original passages of the classics and ask the test takers to provide the deleted words. Another common format was to have the test takers paraphrase sentences taken from the classics. The format became even more rigid during the Ming and Qing dynasties, after *baguwen* became the only acceptable format of responses. *Baguwen* asked the test takers to write an interpretation of original sentences from one of the Confucian classics. The interpretation had to be either 300 or 500 Chinese characters long and contain eight predefined parts.

Memorization of the classics thus became the most important education activity in preparation for the *keju*. In fact, for thousands of years the commonly used phrase for education has been *dushu*, which literally means "reading the books." Even today, many Chinese use *dushu* to refer to education, as in "Have your children begun *dushu*?" meaning "Have your children started school yet?" An educated person is called *dushu ren*, which literally means "people who are reading or have read books." A well-known poem by Emperor Zhenzong of the Song dynasty titled "Advice for Learning" highlights the utmost importance of the classics:

> Wealthy families do not need to buy land, for there are abundant grains in the books; nor do they need to build fancy houses, for there are golden palaces in the books; nor do they need to worry about transportation means, for there are plenty of horses in the books; nor do they need to worry about not having a matchmaker, for there are beautiful women in the books. If a man wishes to realize his lifetime dream, he should be diligently reading the *Six Classics*.

In its early years, especially during the Tang dynasty, when the society was much more open and tolerant of different talents, the *keju* included many more subjects. It began as an effective mechanism to identify and recruit talent from the commoners and in effect broadened the pool and provided the rulers with diverse talent to run the country. Later it became mechanical and narrow, resulting in individuals with only one type of talent—those who could memorize and regurgitate the classics—being valued and selected to join the social elite. The consequence was "talent cleansing." Those who were otherwise excellent and creative were not valued and were excluded from the bureaucracy. For example, one of the most imaginative writers in all Chinese history, Pu Songling, author of *Liaozhai Zhiyi* (*Strange Tales from Make-do Studio)*, failed the *keju* numerous times and eventually gave up.

Because of its exclusive focus on memorization of Confucian classics, the *keju* instilled a worship of the past and of book knowledge, and hence a disdain for physical labor, technology, and natural sciences. Scientific or technological contributions were not valued, and those who excelled in these areas would not be selected into the ruling class. Song Yingxing, author of a comprehensive encyclopedia of agricultural technology and crafts, wrote in the preface, "This book has nothing to do with seeking promotion to the bureaucracy" (Y. Song, 2003, p. 1). The book was first printed in 1637, during China's Ming dynasty.

The *keju* was at least a significant partial answer to the "Needham question": Why didn't China, once so advanced in scientific and technological innovations, continue to develop in these areas in the modern age? The question came from the British scholar Joseph Needham, who devoted his life to studying science and technology innovations in premodern China. By the time he died in 1995, he had published 17 volumes of his *Science and Civilization in China* (Needham, 1954). In this series, Needham and his colleagues at Cambridge University documented the spectacular scientific and technological achievements in China and how these innovations influenced the development of science and technology in Europe. For example, the Chinese began using the movable-type printing technique 400 years before Gutenberg introduced it in Germany. They used the magnetic compass at least a century before it was used anywhere else in the world. The Chinese also invented gunpowder. But somehow, after the 15th century, China's scientific innovations suddenly stopped, and as a result, China became a scientific and technological backwater. Needham asked why. He never did come up with a complete answer, but his question has prompted many discussions and suggestions.

The *keju* was certainly a major factor. Lin Yifu, formerly professor of economics and founding director of the Research Institute of Chinese Economy at Peking University and currently chief economist and senior vice president of the World Bank, suggests that the content and format of the *keju* discriminated against individuals who were talented in science and technology and thus discouraged the vast majority of intellectuals from pursuing scientific and technological work (Lin,

1994). Lee Kuan Yew, the leader of Singapore, said the same thing more directly: "[The] *keju* kept China outside the door of industrial and technological revolutions" (G. Li, 2005).

The *keju*'s exclusive focus on the classics and its rigid format resulted in a class of leaders who were familiar with Confucian morals, could recite the classics and write elegant but rigid essays, were obedient, and perhaps even had great penmanship, but they were not trained in anything else. "*Siti bu qin, wugu bu fen* (the four limbs are not labored and do not know the five grains)" was a common criticism of the followers of the *keju*. The vast bureaucracy was essentially run by these physically weak "bookworms" who were steeped in ancient times but ignorant of their own society. Some scholars in China blame the fall of the Ming dynasty, an empire with a long history of sophisticated civilization, to the Qing rulers, a tribe of "barbarians," on the weak and corrupt bureaucracy selected through the *keju*. Ironically, the Qing emperors continued the tradition, although one of the wiser, earlier emperors, Kang Xi, did discontinue the system for a short period of time and tried to reform it, having realized its problems. Nonetheless, the *keju* had such a strong cultural root it continued until the Middle Kingdom (the literal translation of *China*) could not bear its consequences anymore.

The Opium Wars in the mid-19th century between China and the British Empire began a century of military defeats for China. Western powers forced the once arrogant Middle Kingdom to acknowledge the importance of modern knowledge and accept the fact that the Confucian classics and the *keju* were not sufficient to keep it strong and fend off foreign aggression. In 1898, shortly after losing the first Sino-Japanese War and being forced to cede Taiwan, the Liaodong Peninsula, and the Pescadores to Japan in addition to a war indemnity of 200 million taels silver, Kang Youwei, a political thinker and reformer, told Emperor Guangxu, "The loss of Taiwan and Liaodong was not caused by the government but by [the] *baguwen*; the 200 million taels war indemnity should not be blamed on the government but on *baguwen*" because it had produced a group of "useless" government workers. Thus a major action of the 100-Day Reform was to abolish the use of the *baguwen* in the *keju*. But the reform did not last long. In 1905, a group of powerful governors and officials sent a request to the crumbling central government to end the *keju* because "the nation is in eminent crisis and every moment is critical. [Saving] the nation must begin with promoting schools and [promoting] schools must start with discontinuing [the] *keju*." On September 2, the emperor issued the order to stop all forms of the *keju* exams (G. Li, 2005).

A century has passed since the *keju* was officially ended. But its spirit lives on, in the body of the National College Entrance Exam, the same one I took in 1982. The National College Entrance Exam (*gaokao* in Chinese) has every element of the *keju* except for the content. The *gaokao* is as powerful as the *keju* was in determining the course of an individual's life. Although, unlike the *keju*, the *gaokao* does not directly select government officials based on the result, a college degree is required for virtually all government positions. According to China's minister of personnel, 99 percent of government personnel recruited since 2003 hold at least a bachelor's degree, 53 percent have a master's degree, and more than 4 percent have doctoral degrees (Hanqing & Wei, 2008).

A college degree is essential not only for social mobility but also for geographical mobility. In China, a person's legal residency (*hukou* in Chinese) is determined by place of birth. One may work and live in a city for all of one's life but not be able to change residency and enjoy the same social services as the legal residents of the city. The millions of migrant workers are a telling example. Despite the fact that they may have worked and lived in a city for many years, their children are not entitled to attend the local schools. Attending college has been a primary way to earn the right to change one's legal residency because many cities make college degrees a minimal requirement for granting residency.

In addition to its practical value, a college degree is also an indication of social status in China, another legacy of the *keju*. The Confucian tradition of valuing mental work over physical work remains strong, and the perception that a college degree will grant the opportunity to use one's mind instead of one's hands is widespread. Thus despite the huge shortage of skilled technicians and professionals and the millions of unemployed college graduates, getting into college is still the dream of the overwhelming majority of Chinese students and their parents.

College admissions are based solely on performance on the *gaokao*, as was the case with the *keju*. (Recently China has allowed a small number of universities—68 out of more than 2,000 in the year 2008—to admit 5 percent of the freshman class using criteria other than or in addition to scores on the entrance exam on an experimental basis.) Regardless of students' performance for all their 12 years in school or their special talents, their fate is determined by how well they do on the tests, which include three core subjects (Chinese language and literature, English, and mathematics), plus other subjects decided by the provinces. The only exceptions are students who have won medals or prizes in national or world contests recognized by the government. The medals or prizes can be converted into a certain number of points, which are then added to the points a student receives on the entrance exam. In the times of the *keju*, the well-known saying to describe its importance was "For 10 years, no one cares about you studying facing cold windows, but one day you become famous and are known all over the world." Today, a similarly well-known saying is "One exam determines your whole life."

Given its critical importance, the *gaokao* affects every aspect of China's education system. Although it takes place only at the end of high school, its effects trickle down all the way to elementary school and even preschool. It affects the whole experience of students in and out of school. It affects what is taught and how it is taught in classrooms. It affects school financing and the fate of school leaders and even local government officials, as well as the social and financial well-being of teachers. It affects parents, grandparents, and relatives. Of course, it affects the types of talent that eventually come out of the system. It is also a very resilient system that has resisted many reforms, policies, and executive orders. Almost all observed educational practices and outcomes, good or bad, are somehow related to the *gaokao*.

High Scores but Low Ability

Qi Ke scored very high on the National College Entrance Exam in 1995, but he did not know what he should study; neither did his parents.

When they were in the position of choosing among some of China's best universities, his father made the decision on his behalf—the nine-year program in engineering physics at Tsinghua University (ostensibly China's MIT)—without knowing what exactly engineering physics was or what engineering physicists did. But the program was attractive because after nine years a student would graduate with a doctoral degree and become a scientist. "Let's add one more scientist to contribute to our nation," said the father. Qi Ke's high scores got him into the program but did not turn him into a great scientist. Today he is without a job. After graduating with a bachelor's degree from Tsinghua University, he was offered a position at the Institute of High Energy Physics of the Chinese Academy of Sciences as part of the program. But after only half a year, he was asked to resign and leave. He then found a job as a porter that paid 600 RMB (less than US$100) a month. But he was not physically strong enough to do the heavy lifting required, so his porter career ended after two months. Then he tried handing out advertising pamphlets in shopping centers and various other odd jobs, but he has been unable to keep any of them for long. He is psychologically depressed and physically weak. His aging mother began pleading through the media for some nice people to give him a job to help him regain his confidence (J. Liu, 2006).

Qi Ke's story is not unique. Before him, another story made national news and flooded online discussion forums in China. The central figure in the story is a graduate of Peking University, the so-called Harvard of China, who became a butcher after many failed career attempts following graduation. Another story told of a Ph.D. graduate from Nanjing University, another prestigious university in China, who could not keep a job and eventually became a beggar.

These stories exemplify a widely recognized problem in Chinese education: *gaofen dineng*, which literally means high scores but low ability. It is used to refer to students who score well on tests but have few skills that are usable in society. There are so many cases of "high scores but low ability" that the term has been widely accepted as shorthand to describe education in China. Following are some often-cited examples of this situation.

The Puzzling Top 10 Phenomenon

In 1999, a news report titled "The Puzzling Top 10 Phenomenon" appeared in a local newspaper in Hangzhou. The report recounts the story of an elementary school teacher who discovered at a student reunion that many of his top students had achieved much less than those who ranked below "10" in the class. (Chinese schools all rank their students based on test scores and grades. The ranking is often made public through posts in the classroom and in teacher-parent conferences.) The teacher then expanded this observation to other students he had taught and ultimately was able to find 150 of his former students and survey their life after graduation. His finding was simple yet resulted in a national discussion about education: the students who ranked above 10 in his classes were not as successful in life as those who ranked below.

What Happened to the *Zhuangyuans*?

Zhuangyuan was the title granted to the top performer on the *keju* in ancient times, and the individual was often selected by the emperor himself. The title continues to be used today for the students who receive the highest score on the National College Entrance Exam in a province. These *zhuangyuans* become immediate celebrities. They appear on TV programs, in news reports, on lecture tours, in books, and on other media outlets to talk about how they achieved such high scores. Their parents are invited to share their parenting experiences. Of course, these are the most desirable candidates for universities, which fight over the students with all sorts of incentives. They are without question the best test takers. But their abilities have recently been questioned.

China Alumni Net released the first study of the career accomplishments of *zhuanyuans* of each province from 1977 to 1998. The study found that "the current career situation of the studied *zhuangyuans* falls far below people's expectations. They are not leaders in their field, and most of them are unknown." Their names do not appear on the list of distinguished entrepreneurs, scientists, scholars, engineers, or statesmen. This finding shows that they were only *zhuangyuans* on tests but not *zhuangyuans* in real life (Ying Zhao, 2007).

More English Speakers in China Than in America?

On more than one occasion, I have heard Americans talking about how there are more English speakers in China than in America, often in the context of showing how Chinese education has surpassed that of the United States. This comparison inspires another myth about education in China. Although it is true that there are more people in China who have studied English or are studying English than the total population of the United States, it is a big stretch to call them English *speakers*. English is now a required subject in the national curriculum starting in 3rd grade. In most big cities, English instruction starts in 1st grade, and some families send their children to private English lessons before they start school. Given the more than 300 million students in China, the number of English learners can easily top the U.S. population. But the Chinese learners' communicative competency in English is very limited, making the number of Chinese who can actually use English as a communication tool much smaller.

For example, Chinese college graduates typically have studied English for at least eight years (three years in middle school, three years in high school, and at least two years in college). English is one of the three core subjects of the National College Entrance Exam, so the graduates must have passed this test. In addition, because the national Band Four College English test has been an unofficial requirement for graduation, they are likely to have passed it as well. But more often than not, they are unable to use English for any real communication purposes. The McKinsey report mentioned earlier in this chapter suggests that only about 10 percent of candidates for positions at multinational companies are qualified; a major reason is the lack of communicative proficiency in English. The performance of Chinese on the International English Language Testing System (known as IELTS) is another telling example of Chinese English learners' true proficiency. IELTS "measures ability to communicate in English across all four language skills—listening, reading, writing and speaking—for people who intend to study or work where English is the language of communication. . . . More than 6,000 education institutions, faculties, government agencies, and professional organizations around the world recognize IELTS scores as a trusted and valid indicator of ability to communicate in English" (IELTS, 2008). About one million individuals take the test each year.

Among the 20 countries with the most test takers, China ranked near the bottom in 2007. The overall mean band score for China was 5.45 out of 9, just slightly higher than Saudi Arabia and the United Arab Emirates. In speaking, China ranked last, with a mean score of 5.26. The minimum score required by most universities is 6 or above.

Is the Center of the Earth Very Hot? Science Literacy

"Is the center of the earth very hot?" is one of the questions used to measure science literacy as part of a report on *Science and Engineering Indicators* produced by the National Science Foundation (National Science Board, 2008). Of those surveyed, 88 percent of Americans answered correctly, compared to 39 percent of Chinese. Brad Kloza of Science Central, a production firm that aims "to increase the number and quality of science stories broadcast to the public," summarized the data from the NSF report "in the spirit of the Olympic games" (which were then taking place in China). Based on the percentage of people in various countries who correctly answered specific science literacy questions, Kloza (2008) awarded the top-ranking countries for each of the 10 questions a gold, silver, or bronze medal. Here are the results:

Country	Medal	Total
United States	4 Gold, 2 Silver, 2 Bronze	8
European Union	2 Gold, 6 Silver	8
South Korea	4 Gold, 1 Silver, 3 Bronze	8
Japan	1 Gold, 2 Silver, 1 Bronze	4
Russia	2 Bronze	2
India	2 Bronze	2
China	1 Silver	1
Malaysia	None	0

Again, Chinese students may test well in science, but their science literacy remains low.

The "high scores but low ability" phenomenon explains Premier Wen Jiabao's concern over China's lack of talent and the McKinsey report on China's looming talent shortage. The phenomenon has been confirmed in many other ways. For example, David Lague (2006) of the *International Herald Tribune* writes the following in an article titled "Chinese Paradox: A Shallow Pool of Talent": "Employers complain that many graduates lack the skills and experience necessary to start work immediately, particularly for foreign companies." In 2006, I participated in a fact-finding mission with the National Center on Education and the Economy, which was working on what eventually became the influential report *Tough Choices or Tough Times* (New Commission on the Skills of the American Workforce, 2007). During the trip, we visited a number of multinational corporations and factories and talked with the general managers and human resources directors about the quality of the Chinese workforce. We were told repeatedly that the engineers, even the ones who had graduated from some of the best engineering schools, lacked the required experience and ability despite their abundant book knowledge and high test scores. In addition, they lacked a sense of commitment and passion for their work. Creativity and the risk-taking spirit are also missing from the Chinese workforce.

Education Can Hurt

The "high scores but low ability" phenomenon in China suggests something that we may be unwilling to admit—namely, that education that is oriented solely to preparing students to achieve high scores on tests can be harmful to both individuals and the nation it is supposed to serve. Professors Sharon Nichols and David Berliner (2007) documented the potential damage of high-stakes testing to public education in the United States in their book *Collateral Damage: How High-Stakes Testing Corrupts America's Public Schools*. The damage caused by the *gaokao* in China is much broader and has been proven because the whole education system is test oriented and all that matters is to prepare test takers (Z. Wang, 2004).

Lost Lives: Student Suicide

Xiaoru, a 14-year-old girl, died of a cerebral hemorrhage on March 14, 2003. Education researcher Wang Zhihe recounted the story (Z. Wang,

2004). The cause was constant overwork and exhaustion. She left behind more than 20 awards and certificates of honor and four diaries telling how hard she worked to earn these honors. Xiaoru was a typical good student. Her diaries tell us that she got up at 4 a.m. and went to bed at midnight every day when school was in session. She had no vacation, as her schedule during one winter break tells us:

6:30 a.m.: Get up

8:00 a.m.–11 a.m.: Homework

1:00 p.m.–2. p.m.: Practice math

2:00 p.m.–2:30 p.m.: Preview English book of next semester

2:30 p.m.–3.00.p.m.: Read Guide to Literature Classics

3:00 p.m.–4:00 p.m.: Read reference books, recite an ancient poem, finish practicing one unit math questions exercise, study *English New Thinking in Class*, study *Math New Thinking in Class*, practice calligraphy

Saturday: Self-study *Target English*

Sunday: Self-study *Target English*

Compose two papers in English per week

Compose two papers in Chinese per week

Xiaoru was ambitious and had a dream, as all good students in China do. Half a month before she died, Xiaoru wrote in her diary, "The new semester will start tomorrow. I must achieve the best marks. My original dream is to become a medical doctor. Now I badly want to become an educator. I will let all parents and children take it easy."

Longlong, a 15-year-old boy in China's Jiangsu Province, died early one Monday morning in September 2006, a few hours before he was supposed to go to school. He did not die from overwork. He killed himself with pesticide after being beaten by his English teacher because he could not remember the English words he had studied. Before he took his life, he had been copying English words—200 times for each word—as he had been told to do by his teacher (Chen, 2006).

Xiuxiu, a 13-year-old girl in China's Ningxia Province, committed suicide on July 10, 2005, for a different reason. She did not want to burden her parents with a hefty school-selection fee. She was going to attend middle school after the summer, but she worried that her grades were not good enough for her to be admitted to a good school and her parents would have to pay more than 100,000 RMB to enroll her. She left her parents a note, apologizing:

> Mom and dad, I am sorry! But I have no other way. This is the only thing I can do. I am not a good student. I am a bad student. You and dad work so hard but I make you angry every day. After I die, you and dad should sell the store and rest at home every day. You raised me for 13 years and have spent lots of money! My death can help you save 100,000 *yuan*. I am sorry. I will go accompany grandpa. Mom, dad, brother, and sister, I am sorry. I let you down. I am a bad student!

But according to her neighbors, teachers, and parents, Xiuxiu was a good student, nice, kind, active, and always ready to help others (Meng, Ma, & Liu, 2005).

Longlong and Xiuxiu were among the tens of thousands of children and youth who commit suicide in China each year. "Suicide is the number-one killer of Chinese people between the ages of 15 and 34," according to an article that cited statistics from the Chinese Association of Mental Health (*China Daily*, 2007). In 2006, suicide accounted for more than 26 percent of the deaths in this age cohort, although no information on the exact number of deaths was provided. The Chinese Ministry of Health recorded more than 250,000 suicides and 2 million attempts in 2003, the last year when such statistics were released. About 26.64 percent of those who killed themselves were between the age of 15 and 26 (Z. Yang, 2008). In the same year, there were 31,484 suicides in the total population in the United States (*China Daily*, 2007).

Many more students have considered committing suicide. The same *China Daily* article reports on a two-year study by researchers at Peking University, which found that 20.4 percent of high school students said they had considered killing themselves at some point. The percentage was 13 percent for all students (elementary and secondary) in Zhejiang Province, one of China's more developed coastal areas, according to a separate study in 2005 (Huicong Net, 2005).

"Increased competition in getting into better colleges and an exclusive focus on test scores are putting unbearable pressure on young students, resulting in ever increasing psychological and mental health risks" (Huicong Net, 2005). Competition is constantly reinforced in schools. Most, if not all, schools in China rank students according to their grades and test scores. These ranks are made public through postings in the classroom, so students are constantly aware of their academic standing. Parents hold very high expectations and communicate these expectations to their children. All of these things put tremendous pressure on students, and often students think that suicide is the way to escape the unbearable pressure (Q. Zhao, 2008).

Fat Children: Declining Physical Condition

"When one after another fat or bean-sprout-like child walks by, we should be worried: as the future of our motherland, will these students have the physical strength and energy needed for building our nation?" Thus begins the editorial note for a series of reports on the physical condition of students in China by Xinhua News Agency (Sheng, 2006). This four-part series was intended to raise national awareness about the declining physical condition of children and how it may threaten China's national competitiveness.

The report included data from the Ministry of Education. A 2004 survey of more than 180,000 7- to 22-year-old students in both rural and urban areas found that Chinese students' physical condition continued to decline on all indicators: fitness, eyesight, dexterity, speed, lung capacity, and muscle strength. More than 60 percent of the surveyed age cohorts showed significant increases in cases of excess weight or obesity. More than 15 percent of 10- to 12-year-old city boys were obese. Thirty percent of elementary school students, 60 percent of middle school students, and 80 percent of high school students had poor eyesight (Sheng, 2006).

Considering that just a few decades ago China was struggling to feed its people and supply sufficient nutrition to its young, it is a sad irony that today it has to battle against the declining physical condition of students despite much improved food supplies. Better nutrition has not resulted in stronger bodies. As early as 1998, an article in China's national newspaper *Guangming Daily* reported that although living standards had risen, students' physical condition had declined. The article cites a national study that found more than 50 percent of college freshmen were physically unfit in 1996, and in 1995 Tsinghua

University found 63 percent of its freshman class failed to meet physical fitness expectations (Ren & Li, 1998).

The pressure of testing, which focuses exclusively on academic subjects, is a primary cause. Schools and families view physical activities as a waste of time and a source of unnecessary suffering for children. Thus students' physical activities are reduced to almost nothing at home and in school. According to a study, the average time children spent on household chores was only 11.32 minutes per day (Ren & Li, 1998). Although national requirements set the amount of time for physical activities, schools typically reduce it and use the time for academic studies. According to a report, 83 percent of interviewed students reported that they have less than one hour of physical activity in school per day (Ao & Zhao, 2005).

The higher the grade, the less time is spent on physical activities, as the pressure increases to focus on academic studies. This might explain why a study found that as Chinese children grow older, their physical condition deteriorates. The study of students in Tianjin found that on the indicator of lung capacity, for example, 25.15 percent of 5th grade boys were excellent, but the percentage dropped to 20.4 percent for 6th graders, and it further decreased to 18.97 percent for 10th graders (Ao & Zhao, 2005).

As noted earlier, what is tested in school is what is considered to be important. At one time, grades in physical education (P.E.) were counted in the total score for admissions, so more time was devoted to physical activities. But in 2000, P.E. grades were no longer included, and schools began to reduce the amount of time devoted to physical activities (Ao & Zhao, 2005). To address the problem of obesity and poor physical fitness, some cities began to reconsider including P.E. grades and physical condition as criteria for admission. For example, the Beijing Municipal Education Commission was reported to be considering a policy to add P.E. grades as a criterion for admission to high school beginning in 2009 (H. Wang, 2007).

Imprisoned Students: Fraud and Crime in Testing

Wenfang took the National College Entrance Exam in June 2008. But she is not going to college; instead, she is going to prison, along with her parents. During the math portion of the 2008 *gaokao*, she was found to be using a wireless transmitter to receive answers from her parents, who were in a car parked outside the test site. The parents bought the answers for 8,000 RMB (about US$1,200) and the transmission equipment for another 4,500RMB (about US$700) from a classmate of Wenfang's. The classmate operated a little side business besides studying for the exams and made a total of 27,000 RMB (about US$4,000) in profit selling test answers and transmission equipment, which he obtained from another source. Eventually a total of 26 individuals were arrested and 12 of them charged for "stealing national secrets" (Kong, Lu, & Shi, 2008).

This was not the only case of fraud and crime related to the *gaokao*. A simple search using the term *"gaokao zuobi* (College Entrance Exam fraud)" on Google found similar cases in the southwestern Yunnan Province, where a government official purchased test answers and equipment for his son (R. Song, 2008); in the northeastern Helongjiang Province, where 19 separate cases of using wireless technology to transmit answers were uncovered (W. Li, 2008); and in the western Gansu Province, where hired test takers were caught taking tests on behalf of students from a different province. And these were only a few cases reported during the 2008 exam. Cases were reported in 2007, 2006, 2005, and the years before. It happens every year, all over China.

Because of its high stakes, *gaokao* test papers and answers are considered national secrets and are governed by criminal laws. Cheating on the *gaokao* is considered a criminal action. The consequences are serious and punishments severe, ranging from imprisonment to being deprived of the opportunity to take the exam in the future, thus erasing any hope of getting into college. Yet students and their parents continue to engage in such unethical and criminal activities because the payoff is high.

Chinese parents have been praised by American observers for their devotion to their children's education. All these cases can be viewed as examples of such devotion, albeit unethical and criminal. But these examples also tell the truth about the seeming dedication of parents. They are more concerned about whether their children can get into a good college than whether they receive a good education.

How Is Creativity Killed?

Another casualty of test-oriented education in China is creativity, one of the most sought-after assets in the 21st century. By all accounts, the United States has been the world leader in scientific innovations for most of modern times. These innovations have powered economic growth not only at home but also elsewhere in the world. Although Asia is considered to have gained prominence in the 21st century, the major players in Asia—Japan, Korea, and China—cannot really compete with the United States in the creativity and innovation department. In his book *The Writing on the Wall: How Asian Orthography Curbs Creativity*, linguist William Hannas (2003) documents the fact that modern development in these countries has relied primarily on technology transfers from the United States and European countries. Leaders of Asian nations are acutely aware of their creativity (lack thereof) problem and have been trying to address it, albeit with limited success; but somehow this fact escapes the attention of leaders and educators in the United States, "where East Asia's technical skills are typically confused with real creativity, and where people have little clue about the degree to which their creative resources are utilized abroad for commercial profit" (Hannas, 2003, p. 4). As a result, Asian nations have been working on closing the creativity gap, while the United States has been troubled by the "achievement gap" revealed by international comparison tests, such as TIMSS and PISA.

The creativity gap is a complex phenomenon and can be attributed to many factors, but it certainly has a great deal to do with individuals who are creative. That is, somehow there are more creative people in the United States than in Asian countries, or people in the United States are in general more creative than those in Asia. Because there shouldn't be any genetic difference in creativity between Asians and Americans, the difference has to be "nurture" rather than "nature." How is creativity nurtured then?

To be creative is to be different. Creative people often have ideas, behaviors, beliefs, and lifestyles that deviate from the norm and tradition. How these people and their ideas are treated by others has a defining effect on creativity and indeed on different social groups—that is, a collection of individuals, be it families, schools, communities, or a whole country.

Research on the social and contextual influences on creativity has found that, in general, tolerance of deviation from tradition and the norm resulted in more creativity (Florida, 2002). For example, a comprehensive study of families with highly creative children found that on average these families have less than one specific rule for their children, whereas families without highly creative members have an average of six. Highly creative families live in uncommonly furnished houses located in uncommon settings. Parents in these families encourage distinctive thinking patterns from early on, and they themselves live a somewhat uncommon lifestyle. Research also found that in individualist cultures such as the United States, creativity is considered the expression of a unique individual and thus should be respected and valued; in collectivist cultures, on the other hand, the emphasis is on continuity and tradition, and thus it is important for an individual not to be different (Sawyer, 2006).

Schools have been generally found to be either indifferent to or suppressive of creativity because they demand conformity and obedience:

> Most young children are naturally curious and highly imaginative . . . after children have attended school for a while, they become more cautious and less innovative. . . . Unfortunately it is necessary to conclude from the investigations of many scholars that our schools are the major culprits. Teachers, peers, and the educational system as a whole all diminish children's urge to express their creative possibilities. (Dacey & Lennon, 1998, p. 69)

Schools demand conformity and obedience for good reasons. They are the agency that prepares citizens to respect the rules of law and certain social norms. Practical matters also come into play. Teachers have to maintain a certain level of control in order to teach a group of students something. Students must also follow certain norms in order to fit in. Thus all schools inevitably work against creativity in order to accomplish their other missions. But there is a difference in the degree to which that happens.

Here lies the answer, or at least a significant partial one, to the "creativity gap" between Asians and Americans. First of all, as some admirers of the Chinese and other Asian education systems point out, "American children spend less time in academic activities than Chinese and Japanese children do in terms of hours spent at school each day and days spent in school each year" (Stevenson & Stigler, 1992, pp. 52–53). In addition, American children spend vastly less time on schoolwork at home than their Chinese peers. Most American children do not view schooling as central to their lives, whereas most Chinese children do (Stevenson & Stigler, 1992). Thus American children generally are less exposed to the creativity-killing machine—the school.

Second, Chinese teachers have been praised for their ability to maintain order in the classroom. "Teachers make an explicit effort during the early months of elementary school to teach children techniques and skills that will allow them to function effectively in a group" (Stevenson & Stigler, 1992, p. 62). Inflexible rules and standard routines are just the right tools to squelch creativity (Dacey & Packer, 1992; Stevenson & Stigler, 1992). Similarly, Chinese teachers, much more than their American counterparts, want the students to think of themselves as a group, to be constantly aware of their obligations to the group, and to not bring shame to the group (Stevenson & Stigler, 1992). Again, conformity is emphasized much more in Chinese schools than in American schools.

Third, American parents and educators have often been criticized by reformers for having low academic expectations of students. Empirical studies show that American mothers do indeed seem to be significantly more satisfied with their children's academic performance and their schools than mothers in China and Japan. Critics have been trying to determine whether this satisfaction is a result of parents lacking information about how to judge their children's academic performance or simply not caring about it (Stevenson & Stigler, 1992). But in reality, research suggests that American parents just do not care as much as their Asian counterparts about external measures of success. For instance, a study of parents of academically talented 6th graders in the United States found that "emphasis on meeting external standards is not predominant among parents of talented students" (Ablard & Parker, 1997, p. 651). Excessive or exclusive focus on external indicators of success such as grades and test scores can pressure children, sending the message that academic success is important not for personal reasons, but to please others (Ablard, 1997). In other words, American parents and educators define success more broadly and strongly emphasize children's individuality and the need to respect their wishes and abilities.

In contrast, Chinese parents place an extremely high value on external indicators: grades, test scores, and most important, admission to prestigious universities. The success of a student is measured by test scores, and consequently the performance of teachers and schools is judged by the number or percentage of students admitted to prestigious universities or high schools. Not surprisingly, parents, students, teachers, and the whole education system inevitably work toward getting good scores in subjects that count on college entrance exams. All other activities—art, music, community activities, and athletics—are considered unimportant unless they can somehow result in an advantage in entering better colleges. As noted earlier, awards in certain national or provincial-level contests in art, music, and sports can be converted into points included in the computation used for the college admission process. Thus parents might force their children to take classes in these areas or even hire private tutors, but the purpose is often not to enrich their children's lives but to enhance their probability of getting into college. As a result, a piano student might practice only the pieces required in the certification audition.

A broader definition of success and an emphasis on internal rather than external standards of success may not lead to high test scores or good grades, but they definitely help to preserve and protect individuality and creativity. American parents' broader conception of success allows students to feel good if they excel in areas other than academic subjects. It also enables, if not encourages, children to pursue their interests and thus preserves and protects individuality and creativity. In contrast, Asian parents' and their education system's emphasis on external indicators and high expectations naturally lead to less self-confidence and the externalization of motivation, which are detrimental to creativity.

Lastly, standardized and centralized curriculum, another feature of Asian education systems that is often praised by reformers, serves to further squeeze opportunities for individual differences. Teaching at the same pace, in the same sequence, and using the same textbooks for all students leaves little room for exploring individual interests and accommodating different learning styles. Researchers suggest that in order to nurture creativity, schools need to set aside physical space for long-term projects and research as well as adopt a generous field trip policy (Dacey & Packer, 1992). Curriculum standardization and high-stakes testing are incompatible with these recommendations.

Creativity cannot be taught, but it can be stifled. It should be clear by now how Asian education systems stifle creativity more effectively than the American system. The creativity gap between Americans and Chinese exists not because American schools teach creativity more or better than their Chinese counterparts. They just do not thwart creativity as much as the Chinese.

Resistance to Change: Abysmal Results of Reforms

China, of course, does not like the outcomes of its education system. From its top leaders to the general public, everyone realizes the damage it produces. The culprit has long been identified and well known: "test-oriented education." In a 1997 policy document, the Chinese Ministry of Education (then the Chinese National Education Commission) officially brought charges against it:

> "Test-oriented education" refers to the factual existence in our nation's education of the tendency to simply prepare for tests, aim for high test scores, and blindly pursue admission rates [to colleges or higher-level schools] while ignoring the real needs of the student and societal development. It pays attention to only a minority of the student population and neglects the majority; it emphasizes knowledge transmission but neglects moral, physical, aesthetic, and labor education, as well as the cultivation of applied abilities and psychological and emotional development; it relies on rote memorization and mechanical drills as the primary approach, which makes learning uninteresting, hinders students from learning actively, prevents them from taking initiatives, and heavily burdens them with [an] excessive amount of course work; it uses test scores as the primary or only criterion to evaluate students,

hurting their motivation and enthusiasm, squelching their creativity, and impedes their overall development. "Test-oriented education" violates the *Education Law* and *Compulsory Education Law* and deviates from our education policy. Henceforth, we must take all effective measures to promote "quality education" and free elementary and secondary schools from "test-oriented education." (Guojia Jiaowei [National Education Commission], 1997)

As noted in Chapter 3, China has launched a series of reform efforts over the past 30 years. These efforts range from massive curriculum reform to governance and financing reforms, from textbook reforms to assessment reforms, and from reforming classroom practices to changing teacher preparation. China has even begun to tinker with the untouchable *gaokao* and college admissions.

But these efforts have not been all that successful. In an article in *China Daily*, the state-run English newspaper of China, psychologist Xu Haoyuan says, "Whether it is the vaunted concept of quality education or the reform of the exam-oriented system, I would say education reform is the most unsuccessful of all reforms in China since the 1980s" (Tao, 2003). A large proportion of the Chinese people share this view. A 2005 survey found that more than 77 percent of the public was either "very dissatisfied" or "somewhat dissatisfied" with education in China. Only 4.1 percent reported being "very satisfied" or "somewhat satisfied" (D. Yang, 2006).

The curriculum decentralization movement and other associated reforms have not achieved their objectives: more flexibility in curriculum, education of the whole child, cultivation of more independent thinking and creative talents, and reduction of student burdens. Today, students and schools continue to be burdened by excessive amounts of academic work and tests, which have been blamed for depriving students of the time to engage in other activities and hurting their health, independent thinking, and overall psychological and mental development. According to a recent national study by the Ministry of Education, although many educators seem to have accepted the concept of "quality education" and some teachers have changed their teaching practices, by and large the focus on the whole child remains only lip service. "Quality education is loudly spoken, but test-oriented education gets the real attention," notes the report. As a result, competition among students remains fierce, schools and teachers continue to teach to the test at the expense of students' physical and mental health, test preparation overrides national curriculum requirements, and some schools resort to militaristic ways of managing their students. Under intense pressure, students spend all their time and energy on schoolwork (Yong Zhao, 2007).

The "intense pressure" is placed on everyone: children, parents, teachers, school leaders, local education administrators, and even local government leaders, but it comes from only one source: college entrance exams. Unless China drastically reforms the college admission system to expand the criteria beyond test scores on a few subjects, it is unlikely that any effort to nurture more creative talents and healthy children will bear fruit.

5

The Challenges, Part I:
Globalization

"Honey," I confided, "the world is flat."

—Thomas Friedman

As electrically contracted, the globe is no more than a village.

—Marshall McLuhan

On a rainy autumn day in 2007, I moved into a flat in Royal Leamington Spa, a city of about 40,000 residents located in central Warwickshire, England. According to the plaque next to the Midland Oak, an oak tree just outside the town, this was the center of England. Just the day before I had been in East Lansing, a city of similar size in central Michigan in the United States, about 4,000 miles away. It took me about 12 hours on cars, jet planes, and trains to cover this distance. I was tired, lonely, and slightly disoriented. But considering that the *Mayflower* took 66 days just to cross the "pond" from Plymouth, England, to Plymouth, Massachusetts (which did not even exist when the ship arrived), I should have been grateful. I should have been even more grateful when minutes later I was reunited with my family back in the United States via Skype on my Sony Vaio laptop through an O2 mobile phone service. I saw them and talked with them just as I had the day before. The distance of 4,000 miles was practically erased!

I was not the only one who traveled to Leamington Spa from faraway places, I soon discovered. A few hours later, I was delivered a Peugeot 305 made by the French automaker with factories across Europe, China, Brazil, and Argentina, by two friendly Englishmen who worked for Avis, an international car rental firm founded in Detroit, Michigan (where I had started my journey), and headquartered in Parsippany, New Jersey. I took a short drive to town to do some shopping. Of course, I ended up in Tesco, the British version of Wal-Mart, which sells everything from groceries to clothes, DVDs to phone cards, and financial planning to health insurance worldwide. Without any problem, I got what I wanted: wines from Australia and Chile, cheese from France, rice from Thailand, coffee from Colombia, and soap from China. Later I realized I could have gotten all of these online, without going to the store at all. But I enjoyed the actual visit because I got to see other people in the shop, and some of them even looked like me.

My global encounters did not end in Tesco. I needed dinner, and I was not prepared to cook. In search of a restaurant, I walked the streets and quickly found many choices of cuisine: Chinese, English, French, Indian, Italian, Japanese, Middle Eastern, and, of course, the quintessential American—McDonald's and KFC. I chose the Leamington Bar and Grill and was waited on by two excellent young men from Poland. Then I was driven back in a taxi by someone from Turkey.

The Death of Distance

In the 24-hour period just described, I had interacted, directly and indirectly, physically and virtually, with people from some 20 countries around the globe. My well-being, both psychological and physical, was taken care of by these individuals, and my action as a consumer had in some way affected them as well. This was by no means an epiphany for me, for I had traveled to many countries before and had migrated from China to the United States. I had also read many works by writers such as Thomas Friedman and Marshall McLuhan about how our world has become "globalized." But for some reason, my understanding of the interconnectedness and interdependency among human beings was stronger, more real than ever before. Physical distance had vanished.

The death of distance resulting from advances in transportation and communication technologies has been a major driving force of globalization, but it is not the only one. Political changes have also played a significant role. Born in a small village in China's Sichuan Province that just received electricity in the late 1990s and is still unreachable by car, I likely would not have been in Leamington Spa had China not opened up to the outside world, had the Berlin Wall not fallen, or had the U.S. Congress not repealed the Chinese Exclusion Act. Political changes in the last century have been more than dramatic. The world experienced two world wars and a similarly damaging cold war that divided the human race into enemies and legalized killings of millions for most of the 20th century. But toward the end of the millennium, miracles happened. Although regional conflicts remain, most of the human race began to exchange goods and services rather than bullets and hostility. Nations that used to be at war with each other laid down their arms and opened their borders to their former enemies. The fall of the Berlin Wall, the formation of the European Union (EU), the signing of the North America Free Trade Agreement (NAFTA), the birth of the World Trade Organization (WTO), and the expansion of the United Nations and its associated organizations have all helped build a new platform for the human race to have a different way of interacting and connecting with each other, through trade, through migration, and through negotiation.

What I experienced in Leamington Spa has been described and documented by many scholars. Almost half a century ago, the Canadian media theorist and communication professor Marshall McLuhan coined the phrase "global village" to highlight his observation that thanks to "electric technology, we have extended our central nervous system itself in a global embrace, abolishing both space and time as far as our planet is concerned" (McLuhan, 1964, p. 3). Events in one part of the world could be experienced in real time in other parts of the world—just like the shared experiences in small villages throughout the ages. McLuhan's insights were revolutionary yet astonishingly correct, as confirmed by subsequent developments in communication and information technologies. Today, the all-encompassing information and communication technology, the Internet, has penetrated more than 20 percent of the world's population. Mobile telephones, nonexistent at McLuhan's time, are used by more than two billion people. Television has now entered 90 percent of the world's households, with news and other programming running 24 hours a day.

What McLuhan did not anticipate is that the technologies that enable people to vicariously experience what happens in distant places have also enabled physical movement of goods, services, and people, with the help of new transportation technologies and political and cultural changes. The increased flow of goods, services, money, and information across national borders led Thomas Friedman to declare the arrival of "the flat world," in which more people on the planet are now participating and experiencing economic, cultural, and political activities on a global scale. In 2004, worldwide trade in merchandise and services contributed to 55 percent of the world's gross domestic product (GDP). Global flows of foreign direct investment have more than doubled relative to GDP since 1990, reaching 28.4 percent of GDP in 2004. Similarly, migration and international travel have increased dramatically. In 2005 more than 190 million people, or 3 percent of the world's population, lived in a country they were not born in. Workers' remittances and compensation of employees—that is, transfers by migrant workers and wages and salaries earned by nonresident workers—reached $227 trillion in the received category in 2004. In the same year, nearly 800 million tourists traveled to another country (World Bank, 2006).

The "global village" and "flat world" are only two of the many different metaphors used to describe globalization. But they capture the essence of this process that has profoundly changed how we live, work, and entertain: "[O]ur lives are becoming increasingly intertwined with those of distant people and places around the world—economically, politically, and culturally. These links are not always new, but they are more pervasive than ever before" (Legrain, 2002, p. 4). These links are the result and forces of the defining characteristic of globalization—the increasing free movement of people, goods and services, information, and money across national borders and physical distances that have traditionally limited their movement within political, economic, and geographical boundaries.

Globalization has a number of important implications for education, which I address at the end of this chapter. But first, let's delve more deeply into some of the economic and cultural implications.

Fragmentation of Production: Outsourcing, Offshoring, and Job Losses

Globalization has consequences, and not all of them are good for everyone. Just before my visit to Leamington Spa, Peugeot closed its plant in nearby Coventry. Along with the closure went 2,300 jobs. Lost were not only jobs, but also other things, spiritual and physical, that used to be an integral part of the local culture, such as sports facilities and teams (*Courier*, 2008). And there was fear that more plants would close and relocate to other countries in the future.

Similar things have happened in my home state of Michigan. Between 2000 and 2006, Michigan lost more than 336,000 jobs; most of them were in manufacturing associated with the auto industry, which has relocated plants to other countries (DeGroat, 2006). As a result, Michigan has experienced the worst economic decline in its history and is rapidly slipping from being one of the most prosperous states to being a poor state. In 2006, Michigan was "the only state with a shrinking gross domestic product, or GDP," according to Dana Johnson, chief economist of Comerica Bank. "GDP is the value of all goods and services produced . . . in 2006 it fell 0.5 percent [in the state], while the national GDP grew 3.4 percent. In 2003, Michigan's GDP ranked 23rd in the United States. Last year it fell to 35th" (Aguilar, 2007). Michigan made national news with its budget crisis and a partial government shutdown in fall 2007, as well as the auto industry bailouts in 2008.

Jobs can be lost without factory closures. The same technological advances and political changes that made my travel to Leamington Spa so efficient enable businesses to distribute their production processes globally. Thanks to the decreased cost of transportation and the increased efficiency of communication, a company can locate its designers, manufacturers, marketers, and managers anywhere in the world and still have them all work together on the same product seamlessly, as if they were located in the same place. In fact, companies do not even have to own all parts of the production cycle. They can hire other companies, wherever they are located, to work on parts of their products. This process is called "outsourcing," which is enabled by the unbundling or fragmentation of the production process. As U.S. Federal Reserve Chairman Ben Bernanke observed:

> The production processes are becoming geographically fragmented to an unprecedented degree. Rather than producing goods in a single process in a single location, firms are increasingly breaking the production process into discrete steps and performing each step in whatever location allows them to minimize costs. For example, the U.S. chip producer AMD locates most of its research and development in California; produces in Texas, Germany, and Japan; does final processing and testing in Thailand, Singapore, Malaysia, and China; and then sells to markets around the globe. (Bernanke, 2006)

The Mini Cooper is built in Britain by a German company (BMW), and its nearly 2,500 parts come from a dozen countries around the world (Gwin, 2005). Legrain (2002) recounts a study that found a particular American car was made in nine different countries: 37 percent of the production value of the car was generated in the United States, 30 percent in Korea for assembly, 17.5 percent in Japan for components, 7.5 percent in Germany for design, 4 percent in Taiwan and Singapore for minor parts, and 1.5 percent in Ireland and Barbados for data processing.

Outsourcing is not new, but in recent years it has become a major concern in many countries because it has become much more global and larger in scale. When outsourcing becomes global or offshore, jobs are sent to other countries. Then it is called "offshoring." Offshoring has been growing at a dramatic rate, and the trend is projected to continue. A study by the research firm Forrester Group (McCarthy, 2002) suggested that more than one million jobs in Europe will move offshore by 2015. Nearly 760,000 of these jobs are in the United Kingdom. In other words, each year about 3 percent of the United Kingdom's total number of jobs will move offshore. The situation is worse for the

United States, which is expected to have about 3.4 million service jobs moved to other countries.

Jobs that can be outsourced are not limited to manufacturing and information technology. Airlines, credit card companies, insurance institutions, accounting firms, medical services, and even education institutions have entered the business of the global production chain. When you call an airline to track your lost luggage, you are likely speaking with one of some 240,000 call center employees in India. Your X-ray images may be first read by a doctor in India, as may your tax documents—even though you think you have employed a local accounting firm (Friedman, 2005). Education, too, can be outsourced. The Assessment and Qualifications Alliance (AQA) exam board in the United Kingdom decided to have General Certificate of Secondary Education (GCSE) scripts marked in India in 2005. A growing number of Indians have been working for American tutoring companies and helping American students master math and statistics. As noted in the *Washington Post*, "Tutoring companies figure: If low-paid workers in China and India can sew your clothes, process your medical bills and answer your computer questions, why can't they teach your children, too?" (Paley, 2006).

One's loss seems to be others' gain. While closing plants and cutting jobs in Michigan, General Motors and Ford have been adding plants and creating jobs in China. General Motors, which already had five plants in China, planned to invest $3 billion in China in 2004–07, and Ford was in the midst of a $1 billion expansion, building new assembly and engine plants in China (McDonald, 2007). Both companies also looked at India as their next place for investment (Joshi, 2007). India has been the primary recipient of jobs outsourced, especially in the information technology sector.

Free Movement of Goods: McDonald's, Starbucks, and Cultural Clashes

Jobs and cars are not the only thing China got from globalization. Although it may have sought the economic growth, it certainly did not expect to have the country embrace coffee over its traditional national drink—tea. However, that is exactly what happened. And worse yet, Starbucks set up a shop inside the Forbidden City, the palace complex that housed China's emperors of several dynasties. After a wave of protest led by a well-known China Central Television (CCTV) journalist who accused the store of ruining China's cultural heritage, Starbucks ended its seven-year residency inside the Forbidden City in 2007.

The battle against Starbucks was not an isolated incident of cultural conflict resulting from globalization in China. In 2006, a group of doctoral students from some of China's most prestigious universities issued a call to boycott Christmas. "Western culture has grown from drizzles to storms in China, and its most explicit exemplification is the growing popularity of Christmas," begins the open letter that was widely published by almost all of China's major Web sites. The authors asked Chinese citizens to "treat Christmas with caution" and suggested that the government should seriously reexamine and regulate the "Christmas storm" that was powerfully sweeping across China (B. Liu, 2006). Responses to the call were more than enthusiastic. Strong support for the call was expressed all over China's online chatrooms, discussion forums, blogs, and opinion polls. In 2007, the Chinese government added three major traditional festivals to the calendar as legal holidays. Before this change, the spring festival had been the only one that was observed as a legal holiday. The first reason cited by the government for making the adjustment was that the previous national holidays did not give adequate consideration to Chinese tradition.

China's battle against Starbucks and Christmas, as fierce as it was, is only a milder version of the battle against McDonald's worldwide. Denounced as an agent of cultural imperialism, McDonald's has been the target of protest around the world. The movement started in England with the environmental group London Greenpeace, which in 1986 distributed a pamphlet titled "What's wrong with McDonald's? Everything they don't want you to know." McDonald's responded in 1990 by bringing libel proceedings against the group. The case, now known as "the McLibel case," turned out to be the longest-running court action in English history, with the trial lasting seven years. "From 1994 to 2003, McDonald's restaurants were subject to violent attacks (including bombings) in Rome, Macao, Rio de Janeiro,

Prague, London, Karachi, Jakarta, Mexico City, Beirut, and Beijing—a complete list would fill most of this page," writes the anthropologist James Watson (2004, p. 160). Today, the movement against McDonald's continues. Every year brings organized and globally coordinated protests against the company.

Protests against Starbucks, Christmas, and McDonald's exemplify a widespread concern about the effect of globalization on local and indigenous cultures. Cultural homogenization and standardization of everyday life seem to be an inevitable consequence of globalization, as evidenced by the global presence of McDonald's, KFC, Wal-Mart, Microsoft, Levis, Google, Coke, Hollywood, Disney, and CNN. While scholars are still debating whether multinational companies, Hollywood and Bollywood movies, YouTube and CNN, World of Warcraft and Second Life, Harry Potter and Madonna are wiping out local cultures and standardizing the way we live, eat, dress, and entertain (Jenkins, 2004; Watson, 2004), the concern over the loss of identity is as acute and widespread as that over the loss of jobs.

Free Movement of People: Migration, Cheap Labor, and National Identity Crises

Jobs, factories, Big Macs, french fries, Levi jeans, *Lord of the Rings*, and YouTube are not the only things that move across national borders and bring challenges to local cultures, lifestyles, and standards of living. Human beings move across borders, too, and they sometimes present even more complex challenges.

Migration is not a new phenomenon in human history, but recent technological, cultural, economic, and political developments have significantly increased its frequency and scale. People move from one locality to another for all sorts of reasons, from escaping from poor living conditions, political turmoil, mistreatment, or lack of opportunities to seeking better jobs, better education, more opportunities, and better living conditions. Globalization has made movement across national borders and geographical boundaries easier and more appealing and hence fueled more migration in recent years.

Political changes in the past few decades have made it possible for billions of people who had been confined to their country of birth to seek education, employment, and other opportunities in another country. The fall of the Berlin Wall in 1989 removed the barriers between the West and the East, freeing millions of people to move to and from countries that had been off limits for almost half a century. Political changes inside China since 1979 gave more than a billion people the potential to move out of their country. The formation of the European Union made it possible for millions of people in more than 20 countries to work and live in any member state of the EU.

Economic and technological developments in recent years have made migration more accessible and appealing. As income rises and education quality improves in many developing countries, more people can afford and have the ability and desire to move to another country. Global information technologies have made people more aware of lifestyles and opportunities in other countries, affecting their desire and decision to move elsewhere. In addition, information and communication technologies help immigrants stay in touch with their own culture, families, and relatives, easing the psychological strain of living in a foreign land.

On the demand side, many countries have begun to intentionally attract certain types of immigrants to help sustain and further develop their own economy. Each year, China imports more than 300,000 "foreign experts" as technical advisors, professors, and consultants (Lin & Wang, 2006). The United States annually issues around 100,000 non-immigrant visas for skilled professionals, in addition to other types of visas for guest workers. In 1987, Japan established the Japan Exchange and Teaching (JET) program to attract foreign graduates to teach language (mostly English) and promote internationalization. The program had nearly 6,000 participants in 2006 (Japan Exchange and Teaching Program, 2007). In 2006, Singapore imported a group of toilet cleaners from Japan to professionalize its own cleaning workers (Kyodo News International, 2006).

The scale of migration has been astounding for some countries in recent years. In 2006, more than 860 immigrants arrived in the United Kingdom every day, and this number counts only those who came legally (Dunnell, 2007; Slack, 2008). Between 1997 and 2006, the United Kingdom has had a net increase of immigrants of 2,337,000. As of 2008, about 10 percent of the population in the United Kingdom was born outside the country, almost reaching the level in the country founded on immigration—the United States of America. In 2003, 11.7 percent of the U.S. population was foreign born (Larsen, 2004). The immigrant population is even higher in Australia, with almost one quarter of its people born overseas, as of 2004 (Australian Bureau of Statistics, 2005). Like the United States, Australia is a country founded by immigrants and has a history of high levels of immigration in its early years. In 1891, about 32 percent of Australians were foreign born, but the percentage fell to 10 percent in 1947.

Migration goes both ways. There is *immigration* and there is *emigration*. While some countries, mostly developed countries, have seen an increase in people moving in, others must have experienced an increase in people moving out. Mexico is perhaps the country that has experienced the most emigration in recent years. According to available statistics, more than 1.6 million Mexicans moved across the border into the United States in the five years between 1995 and 2000 (Gutiérrez, 2006). China has seen many of its citizens moving to work and live in other places, too. In 2007, an estimated 750,000 Chinese were living in African countries, 600,000 in Russia, and nearly a million in Europe, the majority of them having moved out of China since the 1980s. India, too, is a country of emigration. Nearly 1.25 million Indians emigrated to the United States, Canada, the United Kingdom, and Australia between 1950 and 2000, with an additional 3 million Indians emigrating to the Middle East since the late 1970s (Srivastava & Sasikumar, 2003).

Increased migration is both a consequence and a cause of globalization. While globalizing forces have significantly increased the level of migration, migration itself is further globalizing the world we live in. The movement of people affects both the home and the host country, and the effect is not clear cut.

Supporters of immigration argue that international migration brings economic prosperity to those who migrate and to their sending, as well as receiving, countries. "History has shown that immigration encourages prosperity," says a special report on international migration published in *The Economist*, for the following reasons:

- The millions of individuals who have migrated to other countries have proven to have a better life.
- They bring back new skills, new ideas, new technology, and savings when they return.
- The money migrants send home helps their home country. At least $260 billion, more than aid and foreign investment combined, was sent to poor countries by migrant workers in 2006.
- They supply the rich countries with fresh workers, both skilled and unskilled. "It is no coincidence that countries that welcome immigrants—such as Sweden, Ireland, America, and Britain—have better economic records than those that shun them" (*Economist*, 2008).

However, one cannot ignore the negative consequences of migration. Immigrants often suffer from prejudice, exploitation, and lack of access to public services and civil rights enjoyed by citizens of the host country. They are treated as second-class citizens and subjected to discrimination and sometimes even violent attacks. They also become scapegoats for domestic problems in the host country. In addition, when skilled workers move to prosperous countries, they take away their home countries' investment and leave behind a talent vacuum. "Brain drain" has been a long-term issue for poor countries with significant migration.

Immigrants can be viewed as a threat to the host community. They may be blamed for unemployment of local residents, seen as an added burden to public services such as health and education, and most serious of all, seen as the cause of a crisis in national identity. The American cultural critic Samuel Huntington, in his controversial book *Who Are We? The Challenges to America's National Identity* (2004), suggests that immigration, particularly from Mexico, may cause the United States of America to disintegrate. These concerns, justified or not, are widespread, as noted by *The Economist*:

> Italians blame gypsies from Romania for a spate of crime. British politicians of all stripes promise to curb the rapid immigration of recent years.

Voters in France, Switzerland, and Denmark last year rewarded politicians who promised to keep out strangers. In America, too, huddled masses are less welcome as many presidential candidates promise to fence off Mexico. And around the rich world, immigration has been rising to the top of voters' lists of concerns—which, for those who believe that migration greatly benefits both recipient and donor countries, is a worry in itself. (*Economist*, 2008)

Challenges for Education

It is clear that globalization has already transformed how we live, work, and entertain, affected our views of relationships, and made us aware of people who live thousands of miles away and were once "out of sight and out of mind." As a social institution, education has been mostly a local entity, funded with local or national taxes, serving the purpose of the local community or the nation, preparing workers for the local economy, and passing on local values. The idea of a local community has already become something of the past. Today we all live in a globally interconnected and interdependent community. We can be certain that our children will live in an even more globalized world. Their lives will be even more affected by others who live in distant lands, belong to different local communities, and believe in different gods or believe in no God at all. Education, the traditionally local social institution, thus faces a number of significant challenges in preparing children to live in the global society.

The first challenge concerns what we can do to help our children secure a job that will provide for them and their families. As discussed earlier, the death of distance has created a global job market. That is, employers can theoretically find the talent they need from anywhere on the globe by either moving their businesses to where the talent is located and outsourcing to operations that have the talent, or directly moving the talent to wherever they need it. In a strictly business sense, businesses use two criteria to decide who to employ: costs and quality, all other things being equal. To maximize profit, all businesses would like to pay as little as possible for their workforce provided that the workforce has adequate knowledge and skills for the tasks. Thus the first thing that matters on the global job market is cost, or salaries, and benefits from the employees' perspective. Cheap labor is responsible for many of the job losses and factory closures mentioned earlier in this chapter. The integration of China, India, and other developing countries into the world economy has provided billions of workers who cost much less than those in developed countries to fill low-level, low-skill, or no-skill positions and thus made it possible for businesses to send jobs to these countries. But China, India, and other countries not only have cheap labor for low-skill jobs; they also have millions of engineers, computer programmers, and other professionals who can competently fill positions that require more sophisticated knowledge and skills, and cost less. That's why we have also seen jobs in the high-tech industry, such as software programming, lost to China and India.

Moreover, China, India, and other developing countries have been working hard at developing their education systems. And as their economic conditions improve, so does the quality of their education. This has caused concern in the developed countries, which certainly do not have the advantage of price compared to the developing countries.

As a result of this situation, education systems in developed countries face a challenging question. The question is one that the New Commission on the Skills of the American Workforce, a group of influential business, education, and political leaders, asked in their 2007 report, *Tough Choices or Tough Times*:

> Today, Indian engineers make $7,500 a year against $45,000 for an American engineer with the same qualifications. If we succeed in matching the very high levels of mastery of mathematics and science of these Indian engineers—an enormous challenge for this country—why would the world's employers pay us more than they have to pay the Indians to do their work? (p. 5)

The second challenge involves what we can do to help our children live, work, and interact with people from different cultures and countries. Another consequence of globalization is increased intensity and frequency of cross-cultural communications. As businesses become global and multinational, so does the workforce. Today, communications within a company often occur across many countries and cultures on a daily basis. External communications with customers, suppliers, government agencies, and other regulation entities are similarly international. Even small businesses need talents that can help them navigate the cultural and linguistic differences when they enter the global economy. In addition, as more and more people move across national borders, communities are becoming increasingly diverse culturally and racially. Communities need to provide services that are culturally sensitive and linguistically competent to assist new immigrants, to attract international investments and tourists, and to get on the global stage. Therefore, the ability to interact effectively with people who speak different languages, believe in different religions, and hold different values has become essential for all workers. That is, what used to be required of a small group of individuals—diplomats, translators, cross-cultural communication consultants, or international tour guides—has become necessary for all professions.

We call the required set of skills and knowledge "global competence." An essential ingredient of global competence is foreign language proficiency and a deep understanding of other cultures. American schools are notorious for not preparing students to cultivate such knowledge and skills. According to a report by a Washington, D.C.-based nonprofit organization, "many American students lack sufficient knowledge about other world regions, languages and cultures, and as a result are likely to be unprepared to compete and lead in a global work environment" (Committee for Economic Development [CED], 2006, p. 14). Most American school systems do not offer foreign languages until high school. Although foreign language instruction starting in high school is already too little too late, not all high school students are even required to take a foreign language, especially a non-Western language.

The third challenge for education concerns what is needed to help our children adopt a global view in their thinking and develop a sense of global citizenship. As economic globalization sweeps contemporary society, it brings both positive and negative effects to different societies and different sectors of a given society. Although it may help spread democracy and lift people out of poverty, it has the potential to lead to more cultural clashes and conflicts, destroy local cultures, breed hostility, create new pockets of poverty, and ruin the environment. Furthermore, what happens in distant places affects communities worldwide. Terrorism, environmental destruction, disease, and political unrest have all acquired a global nature. To ensure a better society for all—actually to ensure the very survival and continuity of human civilization—requires us to prepare our students to become global citizens.

As citizens of the globe, they need to be aware of the global nature of societal issues, to care about people in distant places, to understand the nature of global economic integration, to appreciate the interconnectedness and interdependence of peoples, to respect and protect cultural diversity, to fight for social justice for all, and to protect planet Earth—home for all human beings. This is a difficult task for American educators. No Child Left Behind has already squeezed out any room for subjects other than what is being tested. The frightening descriptions of job losses, trade deficits, foreign terrorists, and the rise of developing countries add to the challenge for educators trying to convince an America-centric public that helping our children develop a sense of global citizenship is a good thing. In reality, it is not only a good thing, but also a necessary and urgent thing to do simply because our well-being is connected to that of people in other countries. We can no longer sustain our prosperity in isolation from others.

To meet these challenges, we need to transform our thinking about education. It may still be locally funded and controlled, but we must think globally in terms of what knowledge and skills our children will need so that they can exercise their inalienable rights to life, liberty, and the pursuit of happiness in the globalized world.

6

The Challenges, Part II:
Technology

It would appear that we have reached the limits of what it is possible to achieve with computer technology, although one should be careful with such statements, as they tend to sound pretty silly in five years.

—John Von Neumann, mathematician (circa 1949)

Here are my strong reservations about the wave of computer networks. They isolate us from one another and cheapen the meaning of actual experience. They work against literacy and creativity. They undercut our schools and libraries.

—Clifford Stoll, author, 1995

The May 2006 issue of *Business Week* features Anshe Chung, a resident of the 3-D virtual world called Second Life (Hof, 2006). Chung does not exist in the physical world. She is the avatar, or virtual representation, of a woman named Ailin Graef in the physical world. Graef, as the *Business Week* cover story tells us, was the first person in the world to make more than $1 million by creating and selling virtual real estate properties in the imaginary virtual space. Born in Hubei, China, Graef married a German and immigrated to Germany. In 2004, she spent $9.95 for a Second Life account and created the character of Anshe Chung, an Asian-looking female wearing a traditional Chinese dress called a *qipao.*

Second Life is a computer game created and operated by Linden Lab, a software company based in San Francisco. It differs from most traditional computer games in its scope, in that it is a vast online diorama in which players can create all sorts of objects, from buildings to golf courses, from cars to flowers, and from food to clothes. It is persistent, as well. That is, even when the user logs off the computer, it still exists, and millions of other players are still there. It is, in essence, a virtual world, or "metaverse."

Players of Second Life, more often called "residents," live in this metaverse as in the physical world. They can create objects and sell or buy them with Linden dollars. Linden Lab has made it a policy that users own the intellectual property rights to the objects they create or purchase. Linden Lab has also made it possible for users to convert their earned Linden dollars into real U.S. dollars. Of course, users can buy Linden dollars with their real money. Registration to play the game is free, but to have a place to "live," the user must buy land or properties. They can buy land from other "residents" or from Linden Lab directly. At the time of this writing, one could buy a 65,536-square-meter private region for $1,000 and would pay a $290 monthly fee to maintain ownership.

Anshe Chung (Ailin Graef in real life) began to accumulate her fortune by making small-scale purchases of properties in Second Life. She subdivided them and developed them into themed properties, such as oriental gardens and country houses. She then sold or rented them to other residents, who apparently found them desirable. In just two and a half years, she had turned her $9.95 into more than $1 million. Today she continues her business on a much larger scale. She now operates the Anshe Chung Studios, which, according to its Web site, "maintains offices in the real world, where it employs more than 80 people full time, and is extended by a huge network of virtual reality freelancers worldwide. It hosts thousands of residents on more than 40 square kilometers of gated communities in virtual worlds."

Anshe Chung's success as a virtual property developer illustrates another transformation brought about by technology: the emergence of the virtual world. Chapter 5 discusses how technology has shortened geographical distances and drastically transformed our lives from physically bounded local experiences to global ones. This chapter provides a glimpse into the virtual world created by technology. Although still in its infancy and by no means physical, the virtual world is real and rapidly expanding. Just as we affect and are affected by people at a distance whom we may never physically meet, the virtual world is quickly evolving into one that will soon affect the physical lives of many of us, although it exists only in cyberspace.

The virtual world is already an all-encompassing reality in the full sense of the word. There are virtual economies, where individuals participate in financial transactions. There are virtual communities, where individuals form relationships and experience the full psychological consequences of those relationships. There are cyber wars, in which enemies attack each other's computer systems in hopes of inflicting maximal damage. There are online crimes, virtual schools, and online marketplaces.

The virtual world, like the global world, poses unique challenges to education. Schools by and large have been trying to ignore it as innocuous entertainment or keep it outside the realm of children's education because it is potentially harmful. But as one dimension of the future world our children will very likely reside in, can we afford not to consider its implications for education?

Real Businesses in the Virtual World: Happenings in Second Life

Second Life is one of the real-life implementations of the metaverse imagined by author Neal Stephenson in his 1992 novel *Snow Crash*. Stephenson created the word "metaverse" out of the words "meta" and "universe" to replace "virtual reality," a phrase he found too awkward. In *Snow Crash*, the metaverse is an urban environment developed along a single road that is 100 meters wide and 65,536 kilometers long, wrapping around the perfectly spherical planet. People use personal or public terminals to gain access to the metaverse, which appears as a high-quality virtual reality display on goggles worn by the user.

There have been various attempts to implement the metaverse on computer systems. Second Life is by far the most successful and influential metaverse implementation for social purposes. There are also a number of highly successful online role-playing games, such as World of Warcraft, that bear some resemblance to the metaverse, but with a specific gaming purpose and more prestructured social organizations.

Second Life was launched in 2003 with the goal of creating a user-defined virtual world in which people could interact, play, and do business. Five years later, one could safely say that the stated goal of Second Life had been met with great success. Second Life had developed into a vast world with a population of more than 15 million as of September 11, 2008. Nearly half a million people logged on during the previous seven days, and more than one million logged on during the previous 60 days. By the end of August 2008, the metaverse had 23,806 privately owned islands (Linden Research, 2008). In June 2008, residents in Second Life spent a total of 33.9 million hours in this virtual world. It has also become an active economy. Total user-to-user transactions in June 2008 were valued at L$7.9 billion (about US$29 million). In June 2007, a total of L$9.7 billion (about US$36 million) of currency circulated throughout Second Life's economy (E. Reuters, 2008).

What the millions of residents can do in Second Life is as rich as, and perhaps even richer than, what they can do in real life. For example, as of September 2008, "you won't have to travel to St. Louis to visit the Gateway Arch or to take a steamboat ride down the Mississippi," according to an article in the *St. Louis Business Journal*. "Once you log on to virtual St. Louis, you'll be able to visit the Gateway to the West, buy real tickets to the attraction and book real hotel rooms. Then you can snag a free St. Louis T-shirt for your avatar, or online persona, and grab a ride on a steamboat" (Volkmann, 2008). St. Louis is not the only city you can tour in Second Life. In fact, it is a latecomer compared with European cities such as London, Copenhagen, Berlin, Amsterdam, Manchester, Barcelona, Liverpool, Salzburg, and many more. Although the replica often does not include the whole city, it gives you a 3-D experience of the major streets, landmarks, monuments, and interesting sites.

In addition to replicas of cities, Second Life has representations of certain important sites, such as the World Trade Center twin towers, the Sydney Harbor Bridge, New York's Times Square, and the Spanish Mezquita Mosque (named the Chebi Mosque in Second Life). You can join other residents around these landmarks for various purposes. For example, "over a period of 24 hours on September 11, 2008, a variety of events took place including speeches, victim name readings, memorial dedications and tribute performances" related to the 9/11 terrorist attacks (Saidi, 2008).

If you prefer shopping, Second Life offers plenty of opportunities. You can buy the latest fashions at many designer stores to dress up your avatar. If you like electronic gadgets, visit the electronics store to browse and purchase. You can also shop for furniture and other items, such as paintings and other artwork, to decorate your virtual residence.

If you want to make money and have the necessary skills and talent, you can build things to sell to other residents, as Anshe Chung did. Second Life provides tools to construct houses, create furniture, develop games, build theme parks, or program race cars or helicopters and sell them to other Second Life residents to enhance their experiences. You can sell services to others, too. Own a restaurant, a tea house, or a pub and offer live music and other entertainment to visitors. Or operate a travel agency and guide visitors through the vast land of Second Life.

If you want something on the lighter side, enjoy some live music. Live concerts and other events are "one of the most popular activities in Second Life. Real-life musicians and DJs use streaming audio to send their sounds into SL, and avatars gather to listen. You can find just about every genre and era of music, from jazz to hip-hop" (Wagner, 2007). About a dozen live music performances take place on a typical day in Second Life. If art is your thing, you can visit some of the hundreds of galleries in this virtual world.

More serious things can happen in Second Life, too. You can try learning a foreign language from native speakers in an immersive environment built to resemble the place where the language is spoken.

If you're interested in learning mandarin Chinese, visit the Chinese Island operated by Michigan State University's Confucius Institute, which features a Chinese museum, markets, and restaurants. Many universities now have a presence in Second Life and are exploring offering courses in this virtual land. About three quarters of the universities in the United Kingdom are actively developing or using Second Life, according to a study (Kirriemuir, 2008).

Besides educational activities, you can also conduct business meetings, attend church services, or visit foreign embassies in Second Life.

Play Money: Gold Farming in the Synthetic World

"On April 15, 2004, I will truthfully report to the IRS that my primary source of income is the sale of imaginary goods—and that I earn more from it, on a monthly basis, than I have ever earned as a professional writer." Writer Julian Dibbell made this "dubious proposal" on March 11, 2003, and immediately set out to work. As of April 14, 2004, he had an annual income of $47,000, which did not exceed the highest annual income he had earned as a professional writer. So he declared: "Game over, I lose" (Dibbell, 2006, p. 284).

Dibbell may have failed to earn more than he had during his best year of writing and thus failed at his own proposal, "but on the other hand, to be honest, it [the $47,000 income] would have topped all other years. And it wasn't exactly hardship pay either: even in that last crazy month, I wasn't putting more than fifty hours a week into the job, all of them in the comfort of whatever I chose to call home" (p. 292). What exactly was his job?

Basically, he played computer games, killed monsters, attacked castles, collected points, and traded weapons, armor, and other valuable items in these games. However, he was not just playing the games for fun. Rather, he sold what he had acquired inside the games to other players for real-world money. That qualified him as a "gold farmer," someone who harvests in-game currency—virtual gold—in a specific type of computer game commonly known as "massively multiplayer online role-playing games" (MMORPG) and sells it for money in the real world.

MMORPG is a genre of computer games in which a large number of players interact with one another in a virtual world. The game is usually hosted by its publisher, and players from all over the world interact within the same environment, which is "persistent," meaning that it continues to exist and evolve while the player is away from the game. In an MMORPG, players assume the role of a fictional character and take control over many of that character's actions. The development of the fictional character is the primary goal in almost all MMORPGs. To develop the character along a prescribed path of progression, the player has to earn experience points. When sufficient points are accumulated, the character reaches a higher level, which often comes with more power, access to new territories and quests, or a more attractive appearance. There are different ways to accumulate points. Some of the common ones include combating monsters, completing quests, or battling with other players. Whatever the method, a player must spend lots of time and develop the skills to move up the levels so as to enjoy the privileges that come with the elevated status.

Although all players want to make their virtual characters more powerful in the synthetic world, not everyone has or wants to spend the time to develop the necessary skills. One solution is to use real money to buy points from other players—sort of like contracting others to do the work for you, which is no different from hiring someone to mow the lawn or clean the house. When there is demand, there is supply. There are plenty of players who love to spend time earning points and then sell them for real money. As a result, a new profession has been born.

Gold farming may have started in the late 1980s when computer game players made cash payments for items or to improve characters within multi-user dungeons (MUDs), the predecessor of MMORPGs (Heeks, 2008). It evolved from a hobby into a profession and from individual acts into a complex organized industry around the year 2000, as MMORPGs grew into a global phenomenon. There is no exact count of the number of MMORPG players in the world today, though one estimate put the number at around 50 million in 2008 (Heeks, 2008). One of the most popular titles, World of Warcraft, surpassed 10 million subscribers on January 22, 2008 (Alexander, 2008). The whole industry of MMORPG is worth about $2.5 billion a year for subscription fees only, excluding hardware and other costs (Heeks, 2008).

Today, gold farming has become an international business. There are an estimated 400,000-plus gold farmers in the world, mainly in China, Mexico, Romania, and Russia. This industry generates about $500 million in annual revenue. The number could be as high as more than a billion U.S. dollars, according to other estimates (Heeks, 2008). Even at $500 million, gold farming is no longer a cottage industry.

The life of gold farmers and the operation of this industry have begun to attract the attention of both the media and serious scholars. Besides Julian Dibbell's personal account of his own gold farming experiment in his book *Play Money: Or How I Quit My Day Job and Made Millions Trading Virtual Loot*, Indiana University professor Edward Castronova (2005) wrote a more scholarly, analytic book on this topic, titled *Synthetic Worlds: The Business and Culture of Online Games*. The *New York Times* has also published multiple articles about this profession (Dibbell, 2007). Ge Jin (2006), a doctoral student at the University of California–San Diego, has produced a documentary film about Chinese gold farmers. Researcher Richard Heeks (2008) of the University of Manchester published a detailed analysis of gold farming as an economic phenomenon.

eSports: Video Game Players Go Pro

"If you want to upset a group of South Koreans, start referring to 'computer gaming,'" writes Liam Fitzpatrick from Seoul for *Time* magazine. "We don't call it 'computer gaming' here. We call it 'e-Sports'" (Fitzpatrick, 2008). In a country where there are TV channels dedicated to video games, tens of millions of devoted fans and followers, famed stars, big corporate sponsorships, professional players and coaches, and specialized training camps, video games are indeed no less of a sport than basketball or soccer.

Vanessa Hua of the *San Francisco Chronicle* wrote about a South Korean professional video game player in 2006:

Choi Yeon-sung avoids going out most days, and when he's on the street, he puts his head down—to dodge the whispers, the stares and the pleas for autographs. Such are the hardships of a celebrity video game player in South Korea. Choi has 90,000 members in his fan club. He pulls down $190,000 a year in salary and winnings combined, in a country where the average annual income is $16,291. At 23, the boyish-looking professional gamer has achieved a level of fame bestowed elsewhere on movie idols, soccer stars and Olympic champions.

Choi was not the only e-sports star admired in South Korea. As Hua discovered, many of the top game players have loyal followers. Some Korean children now are aspiring to become Choi, just like many American children aspire to become Magic Johnson or Kobe Bryant. The stardom is also shared by TV commentator Paul Chong, who broadcasts video game competitions. "If he [Chong] decides that he likes you, your Seoul entrée is assured. He can get you an audience with the mayor" (Fitzpatrick, 2008). "An estimated 18 million South Koreans, more than one-third of the country's 48 million people, play video games online," writes Hua (2006). That's a healthy base for any sport. In addition, big corporations like Samsung, AMD, IBM, and Microsoft have become major sponsors of video game competitions.

But e-sports is not only a Korean phenomenon. The World Cyber Games, one of several international video game competitions, was launched in Seoul in 2000, with 174 players from 17 countries. The 2007 games held in Seattle had 700 players from 75 countries. The prizes totaled $448,000, more than double what was offered in 2000.

The World Cyber Games is not the only international video gaming tournament. Several other organizations operate annual competitions, such as the Cyberathlete Professional League, the World e-Sports Games, the Electronic Sports World Cup, the Championship Gaming Series, and Major League Gaming.

Invisible Attacks: Cyber Wars and Cyber Terrorism

On April 27, 2007, the cyberspace of the small Baltic state of Estonia was invaded. For the next three weeks, Web sites of the country's government agencies, including those of the Estonian presidency and parliament and almost all of its ministries, were attacked. Also attacked were Web sites of the country's political parties, major banks, and news organizations. The attacks took the form of distributed denial of services (DDoS), a commonly used method in cyber attacks that aims to disable or disrupt the targeted Web sites by overcrowding the bandwidths of the servers with tens of thousands of simultaneous visits. The attacks rendered these Web sites inaccessible to their users and caused significant damage to computer-dependent Estonia, a small country of about 1.4 million people but a pioneer in the development of "e-government" and "e-business."

These attacks were considered "a barrage of cyber warfare" launched by Russia against Estonia, according to a report by the U.K. newspaper *The Guardian* (Traynor, 2007). What prompted the attacks, according to the *Guardian* report, was the removal of the "Bronze Soldier," a Soviet war memorial in central Tallinn, Estonia's capital city. NATO, of which Estonia is a member, took notice of these attacks and dispatched top cyber-terrorism experts to Estonia to investigate the attacks and help the country improve its electronic defense. Although NATO does not currently consider cyber attacks as military action, the Estonian case may push its member states to reconsider. As the *Guardian* article suggests, "If it were established that Russia is behind the attacks, it would be the first known case of one state targeting another by cyber-warfare" (Traynor, 2007).

Russia was accused again in 2008 for another cyber war against another former state of the Soviet Union, Georgia. This time, the cyber attacks were reported to have both preceded and accompanied the physical attacks that occurred when Russian military forces moved into the disputed South Ossetia region on August 8, 2008 (Leyden, 2008; Markoff, 2008). The attacks were similar to those against Estonia in 2007, using DDoS to render important government Web sites inaccessible. Georgia eventually moved some of its Web sites, including the site of its president, to servers in other countries to avoid the attacks.

It is uncertain whether the Russian government organized the attacks. As Gadi Evron (2008), a well-known expert in Internet security and cyber crimes, suggests, the attacks may not have been state sponsored, but rather "just some unaffiliated attacks by Russian hackers and/or some rioting by enthusiastic Russian supporters." The same can be said of the attacks on Estonia. But whether these attacks were state sponsored or not is not important for Estonia or Georgia in terms of the damage done. In either case, their national interests were damaged by seemingly coordinated attacks associated with national and ethnic conflicts.

Compromising the interests of other nations or groups of people in cyberspace or via the Internet has become an increasingly likely threat as our societies become more dependent on technology. As early as 1997 the French journalist Jean Guisnel wrote about government intelligence gathering on the Internet in his book *Cyberwars: Espionage on the Internet*. In 2003, Dan Verton, a journalist with *Computer World*, published a book revealing another aspect of modern warfare: cyber terrorism. Titled *Black Ice: The Invisible Threat of Cyber-Terrorism*, the book presents the possibility of terrorist attacks in cyberspace:

> The next terrorist attack may well be launched—at least partially—in cyberspace. Much of our economy depends on the proper functioning of this digital medium. Typically, we think of cyberspace as "the Internet"—the global interconnections of computers that facilitate commerce (e-banking, securities trading, and online sales) and electronic communications. If this were the only function of the new digital medium, this nation would remain at risk. However, much more than the World Wide Web is at risk of a terrorist attack. Virtually everything we do is in some way impacted by the new electronic world. (p. viii)

Cyber attacks are appealing means for governments, terrorists groups, and individuals who wish to inflict damage on others because the cost is relatively low and the damage can be significant. For example, in 2000, the I Love You virus affected more than 20 million Internet users and caused billions of dollars in damage. The Code Red worm, another computer virus, infected about a million servers in 2001 and caused $2.6 billion in damage (Weimann, 2004).

Creating a computer virus and unleashing it on the Internet is relatively easy and can be done by a few individuals or even one person, as in the case of Sven Jaschan, a German teenager and high school student who sent the Sasser computer worm on his 18th birthday,

April 29, 2004 (CNN, 2005). Jaschan created the virus on his own. But the damage it caused was significant and global. "It was blamed for shutting down British Airways flight check-ins, hospitals and government offices in Hong Kong, part of Australia's rail network, Finnish banks, British Coast Guard stations, and millions of other computers worldwide" (CNN, 2005). The estimated damages were in the millions of dollars.

The damages caused by cyber attacks are almost impossible to tally because they come in so many different forms, some of which— defamation, oppressed freedom of expression, and services denied to customers or citizens, for example—cannot be calculated in monetary terms. But a report by the British–North American Committee (2007), a group of business leaders and academics in Britain, the United States, and Canada, gives some numbers for the business sector. The report, *Cyber Attack: A Risk Management Primer for CEOs and Directors*, says that "globally, malware and viruses cost businesses between US$169 billion and US$204 billion in 2004, and the trend is rising sharply. . . . Even the cost of spam is significant: costs associated with spam in the United States, United Kingdom, and Canada in 2005 amounted to US$17 billion, US$2.5 billion, and US$1.6 billion, respectively" (p. 2).

The Back Dorm Boys and the People Formerly Known as the Audience

Remember William Hung, the celebrity created by *American Idol*? Hung, an engineering student at the University of California–Berkeley, auditioned for the Fox TV show in January 2004. After the show aired four months later, Hung became an instant celebrity for his talents, or lack thereof, in singing and dancing. Since then, he has recorded albums, appeared on national TV shows, acted in films, and become perhaps the most famous star uncovered by *American Idol*, for whatever reason.

Hung is a telling example of what modern technology is capable of in transforming the value of talent and creating instant celebrities. Television and other media technologies are certainly powerful in making or breaking individuals. But the Internet is even more so. It has a much broader audience than traditional TV, and more important, it is much more accessible in terms of who gets on the show. Thus the Internet has created many more celebrities and entrepreneurs—many of them self-made, without the control of a big business or the assistance of a large group of professionals.

Wei Wei and Huang Yixin, more commonly known as the Back Dorm Boys, are an excellent example of the grassroots nature of the Internet in this regard. Two students at the Guangzhou Art Institute, Wei and Huang gained fame from a video they made in 2005 that showed them lip-syncing a song originally recorded by the Backstreet Boys. They initially made the video for fun and uploaded it to their college network; it quickly made it onto the international scene through YouTube, the popular video-sharing Web site. Their first video on YouTube was viewed more than 7 million times in the first few years after it was uploaded. They gained instant fame all over the world, and their fame led to new job offers and a new career. They were signed as spokespersons for Motorola cell phones in China and eventually became hosts of Motorola's online lip-sync contests. They also signed a contract with Sina.com, one of China's largest Internet portals. All this while still in college. After graduation in 2006, the two boys founded their own studio in Beijing, continuing to produce lip-sync videos and expanding their business to filmmaking.

The story has been repeated elsewhere. Matt Harding quit his job as a video game developer in February 2003 and used his savings to travel around Asia because he "eventually realized there might be other stuff he was missing out on," according to his Web site, wherethehellismatt.com. During this trip, Harding made a video of his now world-famous dance in Hanoi, Vietnam, at the casual suggestion of a friend. Matt obliged and danced "the only dance he does"—and he does it badly.

That video was put on the Internet and became a big hit in 2005. The popularity of the video led the company that makes Stride Gum to offer Harding the opportunity to travel and dance around the world. Harding accepted the offer and took six months to travel and dance in 39 countries on all seven continents in 2006. The resulting three-and-a-half-minute video quickly became another hit. The video had been viewed more than 11 million times on YouTube as of September 2008.

The success led to many invitations from people around the world who wanted Harding to dance with them. So he made a proposal to Stride Gum, which agreed to sponsor another around-the-world dancing tour. The video of the second tour was posted on YouTube, and within three months it had received more than 10 million views.

The Back Dorm Boys and Matt Harding are among the tens of millions of ordinary people who have turned the tables on the traditional media. Or, in the words of writer and New York University journalism professor Jay Rosen (2006), they are examples of "the people formerly known as the audience." Rosen writes the following in his award-winning blog, ThinkPress:

> Think of passengers on your ship who got a boat of their own. The writing readers. The viewers who picked up a camera. The formerly atomized listeners who with modest effort can connect with each other and gain the means to speak—to the world, as it were. . . . The people formerly known as the audience are those who *were* on the receiving end of a media system that ran one way, in a broadcasting pattern, with high entry fees and a few firms competing to speak very loudly while the rest of the population listened in isolation from one another—and who *today* are not in a situation like that *at all*.

Theoretically, anyone can be a news reporter, a book author, a radio station host, a TV anchor, or an encyclopedia editor thanks to the wide reach of the Internet and the advent of new technologies and services that have made it much easier and affordable for ordinary people to create, post, and share texts, images, audio, and video. Some of the common new technologies include Weblogs (blogs); podcasting (from "iPod" and "broadcasting"); social networks such as MySpace and Facebook; Web forums; Wikipedia; and video-sharing sites such as YouTube. Ordinary people have taken advantage of these possibilities.

According to a study by the New York–based global communication agency Universal McCann (2008), there are more than 457 million active Internet users in the age bracket of 16 to 54, of which about 100 million reside in the United States. Globally, 77 percent of them read blogs, and 45 percent of them have started writing blogs. In early 2008 there were 42 million bloggers in China and 26.4 million in the United

States. More than 47 million Americans have uploaded photos for sharing, and 25.3 million Americans have uploaded videos for sharing as of early 2008. An estimated 394 million people have watched video clips posted on the Internet. YouTube recorded 2.5 billion video views in June 2006, and more than 65,000 videos are uploaded daily, according to a report by Reuters (2006). The top seven social networking Web sites had more than 580 million unique visitors in June 2008, according to a report by comScore (2008), a Virginia-based firm that studies the development of the digital world. The two most popular, MySpace and Facebook, had 117 million and 132 million unique visitors, respectively, in the same period (comScore, 2008).

Challenges for Education

What's described in these paragraphs is just the tip of the iceberg in terms of the massive changes technology has brought to our society. Some of these new phenomena are just beginning to take shape and some will be replaced by even newer technologies. I mention them to make one point: the virtual world is as real as the physical world, psychologically, economically, politically, and socially. What happens in the virtual world has a significant effect on the physical world. It is not an overstatement to say that many of us now live in both the physical world and the virtual world. It would be a mistake to think the virtual world is unreal or imaginary. It may not be tangible, but surely it is real in terms of its psychological consequences, economic effect, political costs and gains, and social connections.

In some way, the virtual world is to me like the world outside my village was to my father when I was growing up. For a period of time, he lived in my village but left it every day. He was a noodle maker and needed to travel to different villages to sell his noodles. His visits to these villages affected other people's lives, but he did not interact with them fully. His visits certainly affected his life and our lives, yet he did not physically belong to those villages. This situation is no different from the lives of many people in modern-day America. Our well-being is affected not only by people we can see, feel, touch, or talk with physically, but also by people and technology we interact with virtually.

Thus the virtual world can be viewed as a foreign culture we must interact with. This foreign culture, like any foreign culture, has some similarities with our own, because we are all human beings. However, it is sufficiently different that we cannot treat it as the same. We cannot assume that because we know how to function in our own culture, we will be able to function effectively in the foreign culture. This foreign culture is also a new one, one that has just come in touch with ours. We are not sure of its full effect on us yet. Is it good or bad, or, in most cases, does that really depend on how we deal with it?

Businesses, governments, academics, and the media have all been working hard to interpret the implications and respond to the challenges of this new world. But the education sector has not. To be fair, many schools have actually embraced new technologies, and some might even argue they have embraced them too much. But they are simply treating new technologies as new tools to help conduct their business more effectively, without recognizing the transformation technology has brought about. This is similar to a peasant in the early days of the Industrial Revolution who bought a steam engine to help improve his farming but failed to notice that a new society was emerging that would alter his or his children's life in an irreversible manner. A majority of our schools have done little more than offer courses on computer keyboarding and other simple computer skills, besides using the new technology to enhance the teaching of traditional subjects.

Schools may not be able to ignore the virtual world any longer because the challenges it presents are becoming increasingly real and the consequences increasingly serious. The challenges of the virtual world to education come primarily from a number of concerns for children's well-being.

My first concern is whether our schools are teaching the skills and knowledge needed for our children to make a living in the virtual world, as Anshe Chung does. We may dismiss the importance of virtual property development, gold farming, or e-sports as a cottage industry, a fringe business, or an interesting but inconsequential phenomenon. However, this could change, and the change may come more quickly than we think. Consider a few simple facts:

• The first graphic Web browser, Mosaic, was released in 1993; but by 2008, just 15 years later, there were more than 1.4 billion Internet users (Internet World Stats, 2008). That is more than 21 percent of the world's population.

• Google was founded in 1998, with $100,000. In less than six years, Google became a company worth $23 billion. More important, its search engine has become an essential tool for virtually every Internet user. It was handling 91 million searches a day in March 2006 (Sullivan, 2006).

• After less than four years, Facebook, a social network site founded by a Harvard student, had more than 132 million users a month and was worth about $8 billion (comScore, 2008).

If the past is an indicator of the future, these examples tell us that we will see the virtual world becoming a significant source of jobs very soon. Workers are needed to continue to develop and improve metaverses such as Second Life; to defend our economy and country against cyber warriors, hackers, and thieves; to develop better video games; to manage huge databases; to deliver customer services; and to deal with the legal and ethical issues brought about by the virtual world. According to the Bureau of Labor Statistics, employment in the category of "Computer Scientists and Database Administrators," an umbrella name for a variety of IT-related professions, is "projected to be one of the fastest-growing occupations over the next decade," with an increase of 37 percent between 2006 and 2016 (Bureau of Labor Statistics, 2007b). Artists, especially those who work in the digital domain, are expected to be in high demand. "Multi-media artists and animators should have better job opportunities than other artists" (Bureau of Labor Statistics, 2007a). In addition, "graphic designers with Web site design and animation experience will especially be needed as demand increases for design projects for interactive media—Web sites, video games, cellular telephones, personal digital assistants, and other technology" (Bureau of Labor Statistics, 2007c). Video game developers, professional video game players, virtual property developers, and many emerging professions are not yet on the list of occupations put out by the Bureau of Labor Statistics.

Our schools have been teaching the skills and knowledge needed for an industrial economy, preparing our children to work only in the physical world. The challenge our schools must face is to begin teaching the skills and knowledge needed for the virtual economy. Certainly the skills and knowledge suitable for the industrial economy may also work well in the virtual world. However, the virtual world also requires different skills and knowledge, as discussed in Chapter 7.

My second concern is whether our schools are preparing our children to live in the virtual world as competent citizens. The virtual world has already become an influential platform for national and local politics. Ordinary citizens and organizations, as well as political leaders, have been using the virtual world to make their views known to others in the hope of influencing important decisions. YouTube, for example, was used to collect questions from American citizens for the CNN/YouTube debates between the candidates during the 2008 presidential primaries. A report titled *The Internet and the 2008 Election*, from the Pew Internet and American Life Project, includes the following statistics:

• Fully 46 percent of all Americans used the Internet to get news about the campaigns, share their views, and mobilize others.

• Thirty-five percent of Americans watched online videos related to the campaign, and 10 percent used social networking sites to engage in political activity.

• Seventy-four percent of wired Obama supporters got political news and information online, compared with 57 percent of online Clinton supporters.

• Thirty-nine percent of online Americans used the Internet to gain access to primary political documents and observe campaign events. (Smith & Rainie, 2008)

The virtual world, as the examples in this chapter illustrate, has also become a major platform for socializing, shopping, education, and entertainment. For example, *Online Dating Magazine* (2008) estimated that more than 20 million people visited at least one online dating service a month in 2007, and the estimated revenue for online dating services could reach $642 million in 2008. In terms of shopping, a report by an independent research firm suggested that online retail sales would reach $33 billion in the 2007 holiday season and more than 30 percent of customers would shop online (Forrester, 2007). In education, a report of the Sloan Consortium, a consortium of online educational institutions, found that more than 3.5 million or nearly 20 percent of students were enrolled in at least one online course in U.S. higher education institutions in the fall semester of 2006 (Allen & Seaman, 2007).

Despite all the activities that take place in the virtual world today, we can expect that the scale will only get larger and affect even more people. Despite all its wonderful benefits and some similarities with the physical world, the virtual world is a new world. The rules of engagement, the indicators of danger and abuse, the tools we use to participate, and the consequences of our actions are different from those in the physical world. To safely and successfully live in the virtual world requires new skills and knowledge. Our children, in spite of the "digital native" label attached to them, are not necessarily knowledgeable enough to fully participate in the virtual world. Yet most of our schools do not teach them the skills and knowledge required for safe and successful living in this new world.

7

What Knowledge Is of Most Worth in the Global and Digital Economy?

In a 21st-century world where jobs can be shipped wherever there's an Internet connection, where a child born in Dallas is now competing with a child in New Delhi, where your best job qualification is not what you do, but what you know—education is no longer just a pathway to opportunity and success, it's a prerequisite for success.

—Barack Obama, 2009

We need to move into niche areas where they will not be able to completely replace us for quite some time.

—Lee Kuan Yew, 2007

At many highway exits leading to major cities in China, one can spot groups of individuals holding cardboard signs with two Chinese characters, *dai lu*, which literally means "road guide." As soon as a vehicle approaches, they quickly swarm around it and tell the driver how much the city has changed, how complex the roads are in the city, and then offer to guide him to wherever he wants to go, for a small fee. They are professional road guides—basically, local residents with knowledge of the city who have decided to make a living by helping drivers navigate through it.

With increased ownership of cars and newly built highways in China, many Chinese have begun to experience the joy of driving. As a result, there is a surge in the number of new drivers traveling to different cities in their own cars. Increased economic activity has also increased the volume of truck transportation in the country. At the same time, almost all cities in China have been going through a construction boom, resulting in dramatic changes in roads and streets. Many cities change so quickly that they are unable to update their maps or put up road signs fast enough to guide out-of-town drivers. Additionally, as many cities in China are adapting to an automobile culture, they enact strict traffic laws, which are even more strictly enforced. Afraid of getting lost or violating traffic laws, many out-of-town drivers appreciate the service of these "road guides."

The road guides are controversial in China. They are certainly a traffic hazard and can pose potential dangers to drivers because they are not regulated or screened. There is also no standard rate for the fees they charge, which basically end up being whatever is agreed upon between the guide and the driver. Thus in some cities they are more welcome than in others, where their profession is considered illegal. However they are viewed, these road guides have found economic value in their knowledge of their city.

Although technology has increased the economic value of knowledge of a city in China, it is threatening the economic value of the same knowledge in London, where black cabs have earned a world-renowned reputation. For more than a century, the black cabs have offered professional, safe, and efficient transportation services in London. But what has truly made the black cabs famous is the cab drivers' knowledge of the city.

In perhaps the most strictly regulated taxi service in the world, licensed taxi drivers must pass a rigorous exam that is simply called "the knowledge." Aspiring drivers must study 320 routes and public buildings, parks, theaters, restaurants, and hotels. According to a report from the Transport Committee of the London Assembly (2005), it takes an average of three years to complete the exam. As a result, every licensed taxi driver in London has a complete mental map of the city. In fact, the London taxi drivers' mastery of the topography and traffic of the city is so amazing that some have concluded that the drivers' brains may be different from other people's. This suspicion was confirmed by a number of scientific studies. For example, the BBC reported in 2008 that "scientists have uncovered evidence for an inbuilt 'sat-nav' system in the brains of London taxi drivers" (Mitchell, 2008). An earlier study using brain scans found that they have "a larger hippocampus compared with other people. This is a part of the brain associated with navigation in birds and animals" (BBC, 2000).

This hard-to-acquire knowledge has made driving a London black cab a very special and exclusive trade, guaranteeing a respected lifelong career for those who possess it. But in recent years, the advent of global positioning systems (GPS) or satellite navigation systems (commonly known as sat-nav in the United Kingdom) has begun to challenge its worth. In 2007, the BBC pitted the new technology against a taxi driver in a real-life race. Acting on behalf of technology, BBC reporter Spencer Kelly used the latest sat-nav device to guide his driving, and cabbie Andy navigated using only his own brain. The race route included traveling through "extremely busy parts of London." And the result? The cab driver beat the sat-nav device by 27 minutes (Kelly, 2007).

The victory of cabbie Andy in this race does not guarantee the future of "the knowledge." There is no question that the technology will get better, and even if it didn't, knowledge that can be acquired instantly for a few hundred dollars is perhaps preferable to knowledge that takes three years to acquire, even though it is not as efficient. In fact, the London Transport Committee's report has already recommended reconsidering "the knowledge" in light of the development of sat-nav, although it still considers "the knowledge" necessary.

These two stories illustrate one obvious truth: useful knowledge changes as societies change. What used to be valuable can become irrelevant today. What is considered necessary in one society may be useless in another. At one time, physical strength may have been the greatest asset for an individual. Knowledge of domesticating and taking care of water buffalos may be essential for a rice farming community, but it is useless in a nomadic one. At one time, the ability to learn Latin or Greek was viewed as necessary for the nobility in England, but it has become much less important today. The invention and spread of the printing press made literacy a necessary skill for anyone who wanted to live successfully in the modern world. The ability to use the Internet was not even heard of 20 years ago, but today it is considered an essential skill for most people.

The massive changes brought about by globalization and technology discussed in Chapters 5 and 6 undoubtedly render some knowledge, skills, and talents less valuable while increasing the value of others. As a summary of the discussions in the previous two chapters, I use eBay to illustrate the potential effects of globalization and technology on the value of knowledge, skills, and talents.

Garage Sales and eBay: How Globalization and Technology Redefine the Value of Knowledge

Garage sales and eBay serve basically the same function: a platform to turn one person's trash into another's treasure, or to turn something of little or no value into something valuable. But they have one fundamental difference: eBay is global and garage sales are local. This difference means that with eBay you have more people working at making the connection between trash and treasure. Consequently, eBay is a much more effective platform for the trash owner and the treasure seeker to realize their goals.

You may be able to sell used books, clothes, cooking pots, golf clubs, or old bicycles in your front yard, but what about your used dentures or wisdom teeth? That can be tough, right? But people sold these items on eBay, according to an ABC News report (Wolf, 2002). You may be able to buy a deck of cards, a painting, or a pair of shoes at a bargain price at your neighbor's garage sale, but what if you want to buy a ghost, some "genuine" dinosaur poop, or two "rare" mutant M&M's joined like Siamese twins? I doubt these items appear very often in your neighborhood, but you can find them on eBay (Walker, 2003; Wolf, 2002).

The magic of eBay lies in its capacity to reduce the distance between trash owners and treasure hunters, resulting in a market visited by a large number of people from very distant places. This capacity does three things. First, it enlarges the number of prospective and real buyers, and thus one can sell to more people. However, by the same token, it enlarges the number of items for sale, and thus one can compare prices for the same objects. Second, it significantly increases the probability of turning one person's trash into another's treasure because the fundamental difference between trash and treasure is a difference in need and taste. People who visit garage sales are often from the same community (it's rare to see people driving more than 50 miles to go to garage sales), which means they are more likely to have the same needs and share similar tastes than people who live in another state or country. In other words, it is more likely that the people who can physically visit your garage sale have the same junk you do, and that makes it difficult to sell to them. Third, a large group of people increases the likelihood of finding those with unique or weird tastes or needs.

Madonna and Soccer: More Customers, More Value

Applying the eBay example to human talent, we find that globalization—the death of distance—has done exactly the same thing. First, it has enlarged the market for certain talents and increased the value of some previously "worthless" talents because they did not have many customers in one local community. Take Madonna, Miley Cyrus, and other contemporary singers as an example. If they lived in a time without modern recording or broadcasting technologies that enable their performances to reach a large audience, their singing talent would at best be rewarded with some applause and perhaps a few free beers in the village bar (if there was one) instead of the millions of dollars they make today. The same goes for Yao Ming, the Chinese basketball player who has a $75 million contract with the Houston Rockets. I don't know what his 7-foot-6-inch body would get him if there were no television screens allowing a large number of people to watch 10 people fighting over a ball. Granted, music and sports have existed throughout human history; but until mass communication technologies made it possible to bring them to many people across huge geographical areas, it was difficult for many people to make a living in these fields—at least not as good a living as today.

Soccer is a telling example. A century ago, it would have been hard to believe that the ability to kick a ball would become a multibillion-dollar business. Today, soccer is played by more than 17 million people in the United States, and the World Cup tournament in 2006 raised several billion dollars. The reason: technology erases geographical distances and brings millions of people together. Of course, it took about 80 years to get to this point. The first FIFA soccer World Cup was held in 1930 in Uruguay, with only 13 nations participating in the event. Many countries did not participate because to do so would require a long and costly trip across the oceans. The final game was watched by 93,000 people in Montevideo, Uruguay. In 2006, the World Cup was hosted in Germany, and a total of 198 nations worldwide attempted to qualify for the tournament. Germany experienced economic growth of 0.3 percent and had an additional 2 million visitors from abroad as a result of hosting the event. Retail sales increased by 2 billion euros, with overnight stays rising by 31 percent (Hweshe, 2008). For the 2006 tournament, FIFA raised 1.9 billion euros in marketing revenue and 700 million euros from sponsorship (*Telegraph*, 2006). The 2006 World Cup had a cumulative TV audience of 26.29 billion, and the final match was watched by a global cumulative audience of 715.1 million viewers (FIFA, 2007).

An expanded market also means more value for the same products. An invention that used to be consumed in one country can now be sold globally. Moviegoers in foreign countries now contribute more to Hollywood products than their U.S. counterparts. For example, the gross earnings of the all-time number-one box-office hit *Titanic* were $600,779,824 in the United States, only half of what it earned outside the country. For another hit, *The Lord of the Rings: Return of the King*, non-U.S. markets earned almost twice as much as the U.S. market ($742,083,616 versus $377,027,325). J. K. Rowling's *Harry Potter* series has been translated into 67 languages and sold more than 400 million copies worldwide since the publication of the first book in 1997. The final book in the series, *Harry Potter and the Deathly Hallows*, was released simultaneously worldwide in July 2007. Its first U.S. edition had a print run of 12 million copies, and its Japanese edition had a first print run of 2 million copies (Dammann, 2008). These astonishing figures would have been impossible to reach when the world was more separated.

Programmers and Toy Makers: Price Matters

But eBay also has expanded the pool of sellers. When two objects of the same quality are offered on eBay, the one with the lower price sells faster. Or in cases when there are hundreds of the same object, the lower-priced ones sell and the higher-priced ones may not sell at all. This situation is what has happened in the market for global talent. As discussed in Chapter 5, when India can provide computer programmers who are as good as those in the United States but cost only a fraction as much to employ, programming jobs are sent to India. The same is true for low-skill jobs in the toy and other labor-intensive industries. When millions of Chinese who are willing to work for one tenth of what an American worker earns for the same job become available on the global market, China becomes the world's factory.

When the job market is global, employers can theoretically find the talent they need anywhere, by either moving their businesses where the talent is found and outsourcing to operations that have the talent or directly moving the talent to wherever they need it. In a strictly business sense, businesses use two criteria to decide whom to employ: costs and quality, all other things being equal. To maximize profit, all businesses would like to pay as little as possible for their workforce provided that the workforce has adequate knowledge and skills for the tasks. Thus the first thing that matters on the global job market is cost or salaries and benefits from the employees' perspective.

Cheap labor is responsible for many of the job losses and factory closures mentioned in Chapter 5. Although many business leaders routinely use the lack of qualified workers in the United States as a reason to justify their outsourcing efforts and as evidence of the "poor quality" of American schools, the real reason is cost. The auto industry is a good example. While General Motors and Ford are closing factories and exporting jobs to foreign countries, Toyota has been expanding its operations in the United States, adding many more plants (Ohnsman, 2005) and tech centers (Krisher, 2008). How could Toyota find enough qualified workers in the United States if the assertion of poor-quality schools were true? Another example is the toy industry. According to a recent *New York Times* article, some of the best-known European toy makers such as Playmobil of Germany and Lego of Denmark resisted the pressure to move to China because "it is clear that Europeans trust Chinese contractors less than their own employees." They believe that "outstanding quality can only be reached when production is carried out under one's own eyes, by people who have developed brand awareness over a long time, and learned to produce the highest quality" (Landler & Ekman, 2007). They cannot find employees of the same quality at lower cost in China, so they kept their jobs at home.

Japanese Toilet Cleaners and American English Teachers: Unique Talents

The ability to speak English is nothing special in most American communities, so in most cases it is difficult to turn it into a valuable commodity. But if you travel to Japan, Korea, or China, you can turn this ability into a commodity by being an English teacher. This illustrates the second aspect of the eBay phenomenon. When distances disappear, people from traditionally isolated communities can benefit by offering what may be common and ordinary in their own communities but is of value in others.

Just as different geographical locations are better suited for cultivating different agricultural products, so have different communities developed specialties in human talents. China, for example, has exported many Ping-Pong coaches and players to other countries. Ireland used to export Catholic priests around the world. And recently Kyodo News International (2006) reported that Singapore imported Japanese toilet cleaners to help train Singaporean toilet cleaners.

The Long Tail Phenomenon: Nothing Is Too Strange to Be Useful

The other thing eBay illustrates is the "long tail" phenomenon explored by Chris Anderson (2006) in his *New York Times* bestseller, *The Long*

Tail: Why the Future of Business Is Selling Less of More. Traditional stores such as Wal-Mart, Best Buy, or Barnes & Noble have to consider carefully what items to put on the shelf based on their potential appeal to local customers. Movie theaters, radio stations, and video rental stores also have to play to their local customer base. These businesses count on "hits"—items that appeal to a large group of local customers. As a result, only a limited number of products make it to the market. But online stores like Amazon, NetFlix, and Rhapsody do not have to follow this approach. They are able to benefit from selling "misses"— items that may appeal to only a small number of people. Given the large number of people they can reach globally, they can always find somebody who is interested in something, however odd it may be. This phenomenon has been proven true by a number of online businesses. Anderson (2004) illustrates the long tail phenomenon with the example of Rhapsody, a subscription-based online music service that offers millions of songs:

> Chart Rhapsody's monthly statistics and you get a "power law" demand curve that looks much like any record store's. . . . But a really interesting thing happens once you dig below the top 40,000 tracks. . . . Here, the Wal-Marts of the world go to zero—either they don't carry any more CDs, or the few potential local takers for such fringy fare never find it or never even enter the store. The Rhapsody demand, however, keeps going. Not only is every one of Rhapsody's top 100,000 tracks streamed at least once each month, the same is true for its top 200,000, top 300,000, and top 400,000. As fast as Rhapsody adds tracks to its library, those songs find an audience, even if it's just a few people a month, somewhere in the country. This is the Long Tail.

The same thing can happen and has happened in the realm of human talent. Certain talents or skills may be needed by only a few people. Constrained by geographical distances, there may not be enough of those "few people" in one location to make the talent or skill a viable business, or there may not be anyone in a local community who needs the available talent or skill. Thus these rare talents are in essence "useless." However, when made available on a global scale, the number of people who may need or appreciate this unique talent or skill can become large enough to make it economically viable. Take the Matt Harding dancing described in Chapter 6 as an example. The majority of people may find the dancing simply silly. But enough people found it interesting and Stride Gum found it so valuable that it sponsored his efforts to do more of his "silly dance" around the globe. The same can be said of the Chinese Back Dorm Boys and Anshe Chung, also described in Chapter 6.

Digital Cameras Versus Cardboard Signs: New Skills in the Digital Age

Plenty of tips are available for successful garage sales and sales on eBay. A review of these tips suggests that success with eBay requires a different set of skills and knowledge than what is required for a successful garage sale. For example, Mark Styranka, owner of Bargain Deals (http://bargaindealsmart.com), a Web site that provides tips for stay-at-home businesses, suggests 10 "simple steps" for effective eBay sales: (1) post a low opening bid; (2) provide accurate shipping and handling costs; (3) offer a simple payment method such as Paypal; (4) use keywords in the title; (5) write a concise item description; (6) use clear photos; (7) provide solid customer communication via e-mail; (8) offer free shipping materials; (9) advertise your expertise; and (10) sell for a cause. Compare these to a list of tips for successful garage sales offered on frugalvillage.com, a Web site that offers tips for "frugal living": (1) choose a day and time to start your garage sale; (2) choose what you want to sell; (3) display your items properly; (4) advertise your sale (5) have lots of change and don't accept any checks; (6) be sure to have an electrical source; (7) be prepared to haggle, so set your prices accordingly; (8) plan some activities such as playing background music; (9) consider selling some refreshments; (10) be sure to have a notice that all sales are final; and (11) do not have your pet with you during your sale. The differences are quite obvious. Effective sales on eBay require more skills and knowledge that support activities in the virtual world, and successful garage sales require skills that are associated more with interactions in the physical world.

Although eBay has not replaced all garage sales or rendered skills for running successful garage sales obsolete, technology has significantly reduced the number of jobs in certain sectors. In fact, "during the seven-year period 1995 to 2002, 22 million global factory jobs disappeared—not due to offshoring but due to increased productivity" (Collins & Ryan, 2007).

Powersellers and the Rise of Self-Employment: The Changing Landscape of Jobs

Technology, like globalization, also creates new jobs. For example, eBay has led to the emergence of professional sellers—that is, people who make a living by selling on eBay. Often these are "powersellers," a label eBay gives to those who maintain certain levels of sales during a certain period of time and have sustained positive feedback from customers. There is even a trade association reserved only for powersellers on eBay: the Professional eBay Sellers Alliance (PeSA), founded in 2003. According to the organization's Web site, PeSA members "sell over $400 million each year on eBay" (PeSA, 2008). A *Forbes* magazine article reports that "more than 724,000 Americans say eBay is their primary or secondary source of income. Millions more sell stuff there from time to time" (Crane, 2006).

What eBay and other technologies have enabled is the growth of individual entrepreneurs who may not work for a big corporation because they now have direct access to their end clients. Writers do not necessarily have to use a publisher to sell their books. Musicians do not have to have a record company. Independent photographers (including amateurs) can sell their photos on Flickr.com. Web designers can independently sell their services online. The result has been a sharp rise in self-employment in the United States and other developed nations. The U.S. Census Bureau (2007) reported that every day an average of more than 2,000 people went into business for themselves in 2005, when individual businesses (without a payroll) reached more than 20 million, making up about 78 percent of all firms in the United States. These self-employment or nonemployer businesses had receipts of $951 billion in 2005. The fastest-growing industries are Web search portals, Internet service providers, nail salons, electronic shopping and mail-order houses, recreational vehicle dealers, and landscaping services. Notice that technology-related industries—Web portals, Internet service providers, and electronic shopping—account for three out of six of the categories of fastest-growing industries.

Starting up and running one's own business requires a different set of skills and knowledge than those needed to be an employee of a large corporation. What helps one succeed as an independent entrepreneur is certainly different from what makes one succeed in climbing up corporate ladders or working on an assembly line. Skills and knowledge that help people successfully operate their own businesses are gaining value.

eBay-Certified Consultants: New Professions

If you are new to eBay and want to quickly sell your junk but are not sure what to do, hire an "eBay-certified consultant." In 2004, eBay began to certify independent individuals who offer advice to eBay buyers and sellers. An examination is required for obtaining the certification to ensure that the certified consultant understands all the features of eBay. In addition to certified consultants, eBay offers a program to certify "eBay education specialists" who can train eBay users.

Technology, while reducing the number of certain types of jobs, creates new jobs and thus increases the value of certain kinds of knowledge. Like eBay's creation of certified consultants as a profession, the advent of Web search engines has created a new profession called "search engine optimization consultants"—people who specialize in helping businesses or individuals attract more visits to their Web sites. Second Life has led to the growth of individuals and companies who design virtual objects for others. Globalization has similarly stimulated the growth of demand for certain types of knowledge and talents. For example, translators and interpreters—specialists who can bridge language and cultural gaps—are in high demand. The Bureau of Labor Statistics (2007d) has projected that employment of interpreters and translators will grow 24 percent between 2006 and 2016, "much faster than the average for all occupations," as a result of increased immigration, national security concerns, and broadening international ties.

What Knowledge Is of Most Worth?
Defining Valuable Knowledge for the Future

In July 1859, the British philosopher Herbert Spencer published an essay titled "What Knowledge Is of Most Worth?" in the *Westminster Review*. In this essay, Spencer set out to "determine the relative value of knowledge" so as to determine "the great thing which education has to teach" (1911). At the time, the world was going through significant transformations brought about by advances in science and technology. In his home country, industrialization was transforming England from a rural society into an urban society. Steam-driven machines not only revolutionized the production of cotton and wool, but also shortened the distances in England through expanded networks of canals and railways. While the society was entering an industrial age, most of the schools at that time were in poor condition and were teaching subjects of no practical use, according to Spencer. He used many examples to show that subjects such as Latin and Greek were prized at the expense of more useful ones. Students were drilled in these subjects only to show that they had received the education of a gentleman—a badge indicating a certain social position that commanded respect. But what was of most worth was science, according to Spencer.

We are in the midst of another revolution that at least rivals the Industrial Revolution. This revolution, as already discussed, is significantly changing our society and thus the value of knowledge and talents. We must then ask the same question: What should schools teach in order to prepare our children for the global and digital economy?

And indeed, this question has been asked and answers have been offered by many organizations and individuals. In the next sections I summarize some of the more influential efforts to define worthwhile knowledge in the new economy.

21st Century Skills

The phrase "21st century skills" has become popular. Policymakers and education leaders all like to talk about "21st century skills" for a

21st century society shaped by globalization and technology. A few organizations have developed frameworks to describe the details of what they view as essential skills for successful living in the 21st century. The most widely disseminated framework is from the Partnership for 21st Century Skills, an organization founded in 2002 with members from national education organizations, major businesses, and education institutions. The organization believes that "every child in America needs 21st century knowledge and skills to succeed as effective citizens, workers and leaders in the 21st century" (Partnership for 21st Century Skills, 2008). According to its framework (Partnership for 21st Century Skills, 2007), "the skills, knowledge and expertise students should master to succeed in work and life in the 21st century" are the following:

• Core Subjects (English, reading or language arts, world languages, arts, mathematics, economics, science, geography, history, government and civics) and *21st Century Themes* (global awareness; financial, economic, business and entrepreneurial literacy; civic literacy; health literacy)
• Learning and Innovation Skills (creativity and innovation skills, critical-thinking and problem-solving skills, communication and collaboration skills)
• Information, Media, and Technology Skills (information literacy, media literacy, ICT [information and communication technology] literacy)
• Life and Career Skills (flexibility and adaptability, initiative and self-direction, social and cross-cultural skills, productivity and accountability, leadership and responsibility)

A similar framework was developed by the Metiri Group, a consulting firm based in California, for the North Central Regional Education Lab in 2003. This framework, as its title, *enGauge 21st Century Skills: Literacy in the Digital Age*, suggests, is more oriented to a future that is altered by technology. According to the authors, the framework was based on two years of research and "represent[s] the fresh, serious, new perspective required in light of recent historical events, globalization, and the idiosyncrasies of the Digital Age" (Lemke, Coughlin,

Thadani, & Martin, 2003, p. 9). In this framework, the skills needed for the 21st century are the following:

> • *Digital-Age Literacy* (basic scientific, economic, and technological literacies; visual and information literacies; multicultural literacy and global awareness)
> • *Inventive Thinking* (adaptability/managing complexity; self-direction, curiosity, creativity, and risk taking; higher-order thinking and sound reasoning)
> • *Effective Communication* (teaming, collaboration, and inter-personal skills; personal, social, and civic responsibility; interactive communication)
> • *High Productivity & Quality, State-of-the-Art Results* (ability to prioritize, plan, and manage for results; effective use of real-world tools; the ability to create relevant, high-quality products) (Lemke et al., 2003, p. 9)

The authors suggest that these skills should be "considered within the context of rigorous academic standards" (p. 9). Two different diagrams have been used to represent this framework, one with academic achievement surrounding the skills (Metiri Group, 2003) and the other with academic achievement sitting at the center, connecting the skills (Metiri Group, 2008). Both, I imagine, are intended to communicate the sense that academic achievement is the context in which the 21st century skills can be developed, although there was no specific discussion about what constitutes academic achievement.

The European Effort

The United States is not the only country that has realized the need to rethink what future citizens will need to know. The European Union has engaged in similar efforts, although the phrase "21st century skills" is not used. The European Parliament and the Council of the European Union, the highest-level governing bodies of the European Union, have worked to "identify and define the key competences necessary for personal fulfillment, active citizenship, social cohesion and employability in a knowledge society." (The European documents refer to *competences* rather than *competencies*.) Their efforts resulted in eight key competences that all European citizens are believed to need in order to "adapt flexibly to a rapidly changing and highly interconnected world" (Recommendation of the European Parliament and of the Council of the European Union, 2006, p. 13). Competences are "a combination of knowledge, skills, and attitudes appropriate to the context" (p. 13). The eight key competences are the following:

1. Communication in the mother tongue
2. Communication in foreign languages
3. Mathematical competence and basic competences in science and technology
4. Digital competence
5. Learning to learn
6. Social and civic competences
7. Sense of initiative and entrepreneurship
8. Cultural awareness and expression

All eight key competences are equally important, "because each of them can contribute to a successful life in a knowledge society" (p. 13). In addition, "critical thinking, creativity, initiative, problem solving, risk assessment, decision taking, and constructive management of feelings" (p. 14) are considered important across all eight key competences.

A Whole New Mind: R-Directed Skills

Although not specifically developed for schools, the American writer Daniel Pink's book *A Whole New Mind: Moving from the Information Age to the Conceptual Age* (2005a) is extremely relevant and has been embraced by many educators. Pink puts skills in two different categories: L-directed thinking and R-directed thinking. The L-directed (left brain–directed) thinking skills are sequential, literal, functional, textual, and analytic—typically functions believed to be performed by the left hemisphere of the human brain. The R-directed (right brain–directed) thinking skills are characterized as simultaneous, metaphorical, aesthetic, contextual, and synthetic—typically functions assigned to the right hemisphere of the brain. In terms more familiar to educators, Pink's L-directed skills are similar to the linguistic and logic intelligences within Howard Gardner's multiple intelligences framework;

or, in terms of school subjects, are associated with math, language arts, and science. Some of his R-directed skills are the other talents proposed by Gardner: kinesthetic, musical, visual/spatial, interpersonal, and intrapersonal intelligences.

Pink suggests that we have entered a new age in which R-directed thinking skills are becoming more important than L-directed thinking skills because of the three *A*s: Asia, automation, and abundance. "Asia" is shorthand for outsourcing or offshoring. As a result of globalization, Asia has become the destination of outsourcing. Many jobs that require L-directed skills have been outsourced to Asia. Technological advancement has led to the automation or computerization of many jobs that require the L-directed thinking skills as well. And abundance, the result of general economic development in the developed nations, has led people to desire more "conceptual" products and services that are beyond simply functional. To illustrate the influence of globalization, technology, and economic development on what is needed in the new age, Pink suggests that all individuals and organizations ask the following three questions to determine if they can survive in the new age:

1. Can someone overseas do it cheaper?
2. Can a computer do it faster?
3. Is what I am offering in demand in an age of abundance?

"If your answer to question 1 or 2 is yes, or if your answer to question 3 is no, you are in deep trouble," says Pink, because "[m]ere survival today depends on being able to do something that overseas knowledge workers cannot do cheaper, that powerful computers can't do faster, and that satisfies the nonmaterial, transcendent desires of an abundant age" (2005a, p. 51). And the ability to do something that cannot be outsourced or computerized or satisfies the desires of the abundant age, according to Pink, is the capability of the right brain.

From the capabilities of the right brain, Pink distills six new essential "high-concept, high-touch senses." They are (1) *design*, the ability to "create something physically beautiful and emotionally transcendent"; (2) *story*, the ability to "fashion a compelling narrative"; (3) *symphony*, the ability to see "the big picture and be able to combine disparate pieces into an arresting new whole"; (4) *empathy*, the ability to "understand what makes their fellow woman or man tick, to forge relationships, and to care for others"; (5) *play*, the ability to laugh and bring laughter to others; and (6) *meaning*, the ability to "pursue more significant desires: purpose, transcendence, and spiritual fulfillment" (pp. 65–67).

Although Pink does not explicitly discount the value of the L-directed thinking skills in his book, his belief that the R-directed skills are becoming much more important is apparent in many statements in the book, such as the following:

> Today, the defining skills of the previous era—the "left brain" capabilities that powered the Information Age—are necessary but no longer sufficient. And the capabilities we once disdained or thought frivolous—the "right brain" qualities of inventiveness, empathy, joyfulness, and meaning—increasingly will determine who flourishes and who flounders. (2005a, p. 3)

Core Assumptions

Taken together, these proposals present a fairly promising picture of the knowledge and skills needed to live successfully in the global and digital economy. The proposed valuable knowledge and skills are indeed desirable responses to the challenges posed by globalization and technology, as illustrated by the eBay example and discussed in Chapters 5 and 6. Underlying these proposals is the recognition of a number of core assumptions, which can be used to guide our decision about what schools should teach.

Assumption #1: We must cultivate skills and knowledge that are not available at a cheaper price in other countries or that cannot be rendered useless by machines. This is mainly Pink's argument but is shared by others such as the New Commission on Skills of the American Workforce and Harvard economists Claudia Goldin and Lawrence F. Katz, both professors of economics at Harvard University. In *The Race Between Education and Technology*, they write:

> Today, skills, no matter how complex, that can be exported through outsourcing or offshoring are vulnerable. Even some highly skilled jobs

that can be outsourced, such as reading radiographs, may be in danger of having stable or declining demand. Skills for which a computer program can substitute are also in danger. But skills for non-routine employments and jobs with in-person skills are less susceptible. (Goldin & Katz, 2008, p. 352)

Assumption #2: Creativity, interpreted as both ability and passion to make new things and adapt to new situations, is essential. All the proposals discussed include creativity as a must for successful living in the new age. "Human creativity is the ultimate source of economic resource," writes economist Richard Florida (2002, p. xiii). "The ability to come up with new ideas and better ways of doing things is ultimately what raises productivity and thus living standards."

Assumption #3: New skills and knowledge are needed for living in the global world and the virtual world. All the proposals discussed (except Pink's) include global competencies such as foreign languages, global awareness, and multicultural literacy as essential skills and knowledge to cope with the global world and digital or technology literacy for the virtual world.

Assumption #4: Cognitive skills such as problem solving and critical thinking are more important than memorization of knowledge. Although the two American proposals organized around 21st century skills include academic content knowledge in core subjects, what is common across all is an emphasis on high-level cognitive skills.

Assumption #5: Emotional intelligence—the ability and capacity to understand and manage emotions of self and others—is important. These proposals all include, to varying degrees, the ability to interact with others, understand others, communicate with others, and manage one's own feelings.

Not Everyone Is a Michael Phelps: The Issue of Feasibility

Together these proposals include a broad range of skills and talents that are indeed necessary or essential for living in an age transformed by globalization and technology. Even Pink, although heavily promoting the R-directed skills, does not want to throw out the L-directed skills. But is it truly possible for every student to develop all these skills and acquire the necessary knowledge? I raise this question not only because each individual has only a limited amount of time to devote to full-time studying before entering the "real world," but also because of the vast individual differences among human beings due to both nature and nurture.

We are not born a "blank slate" waiting to be scripted, as the MIT cognitive scientist Steven Pinker convincingly argues in his 2003 book, *The Blank Slate: The Modern Denial of Human Nature*. Evolution has granted all members of *Homo sapiens* some common capacities, and that certainly includes the potential to learn all the suggested knowledge and develop the R-directed skills. Thus Daniel Pink is correct to assert that "the abilities you'll need—Design, Story, Symphony, Empathy, Play, and Meaning—are fundamentally human attributes. They reside in all of us, and need only be nurtured into being" (2005a, p. 234).

However, for some reason, we are not all born the same. We may have the same set of innate abilities, but the strengths of these abilities are variable. Some are born extremely skilled in music, others in math, still others in making things. These are the people we call geniuses or child prodigies. Mozart was a genius in music, Gauss in mathematics, and Picasso in art. Most of us are not geniuses, but we do have areas in which we are strong. The flip side of this coin is weakness. We are not equally strong in all domains. One person may be great with words but not as good at painting. Another may be talented in dancing but have great difficulty with numbers. We also differ in the affective domain. Some are more adventurous, willing to take risks, and tolerant of uncertainty; some seem to be more cautious and risk-averse.

Nature is only half of the story. Nurture plays an equally if not more important role in the development of an individual. Although nature provides the potential, the environment affects what potentials are realized and to what degree, as well as what talents are suppressed and thus not fully developed. Families, friends, and schools all affect how one turns out to be. A person may have a strong inclination for music, but without the opportunity to learn or if music is forbidden, her musical talent will not be developed. Similarly, a child born with a more adventurous nature can be taught to be timid and cautious. Consequently, depending on the environment (country, neighborhood, schools, and families) one grows up in, innate propensities can be amplified or suppressed.

The dynamics between nature and nurture also play a significant role in what a person ultimately can be or can do. Early experiences may accelerate or slow down the development of certain innate abilities. At the same time, those accelerated abilities gain more attention and change the environment in their favor, which will then further support their development and suppress the less developed ones. This is the "Matthew effect" at work in psychological development: the rich get richer and the poor poorer, just like the Lord said: "For unto every one that hath shall be given, and he shall have abundance: but from him that hath not shall be taken away even that which he hath" (Matthew 25:29).

Tremendous disagreement divides scientists and educators as to which factor determines or plays a more significant role in the development of human abilities. Some tend to attribute more to nature, others more to nurture. Still others point to something else. For example, Harvard biologist Richard Lewontin (2001) writes, "The organism is determined neither by its genes nor by its environment nor even by the interaction between them, but bears a significant mark of random process" (p. 38).

Whatever the determinant, we all agree that human beings are different. We have different strengths and weaknesses. We have different wishes and desires. Thus, although Pink may be right in asserting that the R-directed skills "reside in all of us," it is not true that we are all equally strong. Nor is it correct to assume that we all can or want to develop R-directed skills at the same rate or to the same extent. No matter how hard I try, there is no way I can become another Michael Phelps, the American swimmer who won eight gold medals at the 2008 Beijing Olympics. Even if I had started painting when I was 3 and had been taught by a great master, I doubt I could become another Picasso. However, I must reiterate that we all, barring some extreme cases, can do the basics. I have learned to swim, and I am certain that I can learn to create decent images.

Similarly, although we all can learn a foreign language, not all of us can learn at the same rate and truly become fluent speakers of the target language. The same is true for the ability to use computers or work on math problems.

The Answer: Your Child's Strengths

It is too bad that we cannot expect each and every one of our children to swim as well as Michael Phelps, paint as well as Picasso, write as well as J. K. Rowling, and solve math problems as well as Gauss—all at the same time. But the good news is that they all have strengths, albeit in different areas. And even better, globalization and technological changes have created a world where all talents, even those "once disdained or thought frivolous" (Pink, 2005a, p. 3) have become very valuable.

In this light, the broad range of skills and knowledge discussed earlier in this chapter should be interpreted in two different ways as an answer to the question "What knowledge is of most worth?" First, they can be considered as skills and knowledge that all students should master and hence schools should teach. Second, they can be considered as a menu of skills and knowledge from which students can choose what to specialize in. What schools should do is to provide opportunities and resources to support students' development in their chosen areas.

The first interpretation is necessary because as members of a common society we should all develop a set of common skills and knowledge. Moreover, this approach also provides opportunities for students to experience and find out where their strengths lie and which areas they wish to specialize in. It is also desirable because, as discussed earlier, all human beings, except for a few extreme cases, have the capacity to develop basic competencies in all domains. So there is no question that all schools should provide opportunities for students to acquire the basics of all the proposed skills and knowledge. The question is, how much is desirable and possible? For example, we all agree that all students should know some mathematics, but does that mean all children should study advanced calculus or algebra? Likewise, all students should study at least one foreign language, but is it necessary for all students to acquire near-native proficiency?

None of the proposals discussed earlier in this chapter specifies to what degree each of the content and skill areas should be mastered. And there is plenty of disagreement even among experts with regard to the amount of content in each subject area or the level of skills in each domain. I know I cannot settle the "how much" question here or anywhere, but I am convinced that no one subject or skill, regardless of its perceived importance, should be elevated to a level that excludes other subjects or skills in the school curriculum, nor should it be allowed to kill children's creativity and drain their curiosity for learning. This is, I believe, also the spirit behind the 21st Century Skills Partnership framework and the European Union's eight essential competences.

In this spirit, schools should offer a comprehensive, balanced curriculum that includes opportunities for students to explore and develop both R-directed thinking and L-directed thinking; to learn math, science, technology, history, economics, geography, government, reading, literature, music, foreign languages, and art; to develop global awareness and appreciation for differences; to develop understanding of and ability to interact within the digital virtual world; and to develop a healthy body and mind.

The second interpretation treats the proposed skills and knowledge as possible areas in which students can develop true expertise. As Chapters 5 and 6 (as well as the eBay example in this chapter) illustrate, globalization and technology have opened up new possibilities that increase the value of traditionally "worthless" skills, knowledge, and talents. We have entered a new age in which industries have become more diversified to meet increasingly diverse human needs. In this age, the job market is also global, which makes it possible to turn knowledge and talents that are of little or no value in one local community into something with great worth in other communities. In this age, with the inclusion of many more workers from different countries and rapid changes in technology, it also is increasingly difficult to predict what new businesses will emerge and what will become obsolete. Thus what becomes highly valuable are unique talents, knowledge, and skills, the ability to adapt to changes, and creativity, all of which call for a school culture that respects and cultivates expertise in a diversity of talents and skills and a curriculum that enables individuals to pursue their strengths.

Educator Jenifer Fox's book *Your Child's Strengths: Discover Them, Develop Them, Use Them* (2008) provides an excellent answer to the question of what knowledge is of most worth. It is what the children are interested in and good at. It is their strengths. It is *not* a government mandate or what is being tested. And here is an account of a personal experience that illustrates the value of unique talents.

Taking Jobs Away from the Chinese: Valuable Knowledge in the Global Market

On a sunny spring day in 2008, I was sitting at Eudora, a bar in Beijing's Lido Plaza, with Jean, Hans, and Anna. We had just finished shooting a video interview in a nearby international school. Jean was the producer and director, head of this makeshift team. Son of Vietnamese immigrants, Jean grew up in America's Deep South and went to college in California. In his early 30s at the time of our meeting, Jean had been living in Beijing for about six years, working as a freelance video producer and independent business consultant. Hans, our cameraman, was a German in his late 20s. Hans had been studying filmmaking in China's Central Drama Academy and Beijing Film Academy for about four years and was working as a freelance videographer. Anna, our makeup specialist, came from England and had been living in China for only about two years. After graduating from a college in Wales with a degree in anthropology, she came to China to first study Chinese and then began teaching English.

I had not planned to invite them for a drink; the decision came in the middle of the shooting. I was there to conduct an interview of a successful Hong Kong entrepreneur and philanthropist who had donated a substantial amount of his money to promoting globalization of education; an international school called 3e International

Kindergarten was the first fruit of his generosity and vision. I was going to bring my own crew from the United States but was convinced by the head of the school, who was born in Hong Kong, educated in the United States, and was now working in Beijing, that he could find excellent talent in China for the project. I was quite surprised when I arrived at the scene. I had assumed that the crew was all Chinese and that Jean was a Chinese girl with excellent English abilities. As a researcher, I am always curious about unusual things. So I asked them why they were there and found that they all had extremely interesting stories to tell.

Over beer, I learned that they all loved living in Beijing. They were making good money, perhaps even better than their friends back home. They were fulfilling their dreams—making movies, staying away from their parents, and chasing new opportunities, which are abundant in China. "But my question is, why do companies hire you instead of the locals, who are apparently much cheaper? There are plenty of people who have learned how to shoot videos here, right?" I asked. As someone who was born and raised in China and now lives in the United States, I had always heard that the Chinese were taking over the world with cheap labor and there were millions of unemployed Chinese college graduates. Just a few miles away from Eudora was a village where thousands of college graduates live on less than a dollar a day, looking for jobs. But here were three foreigners who were happily self-employed and earning an income many times higher than the average Chinese college graduate.

"We have something they don't have" summarizes the essence of their answers. And this "something" is "a better sense of the composition of images," according to Hans; "attention to details because we are passionate about what we do," according to Jean; and "more experiences with moving images as we grew up," according to Anna.

This "something" they (the Chinese) don't have has given Jean, Hans, and Anna the relative advantage that enables them to live comfortably and happily in China, a nation that has often been said to have taken jobs away from the developed countries. What is worth noting is that Jean, Hans, and Anna had not necessarily received a formal education that prepared them for their adventure in China.

Judging from what they told me, their talents and pursuits were tolerated at home and in schools. Although that tolerance is critical, of course, a more active celebration and explicit support would be even better.

Tolerance and Diversification: Education with a Global Mindset

In the story of Jean, Hans, and Anna lies the simple yet very important answer to one of the greatest challenges to education brought about by globalization; and that is, in the increasingly globalized world, what is needed is a diversity of talents rather than individuals with the same competencies. If we adopt a global mindset, rather than a local, nationalist one, we will find that historical, cultural, and political factors have resulted in a variety of educational systems that have developed varying practices to cultivate talents valued in different societies. These talents are different, but from a global market perspective they can complement one another, commented Sim Wong Hoo, founder and CEO of Singapore-based Creative Technology. When asked in an interview with *Newsweek* about the advantages and disadvantages of having his company based in Singapore, Sim answered, "[T]he advantage is we come from a very conscientious culture. You tell our people what to do, they'll follow the rules, they'll do it. The downside is they are not as creative. We fixed that by having a U.S.-based R&D team that's doing more advanced research" (Levy, 2005).

A truly global mindset about education suggests that we seriously examine our traditions and identify our strengths in relation to others—not only other countries, but also other communities in our own society. This requires us to move away from not only adopting international standards but also national standards and testing. Each local community may have something special, something unique to offer on the global market. An international uniform curriculum or national curriculum can only serve to destroy local traditions and strengths.

A truly global mindset about education also suggests that we seriously consider the effect of "the death of distance." Our children will become more mobile globally—their talents globally traded. Like Jean, Hans, and Anna, our children can find employment in foreign countries, as long as they have the needed skills and knowledge.

A truly global mindset about education further suggests that developed nations must take responsibility for deliberately cultivating new talents because they are endowed with more resources. They must not fall back to compete with developing nations in the same domains, for both their own sake and the benefit of the world.

Finally, a truly global mindset about education suggests that tolerance for multiple perspectives, different talents, and a respect for diversity are key to a brighter future for all. As we enter a new era of human history, we cannot be certain of what specific talents, knowledge, and skills will be of value, and globalization has expanded the market; therefore, we must accept the idea that all talents, all individuals are worthwhile. Education is thus intended to help every child realize his or her potential. Every child counts!

8

Global Competence and Digital Competence:
The New Universal Knowledge and Skills

I am not an Athenian or a Greek, but a citizen of the world.

—Socrates

Computer science is no more about computers than astronomy is about telescopes.

—E. W. Dijkstra, computer scientist

Technology: No place for wimps.

—Scott Adams, creator of *Dilbert*

Alaska Governor Sarah Palin, the 2008 Republican vice presidential nominee, was criticized for her lack of experience in international affairs. She had to defend why her comments, delivered on national media, about Alaska's geographical proximity with Russia lent credibility to her claims of expertise in international affairs. She also had to explain why her first passport had been issued just two years earlier. Other than visits to Canada, she had made only one international trip in her entire life before the nomination, visiting the Alaska National

Guard stationed in Kuwait and Iraq in her role as governor (Bender & Issenberg, 2008). On this trip she also visited Germany and Kuwait, but later it was said that a fuel stop does not really count as a visit, so Ireland was taken off the list.

Costs of Global Incompetence

Certainly Governor Palin's international experience or lack thereof does seem inadequate for a potential vice president of the United States; but in fairness, she was not that bad in terms of foreign experience when compared with average Americans. Only 25 percent of Americans had a passport in 2006, according to a report of the Committee for Economic Development (CED), a Washington D.C.-based nonprofit organization. The report, *Education for Global Leadership: The Importance of International Studies and Foreign Language Education for U.S. Economic and National Security* (2006), says, "many American students lack sufficient knowledge about other world regions, languages and cultures, and as a result are likely to be unprepared to compete and lead in a global work environment" (p. 1). This assessment is backed up with a long list of compelling evidence, including the following:

- More than 80 percent of New York City eighth graders did not meet the state standards in social studies in 2004. Moreover, the number of students meeting the social studies standards has decreased by almost 20 percentage points since 2002.
- The National Commission on Asia in the Schools analyzed the growing importance of Asia—home to 60 percent of the world's population and most of the fastest growing economies—and what American students know about this vast region of the world. The Commission concluded that young Americans are "dangerously uninformed about international matters" and in particular about Asia.
- Most young Americans lack geographic knowledge. Surveys conducted by the Asia Society in 2001 and by the National Geographic Society in 2002 found that:
  - 83 percent could not locate Afghanistan;
  - 25 percent of college-bound high school students could not name the ocean between California and Asia;

– 80 percent did not know that India is the world's largest democracy;

– 37 percent could not locate China on a map of Asia and the Middle East; and

– 56 percent could not find India, despite the fact that China and India are the world's most populous countries, and major emerging markets.

• In Sweden, the top performing country, 89 percent of young adults spoke at least two languages, and 92 percent had ventured outside of their home country within the previous three years. In stark contrast, at the time of the survey, only 36 percent of young Americans spoke more than one language and a mere 21 percent had left U.S. soil in the preceding three years. (p. 14)

The list could go on, but adding to it is not necessary because Americans' lack of global knowledge and skills and the failure of American schools to teach them is an open secret. "Seventy-seven percent of the public believes that high school programs in the United States are not adequately preparing students to understand current international affairs" (CED, 2006, p. 14). The RAND Corporation surveyed respondents from 16 global corporations and found that many were highly critical of U.S. universities' ability to produce graduates with international skills. "Compared to their counterparts from universities in other parts of the world, U.S. students are 'strong technically' but 'shortchanged' in cross-cultural experience and 'linguistically deprived'" (CED, 2006, p. 6).

Why is this a big deal? The CED report says global awareness is vital to our economy, our national security, and our multicultural society. The future of the U.S. economy depends on its capacity to interact with other economies in the world. Nearly 60 percent of the growth in earnings of U.S. businesses came from overseas in 2004; one in five U.S. manufacturing jobs is already tied to exports. Trade between the United States and Asia is already approaching $800 billion annually. In 2002, U.S. affiliates of foreign companies directly employed more than 5.4 million workers in the United States (CED, 2006).

The lack of global knowledge and skills has already resulted in lost opportunities and revenues. American companies lose an estimated $2 billion a year due to inadequate cross-cultural guidance for their employees in multicultural situations. A 2002 survey of large U.S. corporations found that nearly 30 percent of the companies believed they had failed to exploit fully their international business opportunities due to insufficient personnel with international skills. In one example of the effect of the lack of global awareness, Microsoft's Windows95 was banned by India because its time zone map put the region of Kashmir outside the boundaries of India (CED, 2006).

National security is a critical challenge facing all Americans. But as history can attest, national security is not guaranteed by military might. Instead, it requires diplomacy, cross-cultural communications, intelligence, and, more important, a positive image across the world. A nation is truly secure when it does not have enemies. Although such a situation is almost impossible in this world, especially for the United States, a more positive image around the world can only help. Unfortunately, this is an area in which the United States has suffered in recent years, especially after the U.S. invasion of Iraq. Anti-Americanism in the Muslim world is well known, but even in Western nations, the United States is not very popular. According to Harlan Cleveland, a prominent political scientist and diplomat, "Anti-Americanism has increased rapidly in Europe" (Cleveland, 2004). In Germany, Russia, and France the percentages of respondents with an unfavorable opinion of the United States doubled from 2002 to 2003. Italy's unfavorable opinions went from 23 percent to 59 percent; they more than tripled in Britain and quadrupled in Poland. In Turkey, where the United States already had a 55 percent unfavorable rating, it soared to 84 percent. According to a report released in June 2005 by the Pew Global Attitudes Project, only 41 percent of Germans and Spaniards held favorable views of the United States, a lower percentage than for their views of China and Japan. In Britain, our historically close ally, only 55 percent of the public viewed the United States favorably, 10 points lower than for their view of China, 20 points lower than for their view of Germany. Our neighbor Canada had 59 percent giving the United States a favorable rating, only 1 point more than the percentage giving a favorable rating to China. But we like ourselves; 83 percent of Americans gave a favorable rating of the country, which is at least 20 points higher than the percentage with a favorable view of any other Western country (Pew Global Attitudes Project, 2005).

American's unpopularity may have many causes, but the nation's foreign policy and arrogance as perceived by others should certainly be on the list. An America-centric philosophy and a lack of understanding of other cultures and the global world are among the chief reasons for our unilateralism and perceived arrogance when dealing with other peoples. This is a result of the nation's education system. Abraham Lincoln once said, "The philosophy in the classroom of this generation is the philosophy of government in the next." More important, the United States needs talented diplomats and a public that understands and respects other cultures so when Americans travel abroad or interact with people from other cultures, they can project a better image and reverse perceptions.

The negligence of American schools in teaching foreign languages and cultures has had a more direct effect on America's national security. "The September 11th intelligence failures provide considerable evidence of our shortage of expertise in Arabic and Asian languages and cultures," states the CED report (Committee for Economic Development, 2006, p. 9), citing evidence showing the extreme difficulties the army, the CIA, the FBI, and other U.S. national security agencies had in recruiting enough experts in critical languages. As a result, the FBI's counterterrorism efforts were hampered. "The FBI did not dedicate sufficient resources to the surveillance and translation needs of counter-terrorism agents. It lacked sufficient translators proficient in Arabic and other key languages, resulting in a significant backlog of un-translated intercepts," according to the 9/11 Commission (CED, 2006, p. 9).

The importance of culturally and linguistically competent individuals in the current war against terrorism is highlighted in a comment by Michael Lemmon, former ambassador to Armenia and dean of the National War College: "Part of the reason for our difficulty is that we simply don't have enough competent speakers of Arabic with credible policy context and an ability to connect with the intended audience so they will at least listen to what we are trying to say and give us a hearing" (CED, 2006, p. 8).

Understanding other cultures and languages is also vital to the continued prosperity of the United States as a multicultural society. The United States will continue to receive immigrants from different countries. Racial and ethnic harmony rests upon mutual understanding and respect. Despite progress made over the years, racial and ethnic relationships remain a critical issue in the United States. The nation must continue to face this difficult problem and keep its society open, which also requires schools to teach about other cultures and languages. Globalization brings many benefits, but it comes with new challenges, as noted in the CED report:

> Despite America's status as an economic, military, and cultural superpower, we risk becoming narrowly confined within our own borders, lacking the understanding of the world around us that is essential to our continued leadership role in the world community. The day has long passed when a citizen could afford to be uninformed about the rest of the world and America's place in that world. (p. vii)

Defining Global Competence

According to a report of the University of Wisconsin Global Competence Task Force (2008), a globally competent person should have "the skills, knowledge, and attitude to work effectively in our increasingly interdependent world" (p. 2). The report further states the following:

> Foremost amongst these "global competencies" are the abilities to communicate effectively across linguistic and cultural boundaries, to see and understand the world from a perspective other than one's own, and to understand and appreciate the diversity of societies and cultures. Students need to appreciate the interdependence of nations in a global economy and to know how to adapt their work to a variety of cultures. (p. 3)

Fernando Reimers, a Harvard University education professor, offers a similar definition:

> I define Global Competency as the knowledge and skills that help people understand the flat world in which they live, the skills to integrate across disciplinary domains to comprehend global affairs and events and to create possibilities to address them. Global competencies are also the attitudinal and ethical dispositions that make it possible to interact peacefully, respectfully, and productively with fellow human beings from diverse geographies. (Reimers, 2009)

Reimers's definition includes three dimensions: the affective dimension, the action dimension, and the academic dimension. The affective dimension, also called the ethical dimension, refers to "a positive disposition towards cultural differences and a framework of global values to engage difference." The action dimension, also called the skill dimension, refers primarily to the "ability to speak, understand, and think" in a foreign language. The academic dimension has to do with academic knowledge of the world, hence is also referred to as the disciplinary and interdisciplinary dimension, which includes "deep knowledge and understanding of world history, geography, the global dimensions of topics such as health, climate, and economics, and the process of globalization itself" (Reimers, 2009).

There are other definitions of global competence. For example, Harvard professor Howard Gardner (2004) proposes, without using the term "global competence," that precollegiate education should prepare students to develop an "understanding of the global system," "knowledge of other cultures and traditions," and "knowledge of and respect for one's own cultural traditions"; and foster "hybrid or blended identities" and "tolerance and appreciation across racial, linguistic, national, and cultural boundaries" (pp. 253–355).

Consistent across most definitions of global competence is the issue of "others." As discussed in Chapter 5, technology, trade, and immigration have led to "the death of distance." People previously separated from us by distance have been brought into our lives, and how to view, interact with, and live with them has become a significant issue facing all of us, thus forming the foundation of our ability to live in the global world. In the following sections I highlight some of the core issues that we must address as part of our efforts to foster global citizens.

Two Grasshoppers on the Same String: Global Interdependence

The Chinese often describe situations of mutual dependence with the saying "We are two grasshoppers tied to the same string. I cannot escape; neither can you." Although it may not sound elegant, the saying tells a fundamental truth about living in the global village: the welfare of all human beings has become so interconnected and interdependent that no individual, organization, or nation can continue to live prosperously forever while their fellow villagers live in misery. As Michel Camdessus (2000), managing director of the International Monetary Fund, said in a speech:

> The widening gaps between rich and poor within nations, and the gulf between the most affluent and most impoverished nations, are morally outrageous, economically wasteful, and potentially socially explosive. Now we know that it is not enough to increase the size of the cake; the way it is shared is deeply relevant to the dynamism of development. If the poor are left hopeless, poverty will undermine the fabric of our societies through confrontation, violence, and civil disorder. We cannot afford to ignore poverty, wherever it exists, whether in the advanced countries, emerging economies, or the least developed nations. But it is in the poorest countries that extreme poverty can no longer be tolerated; it is our duty to work together to relieve suffering.

Poverty, diseases such as HIV/AIDS, conflicts, resource shortages, or any other forms of human suffering in one country or one region anywhere on the globe can affect other countries, no matter how far away they are. Conflicts in the Middle East can cause gas prices to rise around the world. Famine in Africa can result in increases in food prices globally. Water shortages in Ethiopia can lead to wars in the region and result in refugees and illegal migration to other nations. Even from a purely selfish perspective, we must learn to help others, to work on raising the living standards of our poor neighbors. It is fairly dangerous to live as the only wealthy family in a poverty-stricken village.

Thus one of the elements of global citizenship is knowledge of the vast economic and social inequalities existing in today's world and how these inequalities may affect our lives. We need to help our children understand that although globalization may have generated more wealth around the world, the distribution has been uneven. Not everyone has enjoyed the same level of economic growth (Stiglitz,

2006). Some have even charged that globalization has increased the misery of many people (Bigelow & Peterson, 2002). Our children, who will live in this village much longer than we will, need to also understand that globalization's negative outcomes—exploitation of poor countries, for example—can affect their own lives.

Jobs for Everyone: Global Economics

Thomas Friedman's advice to his daughters ("Finish your homework; people in India and China are starving for your jobs") may motivate them to complete their homework because they do not want the Chinese and Indians to take their future jobs, but it is a damaging statement concerning globalization. It unnecessarily fans fear of and hatred toward other countries and peoples. One of the consequences of economic globalization is the movement of businesses from developed nations to developing ones, which results in vast job losses, as discussed in Chapter 5. This loss of jobs has already created panic and anxiety in developed nations. Words like Friedman's add to the panic and paint foreigners as job robbers, as the cause of economic hardship in countries where jobs are lost.

The Indians, the Chinese, and all others have a right to jobs. The "pursuit of happiness" mentioned in the United States Declaration of Independence should apply to everyone, not just Americans.

Moreover, the view that the developing countries are taking jobs away from the developed nations is inaccurate from an economic standpoint. First, jobs are lost as industries change. As Robert Thompson (2007), a University of Illinois professor and chairman of the International Food and Agricultural Trade Council, has pointed out:

> Countries' competitive positions change all the time. No economy stands still. New mineral deposits are found, and others are depleted. Some countries' populations grow, and others decline. Research may find new technologies that provide a greater advantage to one country than another. New technologies can completely wipe out previous industries. How many buggy whip manufacturers can you find in the U.S. today? (p. 6)

Even without globalization, what powers a nation's economy can change and force people to transition to other types of jobs. Take the United States, for example. The common perception is that China and India have caused massive job losses in the manufacturing and service sectors, but a study by McKinsey found this is not the case. Based on an analysis of detailed trade and industry data, the study found that

> trade, particularly rising imports of goods and services, didn't destroy the vast majority of the jobs lost in the United States since 2000. [O]nly about 314,000 jobs (11 percent of the manufacturing jobs lost) were lost as a result of trade . . . falling exports, not rising imports, were responsible. Service sector offshoring destroyed even fewer jobs. These figures are tiny relative to the millions of positions lost and created every year in the United States by normal market forces . . . manufacturing's share of total U.S. employment has been falling for at least half a century—a trend that is typical not only of developed economies but also of many developing ones. (Baily & Lawrence, 2005)

In fact, trade and investment with China has benefited the United States, according to a study released by the China-U.S. Business Forum. The study found that trade and investment with China will result in a 0.7 percent increase in U.S. GDP and a 0.8 percent decrease in prices by 2010. Trade and investment with China will also lead to an increase of 0.7 percent in output per worker across the U.S. economy (Britton & Mark, 2006).

But the public and the media often misunderstand the effects of globalization because of their lack of understanding of global economics. For instance, a report based on the 2008 Pew Global Attitudes Project indicates that 53 percent of Americans believe that trade is good and 53 percent say China's growing economy is a bad thing, contrary to what expert analysts have found about the benefits of China's growth to the United States (Pew Research Center, 2008).

Therefore, it is crucial for citizens of the global village to develop a good understanding of economics from a global perspective. Such an understanding not only will help global citizens to actively participate in and contribute to the global society, but also will reduce negative feelings toward other countries and enhance harmony in the global village.

Climate Change and Bird Flu: Global Problems

The earth is getting hotter, and the consequences could be dire. Global warming has already caused the Arctic to shrink, glaciers to retreat, and sea levels to rise. Associated changes have occurred in the amount and pattern of precipitation, resulting in flooding and drought. Global warming also causes extreme weather, affecting agricultural yields, extinction of species, and the spread of life-threatening diseases. These changes can result in great economic costs and threats to human lives.

Human activities have been generally recognized as a major cause of climate change, and increased economic development resulting from globalization has certainly accelerated global warming. But climate change is not the only serious problem facing all human beings that has been exacerbated by increased globalization. Environmental degradation, deforestation, desertification, oil depletion, and destruction of wildlife habitats are all consequences of modernization brought about by globalization. The economic growth resulting from globalization has significantly increased consumption of natural resources and caused irreversible damage to our environment.

These problems are global in nature. When China imports timber from Indonesia, it in essence exports deforestation. When India's middle class expands and an increasing number of Indians begin to drive, they are essentially contributing to the worldwide energy crisis and global warming. When Brazilians replace forests with coffee fields in the Amazon region, they too are affecting the global temperature. Similarly, when the United States sends its manufacturing industries overseas, it also sends pollution. When the British buy petroleum from Africa, they consume global energy resources.

Global problems can only be solved globally. One country can change its energy policy, impose greenhouse gas taxes, or promote conservation; but unless all countries adopt the same approach, unless everyone is aware of the problems and contributing to their solutions, it is impossible to address these problems. However, therein lies a moral difficulty. If all people have the same right to pursue a better, more modern life regardless of where they live, how can we tell the developing nations not to pursue economic development, even though it leads to pollution and environmental destruction? On the other hand, it would be impossible to sustain an American lifestyle for everyone on earth.

Part of the answer probably lies in scientific and technological innovations that will deliver an American lifestyle but consume fewer natural resources. Automobiles that are more energy efficient or that use replaceable energy, for example, can probably allow more people to drive with the same amount of gas or less. Changes in human behavior must also be part of the solution. Turning off the water while brushing your teeth is as important to saving water as more efficient irrigation technologies. Recycling, turning off lights when not in the office, and simply consuming less can significantly reduce humans' impact on the earth.

All of these efforts require everyone to understand the nature of global problems, to understand their causes, their potential effects, their complex moral, economic, and political implications, and possible solutions. Hence, knowledge of global problems should be an essential component of what makes a contributing citizen in the global village.

"Us" and "Them": Human Conflicts and Peace

Wars and other smaller-scale conflicts among human beings are perhaps the most costly, self-destructive human activities in the world. Basically, they start from the desire to protect or enhance self-interest, be it natural resources, ideological superiority, material wealth, or human resources; or to gain advantage over others, to wipe out or weaken potential competitors. Killing others and destroying their property are often justified through demonizing others, through drawing a distinct line between us and them.

It is a natural human tendency to separate people into "us" and "them," although the "us" and "them" (or "we" and "they") merely serve as constantly evolving containers. There are many ways human beings make the separation: race, gender, belief, skin color, birthplace, language, interest, political entity, or any other distinguishable features human beings may bear. Those who look like ourselves are "we," as are those who believe in the same God, attend the same church, share the same country, or have the same level of income. "We" are always better than "they" are and should enjoy a better life. "We" are hardworking, honest, clean, and moral, whereas "they" are lazy, dishonest, dirty, and evil, so they do not deserve the same life, the same respect and dignity. "We" should always be wary of "them" because "they" always want to destroy "us." For all sorts of psychological, technological, political, and cultural reasons, most of "us" do not have direct experiences with "them" or have much knowledge about "them" and their real intentions. This lack of knowledge and understanding feeds the powerful feeling of fear, which has been used to start wars and war-associated activities, such as building up a threatening military arsenal.

Globalization has the potential to both increase the likelihood and scale of destructive conflicts and help reduce the possibility of conflicts. On the one hand, globalization intensifies competition for resources, engenders a sense of invasion by other countries through their goods and migrants, and has resulted in dissatisfaction because of increased income disparities, exploitation, and destruction of local resources and cultural traditions (Galtung, 2002; Stiglitz, 2006). Advances in information and communication technologies further heighten the sense of injustice and exploitation when people around the globe are more aware of the huge differences in living standards between the rich and the poor. Furthermore, advanced technologies have made conflicts more violent, more destructive than ever before. On the other hand, global economic integration binds people and makes their interests more interdependent so they are unlikely to go to war because it causes damage to both parties, as Thomas Friedman explains in his book *The Lexus and the Olive Tree* (1999). Migration, tourism, and information and communication technologies all provide more opportunities for people to interact with and to learn about one another, possibly reducing mistrust and fear.

We need citizens who can lead global efforts to reduce distrust and fear among different people. To do so requires a new mindset, a mindset that considers all human beings as "us," that helps transcend traditional racial, religious, political, and other boundaries that have been used to divide human beings into "us" and "them."

Understanding Others: Foreign Languages and Cross-Cultural Competency

An effective way to develop a global mindset is to understand others as human beings. Such understanding requires direct interaction; and interaction, in turn, requires the ability to move across cultures comfortably and fluently. I refer to such ability as cross-cultural competency. It includes both the ability to use the language and a deep understanding of the culture. Cross-cultural competency is also a necessary ability for all global citizens in their professional life, as they will need to work together with individuals from different cultural backgrounds. And to perform the basic functions of citizens, they will need to make decisions about and interact with people from other cultures, such as people who have immigrated into their communities.

Cross-cultural competency first and foremost includes a deep understanding and appreciation of different cultures. There are many definitions of culture, but the more generally accepted one is proposed by anthropologists Daniel Bates and Fred Plog (1990): "A culture is the system of shared beliefs, values, customs, behaviors, and artifacts that the members of society use to cope with their world and with one another, and that are transmitted from generation to generation through learning" (p. 7). This definition contains a number of important points about culture. First, it includes not only factual knowledge, such as a country's capital city, history, or political system. It also includes beliefs, values, customs, and behaviors, things that cannot necessarily be explicitly described. Second, culture is learned, which means that it is not genetically transmitted and others can learn the system. Third, it is shared by the members of a society and transmitted from generation to generation so it is fairly stable and ubiquitous, which makes a large part of the system unconscious. That is, members of the culture know the values, beliefs, and customs so well that they do not consciously think about them, making it difficult for them to explain their culture to others.

True understanding of other cultures requires one to "penetrate below the surface" of other cultures (Dewey, 1983, p. 263). It does not arise from simple fact telling in international education classes, which are easily colored by superficial emotion, ignorance, fear, and prejudice (Saito, 2003). The understanding needs to reach "the inner spirit and real life of a people" (Dewey, 1983, p. 267). Thus to develop real understanding of other cultures requires us to experience the culture in context, rather than simply memorizing some facts or imitating stereotypes.

Cross-cultural competency also means the ability to live in and move across different cultures easily. In the globalized world, we will be interacting with many cultures, but it is impossible to be competent in all the cultures of the world. Thus cross-cultural competency can be viewed as a general psychological ability that includes attitudes, perspectives, and approaches to new, different cultures. Again, John Dewey suggests such competencies can be developed by confronting and surmounting differences in ways of thinking, value systems, and habits of mind. According to Dewey, education for global understanding must be supported by the notion of unity in diversity, a solidarity among human beings that is made possible only through interaction between different perspectives (Saito, 2003).

Proficiency in foreign languages is an essential component of cross-cultural competency. Today, many education systems teach foreign languages for economic reasons and thus focus on only communicative competency. Although communicative competency is important, language also serves as a window into the "shared beliefs, values, customs, behaviors, and artifacts that the members of society use" (Bates & Plog, 1990, p. 7). Foreign language teaching can also be the avenue for understanding cultures.

In summary, we now live in a "flat" world, or "global village." As residents of this global village, what do we need to make this a happy and prosperous place for all its residents? The answer is simple: global citizenship. For the global village to become a happy and prosperous place for all its residents, everyone in this village must accept the fact that their well-being is intricately interconnected and dependent on others; they must understand and be willing to tackle common problems facing the village; they must treat each other as equals; and they must try to understand and appreciate each other's beliefs, values, behaviors, and customs. And finally, of course, they must be able to talk with each other, using a common language.

Defining Digital Competence

If you are like me, you have received e-mail messages like the following at least once, but more likely many times a day:

> From: jhbeverdam@hetnet.nl
> Subject: Greetings from James O'Brien
> Hello friend,
> My name is James O'Brien, a citizen of wales in the united kingdom. I am contacting you because I need your help to solve a problem. I need your help as a beneficiary to help collect some funds from a security company in Holland. Since the death of my father, I have been unable to do so and the security company wants me to present a foreign beneficiary. The amount involved is Twenty Million Dollars and you shall have Seven Million Dollars, please reply me back at jamesobrienuk5 @yahoo.com.hk I shall give you the whole details. Have a nice day.
> James O'Brien

If you are like me, you probably never respond—not because you are not interested in the $7 million but because you know you actually have no chance of getting it. The sad thing, however, is that there are still people out there who think they can actually get the promised millions of dollars—not many, but enough to encourage the scammers to continue their tricks. This particular form of scam, commonly known as the Nigerian Scam (because it originated in Nigeria) or the 419 Fraud (after the article number of the Nigerian Criminal Code that describes it), has been around for decades. According to Snopes.com, a widely referenced Web site that debunks frauds and urban legends, the scam can be traced back to the Spanish Prisoner con game in the 1920s, when businesses were contacted to rescue wealthy prisoners in Spain and promised a reward of tremendous wealth afterward (Snopes.com, 2003). Of course, the wealth was never distributed and the conned businesses would have given lots of money to the scam operatives. The new version of the Spanish Prisoner con was revived in oil-rich Nigeria in the 1980s. Scammers sent out letters via mail or fax to businesses, asking for assistance to help move millions of dollars out of a bank in Nigeria and, of course, offering the business a healthy chunk of the money. But to access the money, the business would have to pay legal fees, bribes to the bank or local officials, or some other fees in advance. Hence the official name of the scam: Advance Fee Fraud. The Internet has made this scam a global phenomenon, and as the letter I received shows, individuals have become the primary target. After so many years, people are still falling for this trick, and victims lose hundreds of millions of dollars each year. Some have even lost their lives (Carothers, 2006).

The Internet, or the virtual world, is full of wonders and dangers, as discussed in Chapter 6. Although the Nigerian Scam existed long before the Internet, the Internet significantly changed its scale and impact. Like the example of eBay as a global garage sale, the Internet has made the scam global, significantly expanding its reach to potential victims and drastically reducing the chances of the scammers being caught and the victims reclaiming their lost wealth. When this type of dangerous trap is so commonplace, avoiding the dangers and exploring the wonders of the Internet has become an issue of digital competence—the knowledge, skills, attitudes, and ability to live a healthy and successful life in the virtual world.

Chapter 6 describes the emergence of a virtual world and poses a number of challenges facing education today, including how schools can equip our children with the necessary competencies to live productively in the virtual world. The competencies can be generally referred to as digital competence, although a variety of other terms have been used for this new set of skills, knowledge, and attitudes. Some of the most frequently used terms include *computer literacy, digital literacy, digital age literacy, technology literacy, media literacy, information literacy,* and *digital citizenship.*

Definitions of digital competence abound. Some of them are very broad, encompassing a variety of cognitive skills and emotional qualities needed to live in a society transformed by technology. For example, the Metiri Group's definition of *digital-age literacy* includes basic literacy, scientific literacy, economic literacy, technological literacy, visual literacy, information literacy, multicultural literacy, and global awareness (Metiri Group, 2003). The 21st Century Partnership's *Framework for 21st Skills* includes information literacy, media literacy, and information and communication technology (ICT) literacy. Some other definitions are generic, basically reiterating the higher-level thinking skills required for the new society, through the means of technology. For instance, the International Society for Technology in Education (ISTE), the most prominent organization in promoting digital literacy in schools, recently published a new version of its *National Educational Technology Standards and Performance Indicators for Students.* The standards list six categories of performance: creativity and innovation; communication and collaboration; research and information fluency; critical thinking, problem solving, and decision making; digital citizenship; and technology operations and concepts (ISTE, 2007). Other than the last two components—digital citizenship and technology operations and concepts—the list looks like a standard list of cognitive skills necessary for anyone in modern society. Other definitions tend to have too narrow a focus, equating digital competence with information literacy—the ability to evaluate, access, and use information in the digital age.

A truly troublesome issue with all the available definitions is their failure to recognize the virtual world as something different from the physical world. Almost all definitions seem to start from the viewpoint that the virtual world is the physical world, only accessed through technology. But as Chapter 6 suggests, the virtual world is fundamentally different. Although some traditional skills and abilities apply, the virtual world functions differently enough to require a different set of skills and knowledge.

One way to explore what is needed for living in the virtual world is to look at what we do there and how we do it. In essence, we engage in three sets of activities in the virtual world: those associated with living in the virtual world, those associated with making a living in the virtual world, and those associated with re-creating and shaping the virtual world. Not all of us engage in all three sets of activities. The physical world and the virtual worlds are interconnected, and each serves as an inseparable part of our whole life. Some of us may make our living in the physical world but live a portion of our lives online. Some of us can be making a living in the virtual world and live there as well.

To live in the virtual world we often take on three roles: consumers, citizens, and community leaders. As consumers, we make use of what's available in the virtual world to meet our needs in both the physical and virtual worlds. We e-mail our friends, buy books on Amazon, sell used cars on eBay, watch YouTube, or search for information using Google. As citizens of the virtual world, we enjoy the privileges and the accompanying responsibilities of participating in virtual communities. As leaders, we influence others in the virtual world or in the physical world by using virtual tools. We convince other players to follow us in World of Warcraft or create a huge network of "friends" in MySpace or Facebook.

We can also become workers in and for the virtual world, earning an income and making a living. Think about Anshe Chung and the Korean professional video gamers described in Chapter 6, or the eBay powersellers described in Chapter 7. Some of us are also engaged in shaping the virtual world by developing new hardware, software, or virtual communities. The virtual world has expanded since its creation, adding new features, new services, and new choices to meet our needs. Serving and re-creating the virtual world have resulted in big businesses such as Google, YouTube, Yahoo, eBay, and Amazon, as well as smaller businesses.

I use the term *digital competence* to describe what is needed to live productively in the virtual world. Here is a model of digital competence:

1. Knowledge of the nature of the virtual world

   a. Understanding the differences and connections between the physical and virtual worlds; the ability to tell fantasy from reality

   b. Understanding that the virtual world is dependent upon technology and that all technology can break and things can go wrong

   c. Understanding that online/virtual activities are fundamentally psychological

   d. Understanding data representation in the virtual world and how different media work together

   e. Understanding data management in the virtual world and basic file structures

   f. Understanding that the virtual world is a global network of individual and collective participants

   g. Understanding that the virtual world is evolving and constantly expanding

2. Positive attitude toward the virtual world

   a. Appreciation of the complexity and uncertainty of the virtual world

   b. Positive attitude toward technical problems

   c. Effective strategies to approach technical problems (knowing where and how to obtain assistance)

   d. Effective strategies to learn new ways of communication and information sharing

3. Ability to use different tools to participate and lead in the virtual world

   a. Ability to use different tools to participate and lead online communities

   b. Ability to use different tools to entertain, learn, and work

   c. Ability to use different tools to obtain and share information

4. Ability to create products for the virtual world

   a. Ability to use different tools to express views in the virtual world

b. Ability to use different tools to create products (such as music, digital games)

c. Ability to use different tools to create, manage, and lead online communities

d. Ability to launch, manage, and promote businesses in the virtual world

As the virtual world further expands, we need our children to become digitally competent so they can live safely and productively in this newly emerging world. They need to have the proper attitude, understanding, skills, and perspectives that can enable them to lead virtual communities, to manage virtual relationships, to defend our nation in cyberspace, to re-create the virtual world, and to direct the development of the virtual world for the betterment of humankind.

Digital competencies may also be the set of abilities and skills that will prove to have a comparative advantage in the global economy. Our students and schools are much better equipped with the facilities, devices, and infrastructure to help our students develop digital competence than those in the developing countries. It would be unwise to abandon this advantage and focus on teaching things that do not take advantage of this asset.

9

Catching Up or Keeping the Lead:
The Future of American Education

The problem [with globalization] is that economic globalization has outpaced the globalization of politics and mindsets.

—Joseph Stiglitz,
Nobel Prize–winning economist

The future ain't what it used to be.

—Yogi Berra

I have used the previous chapters to show how the current reform efforts are the result of a history of flawed reasoning based on incomplete information, driven by unfounded fear, and influenced by politics. Moreover, the chapters have shown that we have entered a new era, an era characterized by increasingly freer movement of information, people, and businesses across national borders, and marked by the emergence of the virtual world. In the new era, we need more diverse talents rather than standardized laborers, more creative individuals rather than homogenized test takers, and more entrepreneurs rather than obedient employees. Furthermore, this new era requires all citizens to think globally, to understand other cultures, to have the ability to interact with others, and to competently handle changes and complexity.

To meet the challenges of the new era, American education needs to be more American, instead of more like education in other countries. The traditional strengths of American education—respect for individual talents and differences, a broad curriculum oriented to educating the whole child, and a decentralized system that embraces diversity—should be further expanded, not abandoned. This is not to say American education is perfect. On the contrary, American education needs major changes, but the changes should be oriented to the future instead of the past or present. The changes should be made out of hope for a better tomorrow instead of fear of losing yesterday or today. And as such, the changes, I suggest, should include expanding the definition of success, personalizing education, and viewing schools as global enterprises.

Expanding the Definition of Success: Input-Oriented Accountability

In 2008, an announcement by the Chinese Ministry of Education quickly caught the attention of the media and the public. On October 7, a spokesperson for the ministry announced that starting in 2008, 68 higher education institutions would be granted the authority to admit students using their own criteria, and the number admitted under this policy would no longer be held to the previously established limit of 5 percent of new admissions. This announcement was big news because it suggests a significant change in the definition of success in the Chinese education system. Starting in 2003, China began to experiment with a new way of admitting college students, which essentially launched the reform of China's most important mechanism for driving educational practices. As discussed in Chapter 4, China has been using one standardized exam to select college students for decades, forcing all students and educators to focus on passing the infamous *gaokao* (National College Entrance Exam). To shake off the negative effect of high-stakes testing, the ministry authorized 22 colleges to admit students using a combination of their own criteria and test scores on the *gaokao* in 2003. Over the years, the experiment was expanded to more colleges while the number of students that could be admitted by each institution remained limited. The 2008 announcement broke the limit. In addition, colleges were granted more autonomy in their use of test scores on the *gaokao*. Although most still use a combination of their own criteria and test scores, some completely ignore the test scores. If this experiment continues, China will see fundamental changes in its education system and perhaps finally move away from test-oriented education.

This move exemplifies China's efforts to reform its education system by expanding the definition of success from test scores in a limited number of subjects—namely, Chinese language, mathematics, English, plus science or social studies—to a more comprehensive collection of abilities and talents in arts, music, critical thinking, social activities, and sports. In recent years, China has engaged in a series of reforms to grant more autonomy to local schools; decentralize its curriculum; add more emphasis on arts, music, and humanities; and change how students and schools are evaluated (Chinese Ministry of Education, 2003; Zhonggong Zhongyan [Central Committee of the Chinese Communist Party] & Guowuyuan [State Council], 1999; & Zhonggong Zhongyang Bangongting [Office of the Central Committee of the Chinese Communist Party] & Guowuyuan Bangongting [Office of the State Council], 2000). The overarching goal of these reforms is to better prepare its citizens for the global world.

How we define success for students, teachers, and schools determines how students, teachers, and schools are evaluated, and it directs their energy, efforts, and resources to what are considered indicators of success. This effect has already been seen in the U.S. reform efforts of the past several years. As a result of No Child Left Behind, many schools have narrowed their curriculum to focus only on what is tested—math and reading—and teachers have been pushed to teach to the test as well (McMurrer, 2007). Thus, expanding the definition of success should be one of the first changes we make in our efforts to ensure a bright future for our children.

Expanding the definition of success first means that we need to elevate the status of other subjects, abilities, skills, and talents to the same level as math and reading. As discussed in Chapters 7 and 8, the range of knowledge and abilities that are of value includes much more than math and reading. However, the current focus of American education reform seems to be exclusively on these subjects, which have received a vast majority of special funding from federal and state sources and have consumed the energy of schools and teachers because the success of a school, a teacher, and a student is judged by test scores in these two subjects.

Expanding the definition of success also means changing how we measure success. Many of the valuable skills, knowledge, abilities, attitudes, and perspectives one needs and schools cultivate do not have widely accepted standardized tests. Some of them may never be easily measured through standardized tests. Thus we need to adopt a broad range of indicators to assess student learning, including student products, teacher observations, classroom performances, and some psychological measures of student motivation, creativity, and perspectives that have not typically been part of mainstream educational assessment.

Expanding the definition of success of schools should not be limited to only outcome measures, because many factors affect student learning. How well students perform on a math test at a given time is affected by their own ability and efforts, their family environment, their peers, and their previous math learning experiences in addition to their current teachers and math learning. It is simply misleading and wrong to use students' performance on tests to judge the degree of a school's success. A more just and useful way to judge the quality of schools is to assess the quality of input and hold schools accountable for providing the best educational environment for all students.

An input-oriented accountability system measures the quality of schools by looking at the quality of educational resources and opportunities they provide to each student. Rather than holding schools accountable for raising test scores, which is partly beyond the control of schools and teachers, we can hold schools accountable for ensuring that all students have the same high-quality educational opportunities.

Here is a sample of indicators of the quality of a school in terms of input:

• Physical environment: Does the school provide a safe, clean, and inspiring physical environment?

• Facilities: Does the school provide adequate facilities to support learning and development of diverse talents?

• Teachers: Does the school have a staff that is highly qualified and motivated to help students learn?

• Curriculum: Does the school implement a broad and rigorous curriculum relevant to all students?

• Leadership: Does the school have strong leadership that inspires teachers and students to achieve their best?

• Innovation: Does the school encourage and support teacher innovation?

• Opportunities to be different: Does the school make arrangements to enable students who have different talents to pursue them?

Personalizing Education: A Path to Talent Diversification

In 2004, the Department for Education and Skills of the government of the United Kingdom published a pamphlet titled *A National Conversation About Personalised Learning*. This publication marked the official support for a movement that had been gaining momentum in U.K. schools: personalizing learning, which, according to the publication, is analogous to providing personalized services to citizens:

> Personalisation is a very simple concept. It is about putting citizens at the heart of public services and enabling them to have a say in the design and improvement of the organisations that serve them. In education this can be understood as personalised learning—the drive to tailor education to individual need, interest and aptitude so as to fulfill every young person's potential. (p. 5)

The publication recognized that personalized learning is not new and "many schools and teachers [in the United Kingdom] have tailored curriculum and teaching methods to meet the needs of children and young people with great success for many years." Now the government wants to "make the best practices universal . . . so that across the education system the learning needs and talents of young people are used to guide decision making" (p. 5).

Personalized learning recognizes that every child has different talents and different needs, and educational institutions and educators should be responsive to individual children instead of treating them as a collection of products that can be churned out like Henry Ford's Model T. This philosophy takes an opposite view to that embodied in U.S. education reform, which tries to standardize education in pursuit of educational excellence. Although many proponents of standards and centralization in the United States may view personalized learning as lacking rigor, endorsing complacency, and holding low expectations of students, this pamphlet from the U.K. government argues that "giving every single child the chance to be the best they can be, whatever their talent or background, is not the betrayal of excellence, it is the fulfillment of it" (p. 6).

Personalized learning is a promising way to prepare citizens for the 21st century and an effective approach to helping students develop the skills and knowledge needed for the future. It is a dramatic departure from the current reform efforts that move toward standardization and centralization. To personalize learning, we need to take action on multiple levels.

David H. Hargreaves, an associate director of the Specialist Schools and Academies Trust, the United Kingdom's major organization supporting secondary school reform, is perhaps one of the best-known scholars on personalized learning among educators in the United Kingdom. He is especially known for his "nine gateways to personalized learning." According to Hargreaves (2004), "there are nine main gateways, each of which provides a distinctive angle on personalising learning by ensuring that teaching and support are shaped around student needs" (p. 2). The gateways are (1) curriculum, (2) advice and guidance, (3) assessment for learning, (4) learning to learn, (5) school organization and design, (6) workforce development, (7) new technology, (8) mentoring, and (9) student voice.

These nine gateways can serve as a useful framework as we consider how we can personalize learning experiences and opportunities so that students follow a path of learning that suits their individual aptitudes, needs, and interests. Personalized learning requires a curriculum that gives learners choices and schools flexibility. Learners also need advice and guidance in making choices and taking advantage of available resources. Personalized learning also necessitates changes in how learning is assessed. Hargreaves strongly advocates formative assessment. In addition, students need to develop the ability to learn how to learn so that they can gain more control and independence in their own learning.

To support personalized learning, schools need to be redesigned so that they no longer are organized around age cohorts, classes, and classrooms. Instead, schools should be organized around the learning needs of students. The educational workforce, according to Hargreaves, needs to be restructured as well. Educators are not only those who are employed as teachers; the field should be enlarged to include experts from outside the school and community. The "enlargement of a more differentiated workforce is crucial to personalization" (Hargreaves, 2004, p. 4).

Personalized learning can be supported and enabled through creative uses of new technologies and the engagement of mentors from both within and outside the school. Student voice—involving students in making educational decisions—is another crucial element of personalized learning. Hargreaves suggests that student voice may be "potentially the most powerful of all [the gateways] for personalizing learning" because

> for many years those who have researched student perspectives on school and learning have been astonished at the mature and serious way the vast majority of students, even the most disengaged and alienated, talk about their experience of learning and schooling. They have usually remained un-consulted about the many changes that have taken place over recent decades. It would be meaningless to say that we are personalising learning without involving them in the process. The evidence is clear: young people are deeply interested in these matters and

are ready to play a constructive role; and when they are encouraged to do so, the teachers benefit considerably. (2004, p. 5)

Personalized learning captures the spirit of the proposal by Jenifer Fox (2008) for an education that focuses on discovering and cultivating the strengths of each individual child instead of focusing on proving and remedying their "deficiencies." It also reflects a significant part of the "partnership education" proposed by Riane Eisler (2000). Introducing her framework for partnership education, which includes three core components—partnership process, content, and structure—Eisler asks some provocative questions about education:

> Are each child's intelligences and capabilities treated as unique gifts to be nurtured and developed? Do students have a real stake in their education so that their innate enthusiasm for learning is not dampened? Do teachers act primarily as lesson-dispensers and controllers, or as mentors and facilitators? . . . Does the curriculum not only effectively teach students basic skills as the three R's of reading, writing, and arithmetic but also model the life-skills they need to be competent and caring citizens, workers, parents, and community members? . . . Is the structure of a school, classroom, and/or home school one of top-down authoritarian rankings, or is it a more democratic one? . . . Do students, teachers, and other staff participate in school decision making and rule setting? (pp. xv–xvi)

Viewing Schools as Global Enterprises: The Road to Preparing Global Citizens

In Beijing's Chaoyan District near the Holiday Inn Lido Hotel stands a small gray brick building. Across the street is a Japanese school, and nearby are an Italian restaurant, a Korean restaurant, a couple of Chinese restaurants, and the Eudora bar where I talked with Jean, Hans, and Anna, the colleagues whose stories I recounted in Chapter 7. This two-story brick building houses the 3e International Kindergarten, an experimental site of Education for Global Citizenship (EGC).

EGC is a curriculum approach developed by the U.S.-China Center for Research on Educational Excellence at Michigan State University, an R&D center established in 2005 and sponsored by the Hong

Kong–based Sun Wah Education Foundation. The mission of the center is to develop an education model that integrates best practices from Eastern and Western education traditions to help students develop the knowledge, skills, attitudes, and perspectives needed to thrive in the age of globalization.

The EGC approach has three essential elements: bilingualism, biculturalism, and duo-pedagogy. First, EGC aims to cultivate fluency in at least two languages, currently English and Chinese. Second, EGC is intended to develop a strong cross-cultural competency through experiencing two cultures: Chinese and American. Finally, EGC adopts two different pedagogical approaches: the child-centered, more individual-oriented Western approach and the knowledge-centered, more collective-oriented Eastern approach. EGC attempts to provide students with a learning program that immerses them in two different cultures and languages daily, enabling them to experience transitions between cultures and languages, forcing them to confront cultural differences and the discomforts of moving across cultures, supporting them in reflecting on their cultural experiences, and enabling them to benefit from two distinctive curriculums. In a sense, EGC provides two school experiences, one American and one Chinese.

The 3e (explore, experiment, and express) school reflects the design of EGC. Physically, there are two sets of classrooms, one designed and decorated like a typical American classroom, the other like a Chinese classroom. In the American classroom, the language of instruction is English, the teacher is from the United States, and the curriculum roughly follows the Reggio Emilia approach. In the Chinese classroom, the language of instruction is mandarin Chinese, the teacher is from China, and the curriculum is Chinese. Students spend half a day in the Chinese classroom and the other half in the American classroom.

3e is a good example of the third recommendation I have for changes in American education: We should view schools as global enterprises. Although schools will continue to be funded and controlled locally, their students will enter a global market in the sense that they will be competing with other students around the globe. As discussed in Chapter 5, employers have already begun to look for and hire talent on a global scale. They can now compare talent and make

employment decisions globally. Thus whether a school's "product"—
its students—can successfully compete in the global market depends on
its quality, fit, and price, just like the product of any global enterprise.

If we accept the proposal that schools are global enterprises, we
can then learn a number of things from global businesses. First, we
must consider what kind of products we want to make, just like Apple
Computer, Microsoft, Toyota, GM, and Peugeot consider what their
next product should be. The big questions here are what kind of products can meet the needs of the global market, what kind of products
can compete with similar products, and what value we can add to our
products. We are thus challenged to reconsider what curriculum we
offer, what talents we want to focus on, and what abilities and knowledge really count. We must consider these questions in the global
context. We can no longer think about what we offer from a local
perspective. (I have already discussed extensively the skills, talents,
and knowledge that will be of value in the age of globalization in
chapters 7 and 8.)

The EGC curriculum reflects this spirit in that it aims to prepare
cross-culturally competent citizens who will be living and working
globally, wherever that may be. But more important, it prepares leaders for globalization. Thus it differs significantly from traditional
foreign language education programs. Its goal is not to prepare individuals who can speak another language and understand another culture. Rather, it prepares individuals who *are* truly bilingual and
bicultural, who can comfortably and competently cross cultural
boundaries, who can live successfully in any different culture, and
who can work with individuals from any cultural background comfortably. Moreover, the EGC approach is an experiment intended to
integrate two very different educational traditions so as to prepare
individuals who are both creative and well disciplined.

The second thing we can learn from global enterprises is making
use of global resources. Global enterprises look for resources, natural
and human, globally. If they need certain talents that are not available
in the organization, they look outside the organization. If the talent is
not available within the country, they go abroad. Schools should and
can do the same. If a school wants to offer a certain course but does not

have the necessary teacher, it should look outside the school. If a school wants to offer certain education activities but does not have the expertise, it should look beyond the school. In fact, many schools have done so, but in general the action is still bounded by geography. That is, schools may have been tapping into the local community for resources, but by and large they have not looked globally. As a consequence, what schools can offer is often limited to what they can find in the school or the local community.

With the availability of advanced and inexpensive communication and information technologies, resources can be brought in from afar. Virtual schools and courses have become increasingly sophisticated and effective. Research has suggested that there is no significant difference in terms of effectiveness between online and face-to-face instruction (Zhao, Lei, Yan, Lai, & Tan, 2005). There is little reason for a school that is truly concerned about its student education needs to not bring in online versions of courses that it cannot offer face to face because it does not have the expertise among its own staff. Barring political and financial limits, a school can offer as many foreign languages as its students desire by taking advantage of technology. The same is true for other courses, such as advanced calculus or algebra, or fashion design, or filmmaking. And, indeed, many schools have begun to take advantage of this option. For example, the Confucius Institute at Michigan State University has begun to offer mandarin Chinese online to high school students globally. Thus far, thousands of students in many states and countries have enrolled in this course. The institute has also helped many schools bring mandarin Chinese language teachers from China to join their regular staff. Moreover, the institute has developed a massively multiplayer online role-playing game (MMORPG) to provide an immersive Chinese language and cultural learning experience for students. In addition to interacting with the game, tutors from China are available inside the game to provide instruction and support. Some schools have already begun to experiment with the idea of having students learn Chinese solely through this game, without hiring a teacher to be physically present on their campus.

The third thing we can learn from global enterprises is to consider what we can offer and who we can serve—that is, our market.

Globalization enables businesses to market their products beyond their immediate physical location. Schools can do the same. Although political challenges still exist, it is desirable for schools to reconsider who they can serve and what they can contribute to the global education discourse. Schools should consider themselves as resources and assets to other schools, including schools throughout the world.

For example, in Australia, public schools already enroll international students. Australian schools, primary and secondary, routinely have students from foreign countries studying on their campuses as regular students, just as universities do. They charge tuition and fees. In some sense, the Australian schools, which may be locally funded and controlled, have made the transformation from a local entity to a global entity by adding students from foreign countries to their own local student body. Why can't American public schools do the same?

Teaching Global Competencies: What Schools Can Do

Chapter 8 of this book highlights the importance of global competency. It suggests that to live in the increasingly globalized world, citizens need to be able to competently negotiate cultural differences and manage multiple identities, comfortably interact with people from different cultures, and confidently move across cultures as well as the virtual and physical worlds. To do so, they need a global perspective—a deep understanding of the interconnectedness and interdependence of all human beings; a set of global skills—cultural knowledge and linguistic abilities that enable them to appreciate and respect other cultures and peoples and interact with other people; and global attitudes—emotional and psychological capacities to manage the anxiety and complexity of living in a globalized world.

To actually make this happen requires determination, effort, and resources at all levels. The federal and state governments will need to recognize the importance of international and foreign language education and the seriousness of the current situation in schools, and allocate sufficient political and financial resources to help schools with this critical yet extremely difficult change. By "sufficient" I mean at least as much as, if not more than, what has been allocated to math, science, and reading, because the majority of schools today do not have even the basic infrastructure to consider incorporating international and foreign language education in their programs.

Many schools will be starting from scratch, and they need to do everything from reconfiguring their curriculum, developing or adopting a curriculum framework, and identifying teaching materials, to recruiting or retraining professional staff in international education and foreign languages, organizing international experiences for students, and offering courses in these areas. Although some of these can only be accomplished with substantial investment and policy changes, schools can take many actions without waiting for such changes. The Asia Society's publication *Going Global: Preparing Our Students for an Interconnected World* (2008) is an excellent guidebook for schools. It provides practical and specific strategies that schools can take to help students develop global competency, with examples from real schools that have pioneered efforts in this area.

The Asia Society guidebook suggests that schools can choose to start either by developing a single international element or by transforming the entire school. Adding a single international dimension is most practical for schools that are just beginning their internationalization journey. The guide suggests that schools can "use international exchanges to promote curriculum change," like Newton North and South High Schools in Massachusetts, which have been operating a student-faculty exchange program with China's Jingshan School in Beijing. Or they can begin by introducing "critical languages to prepare for the global economy." Creating one or two international courses like what Evanston Township High School in Illinois has been doing is also a good idea (Asia Society, 2008, pp. 10–11).

Achieving whole-school change requires more than effort and resources. It involves changes in the school mission, expected learning outcomes, curriculum arrangement, professional development for staff, working and communicating with the community, and creative use of resources. But it is doable and has been done. The guidebook profiles a few internationally themed schools that have begun the transformation into schools that prepare students for the global future.

Finding globally minded and competent teachers is crucial. But they are difficult to find because schools of education in the United States have historically not been preparing teachers to be internationally oriented, according to a recent report titled *Teacher Preparation for the Global Age: The Imperative for Change* (Longview Foundation, 2008). The report reiterates the call for more internationally minded educators and challenges the nation's teacher education institutions to recruit and educate teachers with global competence. Some schools of education have already begun to take action. For example, Michigan State University's College of Education has recently added a global educators theme to its teacher education program (Asia Society, 2008), and Indiana University's School of Education has been placing student teachers in foreign countries (Longview Foundation, 2008). However, schools do not have to wait for the new graduates. The Asia Society's guidebook suggests other ways to find teachers to help address the immediate need. For example, teachers who served as Peace Corps volunteers have abundant international experience. Teachers can also be brought directly from foreign countries as visiting teachers. Additionally, schools that are near a university can take advantage of what the university offers. And, of course, technology is a great way to bring in teachers from other locations.

Internationalizing the curriculum is another major component of a globally oriented education. Besides adding courses that specifically focus on global issues as suggested in Chapter 8, the Asia Society's guidebook suggests that "international knowledge and skills can be integrated into every curriculum area, from math and language arts to visual arts and science" (2008, p. 24). The book provides examples of how educators in the United States have infused an international dimension in science, math, language arts, social studies, world languages, visual and performing arts, career and technical education, health and physical education, and interdisciplinary courses.

Globalizing student experiences is another effective and necessary way to prepare globally competent citizens. This can be achieved in a number of ways. Ringwood Secondary College in Melbourne, Australia, organizes its senior students for a world tour. They take a show that features music, singing, dance, drama, puppetry, projection, and audience interaction to their partner schools around the globe. Students in the performance group not only perform, but also stay with host families and attend regular classes at the partner school. This is a semester-long project, and students normally visit six or seven countries. This example may be at the more intensive end of the spectrum of global experiences schools can provide, but there are other, less demanding options. The Asia Society guidebook suggests using technology to conduct virtual visits to online museums, art galleries, or historical sites in other countries; to interact with peers in foreign countries via video conferences; or to work on joint projects online. It also suggests short-term international travel, international service learning, and international internships.

Preparing for the Virtual World: Technology and Digital Competencies

Schools can no longer ignore the importance of digital competencies or what our children are already doing in the virtual world, with or without the involvement of educators. Chapters 7 and 8 discuss the importance of digital competencies as potentially valuable skills and knowledge for our students. But the already prevalent use of technology by students may be an important factor in their feeling that what schools teach is irrelevant. The high dropout rates and disengagement found among many students can be partially attributed to schools not moving into the "digital age," as Jim Craig, a retired teacher, wrote in a local newspaper:

> The fact is, more and more bright, otherwise motivated, talented kids are becoming disengaged by the old-fashioned school process. Their digital-native minds don't work the old way. They are bored out of their minds. I have experienced this with my own children. My oldest is a freshman. She gets straight As, plays sports, joins clubs, is respectful to adults and loves her friends and most of her teachers. Any adult would say this is a kid who should be able to accomplish anything. There is a problem. She hates school. Absolutely detests it. Dreads each day. Why? She is a true digital native and, as such, is bored to tears with the way that we are

running school in our 40-plus-year-old buildings that were designed 100-plus years ago. Her mind doesn't work that way. (Craig, 2006)

Craig's view is shared by more experts in this area. Consider, for example, Marc Prensky (2001), an internationally known expert in digital gaming and learning who claims to have coined the term "digital natives" in reference to today's students, who grew up with digital technology. He has repeatedly argued that schools are being run by "digital immigrants" who do not organize learning or teach the way the digital natives are used to and thus enrage and disengage them very quickly. Similar observations have been made by a team of researchers at Harvard University (Palfrey & Gasser, 2008). The Harvard group goes even further to argue how our schools and society may be constraining our children:

Digital Natives will move markets and transform industries, education, and global politics. The changes they bring about as they move into the workforce could have an immensely positive effect on the world we live in. By and large, the digital revolution has already made this world a better place. And Digital Natives have every chance of propelling society further forward in myriad ways—*if we let them* [emphasis added]. (p. 7)

To make schools more relevant and to develop digital competencies, schools must and can take a number of actions to change their mindset, policy, and practices around technology. We should acknowledge that technology is not only a tool for the teacher to use to raise test scores, but also an important tool for students to develop digital competencies, to be creative in art and music, to develop social skills in virtual worlds, and to stay engaged with school. Thus our decisions to invest in technology should be based on more than its effectiveness in improving academic achievement. Instead of banning MySpace, blocking Skype, or forbidding the use of cell phones in schools, we should actively create technology-using experiences for students, under the supervision of teachers, for productive purposes. The best way for students to learn to avoid being taken advantage of by an online pedophile or cyber stalker is to teach them how to recognize and deal with the criminal, not hide them behind a blocked network.

Schools should thus change their policies about students' use of technology in schools. Students should not only be allowed to use their own technological devices for learning, but more important, they should also be given the opportunities to learn how to use technology across the curriculum, for handing in assignments, communicating with friends and teachers, developing multimedia products, and designing video games. Schools should consider digital products as valuable and authentic indicators of student learning for assessment purposes.

Schools should offer courses and other learning opportunities to help students acquire digital competencies. These offerings should move beyond basic technology skills to include authentic projects. Authentic products—that is, products that can be used by others or that have personal meaning—are effective in motivating students. For example, students can work on building a virtual school or community in Second Life, or operate a radio/TV station online using podcasting, or maintain the school Web site. Schools can also organize video-game clubs for game playing and designing.

How we use digital technology and treat our digital native students has significant implications for their future. A quote from the book by the Harvard Digital Citizenship project team *Born Digital* says it best:

> [M]ake no mistake: We are at a crossroads. There are two possible paths before us—one in which we destroy what is great about the Internet and about how young people use it, and one in which we make smart choices and head toward a bright future in a digital age. The stakes of our actions today are very high. The choices that we are making now will govern how our children and grandchildren live their lives in many important ways: how they shape their identities, protect their privacy, and keep themselves safe; how they create, understand, and shape the information that underlies the decision-making of their generation; and how they learn, innovate, and take responsibility as citizens. On one of these paths, we seek to constrain their creativity, self-expression, and innovation in public and private spheres; on the other, we embrace these things while minimizing the dangers that come with the new era. (Palfrey & Gasser, 2008, p. 7)

American education is at a crossroads. Two paths lie in front of us: one in which we destroy our strengths in order to catch up with others on test scores and one in which we build on our strengths so we can keep the lead in innovation and creativity. The current push for more standardization, centralization, high-stakes testing, and test-based accountability is rushing us down the first path, while what will truly keep America strong and Americans prosperous should be the latter, the one that cherishes individual talents, cultivates creativity, celebrates diversity, and inspires curiosity. As we enter a new world rapidly changed by globalization and technology, we need to change course. Instead of instilling fear in the public about the rise of other countries, bureaucratizing education with bean-counting policies, demoralizing educators through dubious accountability measures, homogenizing school curriculum, and turning children into test takers, we should inform the public about the possibilities brought about by globalization, encourage education innovations, inspire educators with genuine support, diversify and decentralize curriculum, and educate children as confident, unique, and well-rounded human beings.

Afterword

We all want to provide our children with an excellent education, but what that looks like divides us. We also all agree that American education must change, significantly and immediately, but there are different views on what changes are needed and how to go about making them happen. I have tried my best to present and justify a proposal that is diametrically opposed to the more popular view of what American education should be like in the 21st century and how to make it happen. I hope I have made it clear why more standardization, increased outcome-based accountability, and narrow focus on a few subjects that we know how to test will not equip American children with what is needed to prosper in the age of globalization. More importantly, I hope I have convinced you about the potential damages of these measures on what our children truly need in the future. Furthermore, I hope that you agree with me that creativity, talent diversity, and global and digital competences are what will make children successful and America strong in the 21st century. And to achieve these goals, American education should continue to lead the way, not to catch up with other countries.

I had hoped that the widely acknowledged problems of NCLB would have caused policy makers to rethink the wisdom of standards, accountability, and equating quality of education to student performances on standardized tests in a few subjects. I had also hoped that the historic election of Barack Obama would bring drastic changes. So I waited until now to write these last pages to see what changes the new administration may bring.

On March 10, 2009, President Obama unveiled an ambitious education agenda in a speech to the Hispanic Chamber of Commerce (Obama, 2009). Ranging from investment in early childhood education to making college more affordable, from raising standards to developing new assessments, from more charter schools to teacher merit pay, the president made it clear that he wants massive reforms to the American education system. He also promised to "make No Child Left Behind live up to its name by ensuring not only that teachers and principals get the funding that they need, but that the money is tied to results" (Obama, 2009). His Secretary of Education Arne Duncan has also toured the nation to talk about the new administration's agenda and hear about NCLB from the field.

As of this moment, I am both encouraged and concerned. I am encouraged because President Obama recognizes we live in a time that is different from the past and that we must give our children "the knowledge and skills they need in this new and changing world." I am encouraged because he recognizes that these skills and knowledge are not the same as the ability to "fill in a bubble on a test," and thus he called for "standards and assessments that [measure] whether they possess 21st century skills like problem-solving and critical thinking and entrepreneurship and creativity"(Obama, 2009). I am also encouraged by his intention to invest in innovations and new ideas for schools. I am further encouraged by his recognition of the problems of NCLB.

But I am also very concerned. I am concerned about how his administration defines "the knowledge and skills" our children need. Although Obama did talk about "critical thinking and entrepreneurship and creativity," all of the examples he cited to show how American students are behind are the test scores and curriculum in math and reading. I am most concerned that his proposal to end the "race to the bottom" problem, that is, states lowering their standards to meet NCLB mandates, serves as the impetus for national standards. As he challenges and motivates "states to adopt world-class standards that will bring our curriculums to the 21st century" with billions of dollars in "race to the top" funding, it may result in national exercises of writing standards for a limited number of subjects.

The probability of another round of standards and testing movement of the Clinton era is very high although neither President Obama nor his Secretary of Education Arne Duncan has uttered the word. Their faith in standards as a solution to America's education problems is well evidenced: "The solution to low test scores is not lowering standards—it's tougher, clearer standards," said Obama (Obama, 2009). And this faith is shared by the nation's state leaders. For example, in December 2008, the state education policy makers pledged to use international benchmarking as a way to make the "efforts to raise standards, advance teaching quality, and improve low-performing schools" more effective (National Governors' Association, Council of Chief State School Officers, & Achieve, 2008, p. 6). A report jointly released by the National Governors Association, Council of Chief State School Officers, and Achieve Inc., called state leaders to take five actions to ensure a world-class education for American students:

Action 1: Upgrade state standards by adopting a common core of internationally benchmarked standards in math and language arts for grades K–12 to ensure that students are equipped with the necessary knowledge and skills to be globally competitive.

Action 2: Leverage states' collective influence to ensure that textbooks, digital media, curricula, and assessments are aligned to internationally benchmarked standards and draw on lessons from high performing nations and states.

Action 3: Revise state policies for recruiting, preparing, developing, and supporting teachers and school leaders to reflect the human capital practices of top-performing nations and states around the world.

Action 4: Hold schools and systems accountable through monitoring, interventions, and support to ensure consistently high performance, drawing upon international best practices.

Action 5: Measure state-level education performance globally by examining student achievement and attainment in an international context to ensure that, over time, students are receiving the education they need to compete in the 21st century economy. (National Governors' Association, et al., 2008, p. 6)

As I have discussed in much detail elsewhere in the book, the faith in high standards as a solution is misplaced. Theoretically national curriculum standards for each subject can be useful, but unless we can develop sound standards for all subjects and knowledge we think our students should have, unless we can develop and implement valid and reliable assessment for all standards, unless we can enable our students to choose from a wide range of offerings, and unless we can attach equal value to a broad range of knowledge and skills, national standards will do more harm than good. As a recent study of the standards-based reform in the United States shows, after some 20 years of experiments, all the expected positive outcomes of standards-based reform remain elusive, while unintended and undesirable consequences have all borne out (Hamilton, Stecher, & Yuan, 2008).

The essence of this book is about what high-quality education is. In my thinking, education is much more than the memorization of prescribed skills and knowledge bits. And education, to slightly modify John Dewey, is not (only) a preparation for life; education is (also) life itself. Furthermore, education is about helping each and every child to realize his or her potential, not molding them into economic working beings for a state. In this spirit, I offer this book to our political leaders, educators, and parents who are designing and implementing education for our sons and daughters, who will live in a time that is different from ours.

May 2009

References

Ablard, K. E. (1997). Parents' conceptions of academic success: Internal and external standards. *Journal of Secondary Gifted Education, 8*(2), 57–64.

Ablard, K. E., & Parker, W. D. (1997). Parents' achievement goals and perfectionism in their academically talented children. *Journal of Youth and Adolescence, 26*(6), 651–667.

Abowitz, D. A. (2005). Social mobility and the American dream: What do college students believe? *College Student Journal, 39*(4), 716–728.

Aguilar, L. (2007, June 13). Worst yet to come for Michigan economy. *Detroit News.* Retrieved March 13, 2009, from http://www. detnews.com/apps/pbcs.dll/ article?aid=/20070613/biz/ 706130416/1001

Alexander, L. (2008, January 22). World of Warcraft hits 10 million subscribers. Retrieved September 17, 2008, from http://www.gamasutra.com/php-bin/ news_index.php?story=17062

Allen, I. E., & Seaman, J. (2007). *Online nation: Five years of growth in online learning.* Needham, MA: Sloan Consortium.

Anderson, C. (2004, October). The long tail. Retrieved October 5, 2008, from http://www.wired.com/wired/archive/12.10/tail.html

Anderson, C. (2006). *The long tail: Why the future of business is selling less of more.* New York: Hyperion.

Ansary, T. (2007, March). Education at risk: Fallout from a flawed report. Retrieved March 15, 2008, from http://www.edutopia.org/landmark-education-report-nation-risk

Ao, T., & Zhao, A. (2005, October 9). Xuesheng nianji yuegao, shenti suzhi yuecha (Higher grade students have worse physical conditions). Retrieved August 30, 2008, from http://politics.people.com.cn/GB/1026/3751956.html

Asia Society. (2006). *Math and science education in a global age: What the U.S. can learn from China.* New York: Asia Society.

Asia Society. (2008). *Going global: Preparing our students for an interconnected world.* New York: Asia Society.

Asia Society, Business Roundtable, & Council of Chief State School Officers. (2005). *Education in China: Lessons for U.S. educators.* New York: Asia Society.

Australian Bureau of Statistics. (2005). *Migration, Australia.* Canberra: Australian Bureau of Statistics.

Baer, J., Baldi, S., Ayotte, K., & Green, P. J. (2007). *The reading literacy of U.S. fourth-grade students in an international context: Results from the 2001 and 2006 Progress in International Reading Literacy Study (PIRLS)* (NCES 2008-017). Washington, DC: National Center for Education Statistics, Institute of Education Sciences, U.S. Department of Education.

Baily, M. N., & Lawrence, R. Z. (2005). Don't blame trade for U.S. job losses. Retrieved July 8, 2008, from http://www.mckinsey quarterly.com/Economic_Studies/Productivity_Performance/Dont_blame_ trade_for_US_job_losses_1559

Baker, K. (2007). Are international tests worth anything? *Phi Delta Kappan, 89*(2), 101–104.

Bates, D. G., & Plog, F. (1990). *Cultural anthropology* (3rd ed.). New York: McGraw-Hill.

BBC. (2000, March 14). Taxi drivers' brains "grow" on the job. Retrieved September 26, 2008, from http://news.bbc.co.uk/2/hi/science/nature/677048.stm

Beijing Youth Newspaper. (2003, January 6). Thin profit from toy exports in 2002. Retrieved August 7, 2008, from http://finance.jrj.com.cn/news/2003-01-06/000000477602.html

Bell, T. H. (1988). *Thirteenth man: A Reagan cabinet memoir.* New York: Free Press.

Bender, B., & Issenberg, S. (2008, September 4). Record shows little foreign experience. Retrieved October 15, 2008, from http://www. boston.com/news/nation/articles/2008/09/04/record_shows_little_ foreign_ experience/

Berliner, D. C. (2006). Our impoverished view of educational reform. *Teachers College Record, 108*(6), 949–995.

Berliner, D. C., & Biddle, B. J. (1995). *The manufactured crisis: Myths, fraud, and the attack on America's public schools.* Reading, MA: Addison-Wesley.

Bernanke, B. S. (2006). *Global economic integration: What's new and what's not?* Paper presented at the Federal Reserve Bank of Kansas City's Thirtieth Annual Economic Symposium. Retrieved September 2, 2006, from http://www.federalreserve.gov/boarddocs/speeches/2006/20060825/default.htm

Bigelow, B., & Peterson, B. (2002). *Rethinking globalization: Teaching for justice in an unjust world.* Milwaukee, WI: Rethinking Schools Press.

Bourke, J. (2006). *Fear: A cultural history.* Washington, DC: Shoemaker & Hoard.

Bracey, G. W. (2006a, July–August). Believing the worst. *Stanford Magazine.* Available: http://www.stanfordalumni.org/news/magazine/2006/julaug/features/nclb.html

Bracey, G. W. (2006b, May 21). Heard the one about the 600,000 Chinese engineers? *Washington Post,* p. B3.

British–North American Committee. (2007). *Cyber attack: A risk management primer for CEOs and directors*. Washington, DC: British–North American Committee.

Britton, E., & Mark, C. T. (2006). *The China effect: Assessing the impact on the U.S. economy of trade and investment with China*. Washington, DC: U.S.-China Business Forum.

Bureau of Labor Statistics, U.S. Department of Labor. (2007a). *Occupational outlook handbook, 2008–09 edition*, Artists and Related Workers. Retrieved September 23, 2008, from http://www.bls.gov/oco/ocos092.htm

Bureau of Labor Statistics, U.S. Department of Labor. (2007b). *Occupational outlook handbook, 2008–09 edition*, Computer Scientists and Database Administrators. Retrieved September 23, 2008, from http://www.bls.gov/oco/ocos042.htm

Bureau of Labor Statistics, U.S. Department of Labor. (2007c). *Occupational outlook handbook, 2008–09 edition*, Graphic Designers. Retrieved September 23, 2008, from http://www.bls.gov/oco/ocos090.htm

Bureau of Labor Statistics, U.S. Department of Labor. (2007d). *Occupational outlook handbook, 2008–09 edition*, Interpreters and Translators. Retrieved September 23, 2008, from http://www.bls.gov/oco/ocos175.htm

Bureau of Labor Statistics, U.S. Department of Labor. (2008). Labor force statistics from the current population survey. Retrieved July 18, 2008, from http://data.bls.gov/PDQ/servlet/ SurveyOutputServlet?data_tool=latest_numbers&series_id=LNU04000000&years_option=all_years&periods_option=specific_periods&periods=Annual+Data

Bush, G. W. (2001, July 3). No Child Left Behind: Transforming the federal role in education so that no child is left behind. Retrieved July 12, 2008, from http://www.whitehouse.gov/news/reports/no-child-left-behind.pdf

Bush, G. W. (2002, January 8). President signs landmark No Child Left Behind education bill. Retrieved March 5, 2008, from http://www.whitehouse.gov/news/releases/2002/01/20020108-1.html

Bush, G. W. (2006, January 31). State of the Union Address. Retrieved January 30, 2009, from http://www.c-span.org/executive/transcript.asp?cat=current_event&code=bush_admin&year=2006

Bush, G. W. (2008, January 7). President Bush discusses the No Child Left Behind Act. Retrieved July 12, 2008, from http://www. whitehouse.gov/news/releases/2008/01/20080107-2.html

Business Roundtable. (2005). *Tapping America's potential: The Education for Innovation Initiative*. Retrieved March 13, 2009, from http://www.uschamber.com/NR/rdonlyres/epivg5lni4pxype7by6h3gl5kpkbr3hyief6oxhbv4dgodcj4kmizkva2oe542sdaq2cx33sxce36i3jgwmflzf2q6b/050727_tapstatement.pdf

Camdessus, M. (2000, February 13). Development and poverty reduction: A multilateral approach. Retrieved July 8, 2008, from http://www.imf.org/external/np/speeches/2000/021300.htm

Carothers, C. (2006, November 29). Victims still falling prey to Nigerian e-mail scam. Retrieved October 17, 2008, from http://www.foxnews.com/story/0,2933,232500,00.html

Castronova, E. (2005). *Synthetic worlds: The business and culture of online games*. Chicago: University of Chicago Press.

Chen, J. (2006, September 18). Chuyi xueshen bei laoshi ouda hou zisha (Junior high student kills himself after being beaten by teacher). Retrieved August 25, 2008, from http://tech.nen.com.cn/73470487954456576/20060915/2013831. shtml

China Daily. (2007, March 27). Suicide the leading cause of death among youth. Retrieved March 13, 2009, from http://www.china.org.cn/english/China/204533.htm

Chinese Ministry of Education. (2003). *Putong gaozhong kecheng gaige gangyao (Shiyan) (A framework for high school curriculum reform [Pilot]).* Beijing: Chinese Ministry of Education.

Chinese Ministry of Education. (2007a). Number of enrollment of schools of all types and level providing formal programs. Retrieved August 9, 2008, from http://www.moe.edu.cn/edoas/website18/56/info33456.htm

Chinese Ministry of Education. (2007b). Size of education. Retrieved August 9, 2008, from http://www.moe.edu.cn/edoas/website18/81/info33481.htm

Chua, A. (2007). *Day of empire: How hyperpowers rise to global dominance—and why they fall.* New York: Doubleday.

Cleveland, H. (2004). American foreign policy: Learning to lead anew. *Issues in Global Education No. 179.* Retrieved March 13, 2009, from http://www.globaled.org/issues/179.pdf

Clinton, W. J. (1998, January 27). State of the Union Address. Retrieved March 26, 2008, from http://www.washingtonpost.com/wp-srv/politics/special/states/docs/sou98.htm

CNA Corporation. (2007). *National security and the threat of climate change.* Alexandria, VA: CNA Corporation.

CNN. (2005, August 17). Sasser author gets suspended term. Retrieved September 19, 2008, from http://www.cnn.com/2005/LAW/07/08/sasser.suspended/index.html

Collins, D. T., & Ryan, M. H. (2007). The strategic implications of technology on job loss. Retrieved October 10, 2008, from http://findarticles.com/p/articles/mi_m1TOK/is_/ai_n25009527? tag=artBody;col1

Committee for Economic Development (CED). (2006). *Education for global leadership: The importance of international studies and foreign language education for U.S. economic and national security.* Washington, DC: Committee for Economic Development.

Committee on Prospering in the Global Economy of the 21st Century (National Academies). (2006). *Rising above the gathering storm: Energizing and employing America for a brighter economic future.* Washington, DC: National Academies Press.

Compton, R. (2008). *Two million minutes: About the film.* Retrieved February 23, 2008, from http://2mminutes.com/about.html

comScore. (2008, August 12). Social networking explodes worldwide as sites increase their focus on cultural relevance. Retrieved September 22, 2008, from http://www.comscore.com/press/release.asp?press=2396

The Courier. (2008, February 11). Sports teams disappeared along with factories. *The Courier Leamington Spa*. Retrieved March 13, 2009, from http://www. learningtoncourier.co.uk/history/Sports-teams-disappeared-along-with.3241986.jp

Craig, J. (2006, February 19). Schools need to meet the needs of the "digital natives." *South Bend* [IN] *Tribune*. Retrieved March 13, 2009, from http:// pqasb.pqarchiver.com/southbendtribune/access/1002825201.html?dids=1002 825201:1002825201&FMT=ABS&FMTS=ABS:FT&date=Feb+19%2C+2006&aut hor=JIM+CRAIG&pub=South+Bend+Tribune&edition=&startpage=1&desc= Schools+need+to+meet+the+needs+of+the+%27digital+natives%27

Crane, M. (2006, October 31). Gaming eBay. Retrieved October 10, 2008, from http://www.forbes.com/entrepreneurs/2006/10/30/ebay-google-yahoo-ent-sales-cx_mc_1031auction.html

Dacey, J. S., & Lennon, K. H. (1998). *Understanding creativity: The interplay of biological, psychological, and social factors*. San Francisco: Jossey-Bass.

Dacey, J. S., & Packer, A. (1992). *The nurturing parent: How to raise creative, loving, responsible children*. New York: Simon & Schuster.

Dammann, G. (2008, June 18). Harry Potter breaks 400m in sales. *The Guardian*. Retrieved from http://www.guardian.co.uk/books/2008/jun/18/harrypotter.news

Day, J. C., & Newburger, E. C. (2002). *The big payoff: Educational attainment and synthetic estimates of work-life earnings*. Washington, DC: U.S. Census Bureau.

DeGroat, B. (2006, November 17). Michigan's job-loss streak is the longest since Great Depression. Retrieved February 10, 2008, from http://www.ns.umich. edu/htdocs/releases/story.php?id=1069

Department for Education and Skills. (2004). *A national conversation about personalised learning*. Retrieved from http://publications.teachernet.gov.uk/ eOrderingDownload/DfES%200919%20200MIG186.pdf

Dewey, J. (1983). Some factors in mutual national understanding. In J. A. Boydston (Ed.), *The middle works of John Dewey* (Vol. 13). Carbondale: Southern Illinois University Press.

Dibbell, J. (2006). *Play money: Or, how I quit my day job and made millions trading virtual loot*. New York: Basic Books.

Dibbell, J. (2007, June 17). The life of the Chinese gold farmer. Retrieved July 9, 2007, from http://www.nytimes.com/2007/ 06/17/magazine/17 loot farmers-t.html?pagewanted=1&ei=5070&en= 8c4b41b73bcbffce&ex= 1184040000

Dunnell, K. (2007). *The changing demographic picture of the UK national statistician's annual article on the population*. London: Office of National Statistics.

Eakin, S. (1996). Forum: National Education Summit. *Technos Quarterly*, 5(2).

Economist. (2008, January 3). Global migration: Keep the borders open. *The Economist*. Retrieved March 13, 2009 from http://www.economist.com/ displaystory.cfm?story_id=10430282&fsrc=RSS

Ed in '08. (2008). *A stagnant nation: Why American students are still at risk*. Washington, DC: Ed in '08.

Eisler, R. (2000). *Tomorrow's children: A blueprint for partnership education in the 21st century*. Boulder, CO: Westview Press.

Evron, G. (2008, August 13). Georgia cyber attacks from Russian government? Not so fast. Retrieved September 19, 2008, from http://www.csoonline.com/article/443579/George_Cyber_Attacks_ From_Russian_Government_Not_ So_Fast

Farrell, D., & Grant, A. (2005). *Addressing China's looming talent shortage*. Shanghai: McKinsey Global Institute.

FIFA. (2007). 2006 FIFA World Cup™ broadcast wider, longer and farther than ever before. Retrieved July 1, 2008, from http://en.fifa.com/aboutfifa/marketingtv/news/newsid=111247.html

Fitzpatrick, L. (2008). The wired bunch. Retrieved September 22, 2008, from http://www.time.com/time/specials/2007/article/0,28804,1815747_1815707_1815675-1,00.html

Florida, R. (2002). *The rise of the creative class and how it's transforming work, leisure, community and everyday life*. New York: Basic Books.

Florida, R. (2005). *The flight of the creative class: The new global competition for talent*. New York: HarperBusiness.

Forrester. (2007). *The state of retailing online 2007*. Cambridge, MA: Forrester.

Fox, J. (2008). *Your child's strengths: Discover them, develop them, use them*. New York: Viking.

Friedman, T. L. (1999). *The Lexus and the olive tree* (1st ed.). New York: Farrar, Straus, Giroux.

Friedman, T. L. (2005). *The world is flat: A brief history of the twenty-first century*. New York: Farrar, Straus and Giroux.

Galama, T., & Hosek, J. (2008). *U.S. competitiveness in science and technology*. Santa Monica, CA: RAND.

Gallup, A. M., & Clark, D. L. (1987). *Nineteenth annual survey of the public's attitude toward the public schools*. Princeton, NJ: Gallup International.

Gallup, G. (1970). *Second annual survey of the public's attitude toward the public schools*. Princeton, NJ: Gallup International.

Galtung, J. (2002, 19 September). Globalisation and Europe-Asia: Risks and opportunities. Retrieved July 8, 2008, from http://www.sopos.org/aufsaetze/3e747cf89a6c7/1.phtml

Gardner, H. (1993). *Frames of mind: The theory of multiple intelligences*. New York: Basic Books.

Gardner, H. (2004). How education changes: Considerations of history, science, and values. In M. M. Suarez-Orozco & D. B. Qin-Hillard (Eds.), *Globalization: Culture and education in the new millennium* (pp. 235–258). Berkeley: University of California Press.

Gates, W. H. (2005, February 26). Prepared remarks by Bill Gates at the National Education Summit on High Schools. Retrieved March 13, 2009, from http://www.admin.mtu.edu/ctlfd/Ed%20Psych%20Readings/BillGate.pdf

Goals 2000: Educate America Act, H.R. 1804 (1994).

Goldin, C., & Katz, L. (2008). *The race between education and technology.* Cambridge, MA: Belknap Press of Harvard University Press.

Goleman, D. (1995). *Emotional intelligence.* New York: Bantam Books.

Goodall, J. (1988). *In the shadow of man.* San Diego, CA: San Diego State University Press.

Guisnel, J. (1997). *Cyberwars: Espionage on the Internet* (G. Masai, Trans.). New York: Basic Books.

Guojia Jiaowei (National Education Commission). (1997). *Guanyu dangqian jiji tuijin zhongxiaoxue shishi suzhi jiaoyu de ruogan yijian (Several suggestions for the promotion of quality education in secondary and elementary schools).* Retrieved March 13, 2009, from http://www.hnedu.cn/fagui/Law/15/law_15_1223.htm

Gutiérrez, J. (2006). *Mexico: Practices used in measuring stocks and flows of international migration.* Paper presented at the United Nations Expert Group Meeting on Measuring International Migration: Concepts and Methods. Available: http://unstats.un.org/unsd/Demographic/meetings/egm/migrationegm06/DOC%209%20Mexico.pdf

Gwin, P. (2005, February). A world of parts: It's a big job to build a Mini. *National Geographic.* Available: http://ngm.national geographic.com/ngm/0502/resources_geo.html

Hamilton, L. S., Stecher, B. M., & Yuan, K. (2008). *Standards-based reform in the United States: History, research, and future directions.* Santa Monica, CA: RAND.

Hannas, W. C. (2003). *The writing on the wall: How Asian orthography curbs creativity.* Philadelphia: University of Pennsylvania Press.

Hanqing, L., & Wei, W. (2008, January 21). 99% of new recruits for central government civil servants hold at least a college degree. Retrieved August 17, 2008, from http://news.xinhuanet.com/newscenter/2008-01/21/content_7466551.htm

Hargreaves, D. H. (2004). *Personalising learning 1: Next steps in working laterally.* London: Specialist Schools and Academies Trust.

Hawking, S. (2009). Life in the universe (public lecture). Retrieved March 2009, from http://hawking.org.uk/index.php?option= com_content&view= article&id=65

Heeks, R. (2008). *Current analysis and future research agenda on "gold farming": Real-world production in developing countries for the virtual economies of online games.* Manchester, UK: Institute for Development Policy and Management (University of Manchester).

Helgerson, J. L. (1996). *CIA briefings of presidential candidates.* Washington, DC: Central Intelligence Agency.

Hitler, A. (1919). Letter to Herr Gemlich (R. S. Levy, Trans.). In E. Jäckel (Ed.), *Hitler: Sämtliche Aufzeichnungen 1905–1924* (pp. 88–90). Stuttgart: Deutsche Verlags-Anstalt.

Hof, R. D. (2006, May 1). My virtual life. Retrieved September 13, 2008, from http://www.businessweek.com/magazine/content/ 06_18/b3982001.htm

Holton, G. (2003, April 25). An insider's view of "A Nation at Risk" and why it still matters. *Chronicle of Higher Education, 49*, B13.

Hu, J. (2006). Speech at the National Science and Technology Conference. Retrieved August 5, 2008, from http://news.xinhuanet.com/politics/2006-01/09/content_4031533.htm

Hua, V. (2006, December 18). Video game players score big money in South Korea. *San Francisco Chronicle*. Available: http://www.sfgate.com/cgi-bin/article.cgi?f=/c/a/2006/12/18/GAMERS.TMP

Huicong Net. (2005, November 23). Diaocha: 13.3% Zhejiang zhongxiao xueshen cheng jihua zisha (Study: 13.3% Students in Zhejiang considered suicide). Retrieved August 26, 2008, from http://info.edu.hc360.com/2005/11/23141185758.shtml

Hunt, H. (2005). The effect of extracurricular activities in the educational process: Influence on academic outcomes? *Sociological Spectrum, 25*(4), 417–445.

Huntington, S. P. (2004). *Who are we? The challenges to America's national identity*. New York: Simon & Schuster.

Hweshe, F. (2008, July 3). 2010 Cup not a get rich quick event. *Cape Argus*. Available: http://www.capeargus.co.za/?fSectionId=3571&fArticleId=vn20080703114345729C702228

IELTS. (2008). IELTS: International English Language Testing System. Retrieved August 22, 2008, from http://www.ielts.org/default.aspx

Internet World Stats. (2008, June 30). Internet World Stats: Usage and population statistics. Retrieved September 23, 2008, from http://www.internetworldstats.com/stats.htm

ISTE. (2007). *The ISTE National Educational Technology Standards and Performance Indicators for Students (NETS.S)*. Eugene, OR: International Society for Technology in Education.

Iwao, S. (2000). Educational reform [Electronic version]. *Japan Echo, 27*(6). Retrieved November 30, 2006, from http://www.japanecho.com/sum/2000/270603.html

Japan Exchange and Teaching Program. (2007). 2006–2007 JET Programme participant numbers. Retrieved April 15, 2007, from http://www.jetprogramme.org/e/introduction/statistics.html

Jefferson, T. (1904). Notes on Virginia. In A. A. Lipscomb & A. E. Bergh (Eds.), *The writings of Thomas Jefferson: Memorial edition* (Vol. 2, p. 204). Washington, DC: Thomas Jefferson Memorial Association.

Jenkins, H. (2004). Pop cosmopolitanism: Mapping cultural flows in an age of media convergence. In M. M. Suarez-Orozco & D. B. Qin-Hillard (Eds.), *Globalization: Culture and education in the new millennium* (pp. 114–140). Berkeley: University of California Press.

Jia, H. (2007, August 15). China hits top three in patent applications. Retrieved August 8, 2008, from http://www.scidev.net/en/news/china-hits-top-three-in-patent-applications.html

Jia, S. (2006, March 20). Keju: A Chinese grand invention. Retrieved August 16, 2008, from http://theory.people.com.cn/GB/49157/49163/4217339.html

Jiaoyubu (Ministry of Education). (2001). *Yiwu Jiaoyu Kecheng Shezhi Fang'an (Curriculum Framework for Compulsory Education)*. Available: http://www.edu.cn/ke_cheng_775/20060323/t20060323_109425.shtml

Jin, G. (2006). Chinese gold farmers. Retrieved September 18, 2008, from http://www.chinesegoldfarmers.com/Index.html

Joshi, D. (2007, May 22). Ford, GM gearing up for India's diesel market. *Hindustan Times*. Retrieved March 13, 2009, from http://www.hindustantimes.com/StoryPage/StoryPage.aspx?section Name=NLetter&id=b9ac6d07-79c3-4a49-8e3b-e2dddee73de5&Headline=Ford%2c+GM+gearing+up+for+India's+diesel+market

Kannankutty, N. (2005). 2003 college graduates in the U.S. workforce: A profile. Retrieved July 18, 2008, from http://www.nsf.gov/statistics/infbrief/nsf06304/#fn1

Kelly, S. (2007, December 14). The sat-nav v. cabbie challenge. Retrieved September 26, 2008, from http://news.bbc.co.uk/2/hi/programmes/click_online/7143897.stm

Kirriemuir, J. (2008, May). A spring 2008 "snapshot" of UK higher and further education developments in Second Life. Retrieved September 17, 2008, from http://www.eduserv.org.uk/upload/foundation/sl/uksnapshot052008/final.pdf

Kloza, B. (2008, August 8). Science literacy Olympics. Retrieved August 22, 2008, from http://www.sciencentral.com/video/2008/08/08/science-literacy-olympics/

Kober, N., Zabala, D., Chudowsky, N., Chudowsky, V., Gayler, K., & McMurrer, J. (2006). *State high school exit exams: A challenging year*. Washingon, DC: Center on Education Policy.

Kong, F., Lu, J., & Shi, L. (2008, August 23). Haizhi gaokao jiazhang "Bangman" Shangdong jinan zuobian 12 ren beibu (Parents help with children's *gaoke*, 12 indicted in Shangdong Province). Retrieved August 30, 2008, from http://news.xinhuanet.com/legal/2008-08/23/content_9637886.htm

Krisher, T. (2008, October 9). Toyota dedicates new tech center in Michigan. Retrieved October 10, 2008, from http://www.businessweek.com/ap/financialnews/D93N85O80.htm

Kyodo News International. (2006, June 26). Singapore enlists Japanese trainers to up skill of toilet cleaners. Retrieved April 16, 2007, from http://findarticles.com/p/articles/mi_m0WDP/is_2006_June_26/ai_n16499792

Lagowski, J. J. (1996). The education summit: A different signal. *Journal of Chemical Education, 73*(5), 383.

Lague, D. (2006, April 24). Chinese paradox: A shallow pool of talent. Retrieved August 23, 2008, from http://www.iht.com/articles/2006/04/24/news/talent.php

Landler, M., & Ekman, I. (2007, September 18). In Europe, some toy makers shun the China label. Retrieved October 10, 2008, from http://www.nytimes.com/2007/09/18/business/worldbusiness/18toys.html

Lane, K., & Pollner, F. (2008, July). How to address China's growing talent shortage. Retrieved August 11, 2008, from http://www.mckinseyquarterly.com/Organization/Talent/How_to_address_ Chinas_growing_talent_shortage_2156#foot1up

Larsen, L. J. (2004). *Current population reports*. Washington, DC: U.S. Census Bureau.

Legrain, P. (2002). *Open world: The truth about globalization*. London: Abacus.

Lemke, C., Coughlin, E., Thadani, V., & Martin, C. (2003). *enGauge 21st century skills: Literacy in the digital age*. Culver City, CA: Metiri Group.

Levy, S. (2005, February 21). The zen of fighting iPod. *Newsweek*. Available: http://www.newsweek.com/id/48794

Lewontin, R. (2001). *The triple helix: Gene, organism, and environment*. Cambridge, MA: Harvard University Press.

Leyden, J. (2008, August 11). Russian cybercrooks turn on Georgia. Retrieved September 18, 2008, from http://www.theregister.co.uk/2008/08/11/georgia_ddos_attack_reloaded/

Li, B. (2006, November 26). Premier Wen Jiabao seeks advice from university presidents on how to prepare excellent talents. Retrieved August 5, 2008, from http://news.xinhuanet.com/school/2006-11/28/content_5400168.htm

Li, G. (2005, September 2). How should we assess *keju* (an interview). Retrieved August 17, 2008, from http://gb.cri.cn/3601/2005/09/02/109@684061.htm

Li, W. (2008, June 11). Helongjiang chahuo 19 qi gaokao zuobi an, moshou zuobi shebei 25 bu (Heilongjian uncovers 19 cases of fraud in *gaokao*, confiscates 25 sets of equipment). Retrieved August 30, 2008, from http://edu.people.com.cn/GB/116076/7370019.html

Lin, L. P., & Wang, Y. (2006). Waizhuanju fayanren: Zhongguo jiang zhuozhong yingjin waiguo gaoshuipin rencai (Spokesperson of foreign expert bureau: China will focus on importing advanced experts) [Electronic version]. *Xinhua News Agency*. Retrieved November 20, 2006, from http://www.gov.cn/jrzg/2006-09/20/content_393748.htm

Lin, Y. (1994). *Zhidu, jishu yu zhongguo nongye fazhan (System, technology, and the development of agriculture in China)*. Shanghai: Sanlian Shudian.

Linden Research. (2008, September 1). Economic statistics. Retrieved September 13, 2008, from http://secondlife.com/whatis/economy_stats.php

Liu, B. (2006, December 21). Our views on Christmas. Retrieved February 10, 2008, from http://culture.163.com/06/1221/12/32S8M1PU00280004.html

Liu, J. (2006). Qinghua jiaozi zhuiru yiyuzheng yinying, Cong Zhongheyuan Cizhi Dang Banyungong (Tsinghua's gifted student fell into depression, resigning from China's Academy of Sciences to become a porter). Retrieved August 20, 2008, from http://news.sohu.com/20060403/n242609421.shtml

London Assembly (Transport Committee). (2005). *Where to, Guv? The Transport Committee's review of the public carriage office*. London: London Assembly (Transport Committee).

Longview Foundation. (2008). Teacher preparation for the global age: The imperative for change. Retrieved November 12, 2008, from http://www.longviewfdn.org/files/44.pdf

Markoff, J. (2008, August 13). Cyber attack preceded invasion. Retrieved September 18, 2008, from http://www.chicagotribune.com/business/technology/chi-cyber-war_13aug13,0,7241513.story

Marks, I. (1987). *Fears, phobias, and rituals: Panic, anxiety, and their disorder*. New York: Oxford University Press.

Mattila, H., & Seeley, T. (2007). Genetic diversity in honey bee colonies enhances productivity and fitness. *Science*, 317(5836): 362–364.

May, W. (1934). *Deutscher National-Katechismus* (R. L. Bytwerk, Trans., 2nd ed.). Breslau: Verlag von Heinrich Handel.

McCarthy, J. C. (2002, November 11). 3.3 million U.S. services jobs to go offshore. Forrester Research. Available: http://www.forrester.com/ER/Research/Brief/Excerpt/0,1317,15900,00.html

McDonald, J. (2007, January 8). GM, Ford: China sales up sharply in 2006. *Washington Post*. Retrieved March 13, 2009, from http://www.washingtonpost.com/wp-dyn/content/article/2007/01/08/AR2007010801039.html

McLuhan, M. (1964). *Understanding media*. New York: Mentor.

McMurrer, J. (2007). *Choices, changes, and challenges: Curriculum and instruction in the NCLB era*. Washington, DC: Center on Education Policy.

McNamara, R. (1998). Robert McNamara: Secretary of Defense. CNN Cold War Interviews.

Meng, Z., Ma, M., & Liu, J. (2005, July 5). Ningxia 13 sui nvsheng danxin yaojiao 10 wanyuan zexiaofei fudu zisha shenwan (13-year-old girl committed suicide, worried about 100,000-yuan school selection fee). Retrieved August 25, 2008, from http://news.sina.com.cn/s/2005-07-25/01256517005s.shtml

Metiri Group. (2003). enGauge 21st century skills for 21st century learners. Retrieved September 28, 2008, from http://www.metiri.com/21/Metiri-NCREL21stSkills.pdf

Metiri Group. (2008). What's so different about the 21st century? Retrieved September 28, 2008, from http://www.metiri.com/features.html

Mid-continent Research for Education and Learning. (2008). Content knowledge. Retrieved March 26, 2008, from http://www.mcrel.org/standards-benchmarks/docs/purpose.asp

Ministry of Education. (2005). *Nurturing every child: Flexibility and diversity in Singapore schools*. Singapore: Ministry of Education.

Ministry of Education and Human Resources Development. (2001). *7th national curriculum*. Seoul: Ministry of Education and Human Resources Development.

Mitchell, E. (2008, September 13). Taxi drivers "have brain sat-nav." Retrieved September 26, 2008, from http://news.bbc.co.uk/2/hi/science/nature/7613621.stm

National Academies. (2005, October 12). Broad federal effort urgently needed to create new, high-quality jobs for all Americans in the 21st century. Retrieved

August 10, 2008, from http://www8.nationalacademies.org/onpinews/newsitem.aspx?RecordID=11463

National Center for Education Statistics. (2001). *Drop-out rates in the United States: 2000*. Washington, DC: National Center for Educational Statistics.

National Center for Education Statistics. (2003a). *Nation's report card: Average mathematics scale scores, by race/ethnicity, grades 4 and 8: 1990–2003*. Retrieved July 12, 2008, from http://nces.ed.gov/nationsreportcard/mathematics/results2003/raceethnicity.asp

National Center for Education Statistics. (2003a). *The Nation's report card: Reading 2003*. Retrieved March 13, 2009 from http://nces.ed.gov/pubsearch/pubsinfo.asp?pubid=2005453

National Center for Education Statistics. (2003b). *Nation's report card: Math 2003*. Retrieved March 13, 2009, from http://nces.ed.gov/pubsearch/pubsinfo.asp?pubid=2005451

National Center for Education Statistics. (2008). *The condition of education*. Retrieved July 12, 2008, from http://nces.ed.gov/programs/coe/2008/section3/indicator23.asp

National Commission on Excellence in Education. (1983). *A Nation at Risk: The imperative for educational reform*. Washington, DC: U.S. Department of Education.

National Governors Association. (1986). *Time for results: The governors' 1991 report on education*. Washington, DC: National Governors Association.

National Governors Association, Council of Chief State School Officers, & Achieve, Inc. (2008). *Benchmarking for success: Ensuring U.S. students receive a world-class education*. Washington, DC: National Governors' Association.

National Science Board. (2008). *Science and engineering indicators 2008*. Arlington, VA: National Science Foundation.

Needham, J. (Ed.). (1954). *Science and civilisation in China*. Cambridge: Cambridge University Press.

Neisser, U., Boodoo, G., Bouchard, T. J., Boykin, A. W., Brody, N., Ceci, S. J., et al. (1996). Intelligence: Knowns and unknowns. *American Psychologist, 51*(2), 77–101.

New Commission on the Skills of the American Workforce. (2007). *Tough choices or tough times*. Washington, DC: National Center on Education and the Economy.

Nichols, S. L., & Berliner, D. C. (2007). *Collateral damage: How high-stakes testing corrupts America's schools*. Cambridge, MA: Harvard Education Press.

Obama, B. (2009, March 10). President Obama's remarks to the Hispanic chamber of commerce. Retrieved May 19, 2009, from http://www.nytimes.com/2009/03/10/us/politics/10text-obama.html

Ohnsman, A. (2005, July 1). North American sales spur Toyota expansion. Retrieved October 10, 2008, from http://www.iht.com/articles/2005/06/30/bloomberg/sxtoyota.php

Online Dating Magazine. (2008). *Online Dating Magazine* media center: Abbreviated online dating facts and stats. Retrieved September 26, 2008, from http://www.onlinedatingmagazine.com/mediacenter/onlinedatingfacts.html

Paley, A. R. (2006, May 15). Homework help, from a world away. *Washington Post*, p. A01.

Palfrey, J., & Gasser, U. (2008). *Born digital: Understanding the first generation of digital natives*. New York: Basic Books.

Partnership for 21st Century Skills. (2007). Framework for 21st century learning. Retrieved September 28, 2008, from http://www.21stcenturyskills.org/documents/frameworkflyer_072307.pdf

Partnership for 21st Century Skills. (2008). Mission: Twenty first century children. Retrieved September 28, 2008, from http://www.21stcenturyskills.org/index.php?option=com_content&task=view&id=188&Itemid=110

PeSA. (2008). Professional eBay Sellers Alliance. Retrieved October 10, 2008, from http://www.gopesa.org/index.cfm?page=about

Petrilli, M. J., & Finn, C. E., Jr. (2006). A new new federalism: The case for national standards and tests. *Education Next, 6*(4), 48–51.

Pew Global Attitudes Project. (2005). U. S. image up slightly, but still negative. Retrieved March 13, 2009, from http://pewglobal.org/reports/display.php?ReportID=247

Pew Research Center. (2008). Global public opinion in the Bush years (2001–2008). Retrieved March 13, 2009, from http://pewglobal.org/reports/pdf/263.pdf

Pink, D. H. (2005a). *A whole new mind: Moving from the information age to the conceptual age*. New York: Riverhead Books.

Pink, D. H. (2005b, May). Why the world is flat. *Wired, 13.05.*

Pinker, S. (2003). *The blank slate: The modern denial of human nature*. New York: Penguin.

Preble, C. A. (2003). Who ever believed in the "missile gap"? John F. Kennedy and the politics of national security. *Presidential Studies Quarterly*. Retrieved March 10, 2008, from http://goliath.ecnext.com/coms2/summary_0199-1230060_ITM

Prensky, M. (2001). Digital natives, digital immigrants: A new way to look at ourselves and our kids. Retrieved November 12, 2008, from http://www.marcprensky.com/writing/Prensky%20-%20Digital%20Natives,%20Digital%20Immigrants%20-%20Part1.pdf

Rado, D. (2004, October 4). Education reforms test the candidates: No Child Left Behind law fuels new debate. *Chicago Tribune*. Retrieved March 13, 2009, from http://www.chicagotribune.com/shopping/chi-0410040270oct04,0,6370636,full.story

Ravitch, D. (2003). A nation at risk: Twenty years later. Retrieved September 28, 2008, from http://www.hoover.stanford.edu/pubaffairs/we/2003/ravitch04.html

Reagan, R. (1984). State of the Union Address. Retrieved March 26, 2008, from http://reagan2020.us/speeches/state_of_the_union_1984.asp

Recommendation of the European Parliament and of the Council of the European Union on key competences for lifelong learning, L394/10 C.F.R. (2006, December 12). Retrieved March 13, 2009, from http://eur-lex.europa.eu/LexUriServ/site/en/oj/2006/l_394/l_39420061230en00100018.pdf

Reimers, F. (2009). Educating for global competency. In J. E. Cohen & M. B. Malin (Eds.), *International perspectives on the goals of universal basic and secondary education*. New York: Routledge Press.

Ren, W., & Li, Z. (1998, July 4). Shenghuo shuiping tigao, shenti shuzhi xiajiang (Rising living standards, declining physical conditions). Retrieved August 30, 2008, from http://www.gmw.cn/01gmrb/1998-07/04/GB/17743%5EGM5-0407.htm

Rentner, D., Scott, C., Kober, N., Chudowsky, N., Chudowsky, V., & Joftus, S. (2006). *From the capital to the classroom: Year 4 of the No Child Left Behind Act*. Washington, DC: Center on Education Policy.

Reuters. (2006, July 16). YouTube serves up 100 million videos a day online. Retrieved September 22, 2008, from http://www.usatoday.com/tech/news/2006-07-16-youtube-views_x.htm

Reuters, E. (2008, July 8). Second Life sees record usage but bleeds paid accounts. Retrieved September 18, 2008, from http://secondlife.reuters.com/stories/2008/07/08/second-life-sees-record-usage-but-bleeds-paid-accounts/

Riley, R. W. (1988). *Speech of Richard W. Riley in Southern Regional Education Board proceedings 1988 joint meeting*. Paper presented at the Annual Meeting of the Southern Regional Education Board and Annual SREB Legislative Work Conference in Observance of SREB's 40th Anniversary.

Romer, R. (2008, April 25). 25 years after "Nation at Risk," education still inadequate. Retrieved July 18, 2008, from http://www.denverpost.com/opinion/ci_9057473

Rosen, J. (2006, June 27). The people formerly known as the audience. Retrieved September 22, 2008, from http://journalism.nyu.edu/pubzone/weblogs/pressthink/2006/06/27/ppl_frmr.html#more

Rushe, D. (2006, December 24). How much does a Bratz really cost? Retrieved August 7, 2008, from http://business.timesonline.co.uk/tol/business/article1264133.ece

Russell, M., & Abrams, L. (2004). Instructional uses of computers for writing: The effect of state testing programs. *Teachers College Record, 106*(6), 1332–1357.

Saidi, N. (2008, September 11). Virtual September 11 memorials bring back memories, emotions. Retrieved September 13, 2008, from http://edition.cnn.com/2008/US/09/11/sl.911.irpt/

Saito, N. (2003). Education for global understanding: Learning from Dewey's visit to Japan. *Teachers College Record, 105*(9), 1758–1773.

Sawyer, R. K. (2006). *Explaining creativity: The science of human innovation*. New York: Oxford University Press.

Schmid, J. (2003, December 30). China engineers its next great leap. Retrieved August 10, 2008, from http://www.jsonline.com/story/index.aspx?id=196593

Sheng, N. (2006, April 19). Zhongguo xuesheng tizhi diaocha: Xuesheng pang er wuli weiji guojia jingzhengli (A survey of student physical conditions in China: Obese but lacking strength threatens national competitiveness).

Retrieved August 30, 2008, from http://news.xinhuanet.com/sports/2006-04/19/content_4446605.htm

Shenkar, O. (2006). *The Chinese century: The rising Chinese economy and its impact on the global economy, the balance of power, and your job.* Upper Saddle River, NJ: Wharton School Publishing.

Simonton, D. K. (2005). Giftedness and genetics: The emergenic-epigenetic model and its implications. *Journal for the Education of the Gifted, 28*(3–4), 270–286.

Sina.com. (2007). Thousands of factories closed, manufacturing industry faces crisis. Retrieved August 7, 2008, from http://finance.sina.com.cn/chanjing/b/20071212/15454282637.shtml

Slack, J. (2008, February 13). More than 860 immigrants enter Britain every day—and two-thirds come from outside EU. *Daily Mail.* Retrieved March 13, 2009, from http://www.dailymail.co.uk/news/article-513949/More-860-immigrants-enter-Britain-EVERY-DAY—thirds-come-outside-EU.html

Smith, A., & Rainie, L. (2008). *The Internet and the 2008 election.* Washington, DC: Pew Internet and American Life Project.

Snopes.com. (2003). Nigerian scam. Retrieved October 15, 2008, from http://www.snopes.com/crime/fraud/nigeria.asp

Song, R. (2008, August 12). Yunnan guanyuan gaojia goumai daan yong wuxiandian bang erzi gaokao zuobi (Government officials purchased answers, helped son commit fraud in *gaokao* with wireless technology). Retrieved August 30, 2008, from http://learning.sohu.com/20080812/n258781298.shtml

Song, Y. (2003). *Tiangong kaiwu [Exploitation of the works of nature].* Lanzhou, China: Gansu Wenhua Chubanshe.

Spencer, H. (1911). *Essays on education and kindred subjects.* Available: http://www.gutenberg.org/files/16510/16510-h/16510-h.htm

Srivastava, R., & Sasikumar, S. K. (2003). *An overview of migration in India, its impacts and key issues.* Paper presented at the Regional Conference on Migration, Development and Pro-Poor Policy Choices in Asia. Available: http://www.gdnet.org/cms.php?id=research_paper_abstract&research_paper_id=8227

Sternberg, R. J. (1998). Teaching and assessing for successful intelligence. *School Administrator, 55*(1), 26–27, 30–31.

Stevenson, H. W., & Stigler, J. W. (1992). *The learning gap: Why our schools are failing and what we can learn from Japanese and Chinese education.* New York: Simon & Schuster.

Stevenson, H. W., & Stigler, J. W. (2006). *The learning gap: Why our schools are failing and what we can learn from Japanese and Chinese education* (2nd ed.). New York: Simon & Schuster.

Stewart E. McClure: Chief Clerk, Senate Committee on Labor, Education, and Public Welfare *(1949–1973).* Oral History Interviews, Senate Historical Office, Washington, DC.

Stiglitz, J. (2006, September 8). Make globalisation work for everyone. [Singapore] *Straits Times,* p. 25.

Stoops, N. (2004). *Educational attainment in the United States: 2003*. Washington, DC: U.S. Census Bureau.

Strong American Schools. (2008, April 21). Ed in '08 unveils new analysis and report card surrounding 25th anniversary of *A Nation at Risk*. Retrieved July 18, 2008, from http://www.edin08.com/uploadedFiles/Issues/A%20Stagnant%20Nation.pdf

Sullivan, D. (2006, August 21). Search engine watch. Retrieved September 22, 2008, from http://searchenginewatch.com/showPage.html?page=2156431

Sun, S. (2006, June 29). Lack of patents restrains China. Retrieved August 8, 2008, from http://www.chinadaily.net/china/2006-06/29/content_628613.htm

Swanson, C. B. (2008, April 1). Cities in crisis: A special analytic report on high school graduation. Retrieved July 12, 2008, from http://www.americaspromise.org/uploadedFiles/Americas PromiseAlliance/Dropout_Crisis/SWANSONCitiesInCrisis 040108.pdf

Tao, X. (2003, June 13). Lessons to learn on education reform [Electronic version]. *China Daily*. Retrieved December 28, 2007, from http://www.china.org.cn/english/culture/67092.htm

Telegraph. (2006, September 6). FIFA is the one sure-fire winner. Retrieved July 1, 2008, from http://www.telegraph.co.uk/money/main.jhtml?xml=/money/2006/06/09/ccup209.xml

Thompson, R. (2007). Globalization and the benefits of trade. *The Chain Letter*. Retrieved March 13, 2009, from http://www.ifama.org/library.asp?collection= chainltr&volume=v6i1.pdf.

Tian, Y. (2008). Cujing daxuesheng jiuye:Wenti yu duice (Improve college graduate placement rate: Problems and solutions). Retrieved August 11, 2008, from http://www.china.com.cn/info/zhuanti/08jylps/2008-05/06/content_15084849.htm

Traynor, I. (2007, May 17). Russia accused of unleashing cyberwar to disable Estonia. Retrieved September 18, 2008, from http://www.guardian.co.uk/world/2007/may/17/topstories3.russia

Turner, R. H. (1960). Sponsored and contest mobility and the school system. *American Sociological Review, 25*(6), 855–862.

Universal McCann. (2008). *Power to the people social media tracker: Wave 3*. New York: Universal McCann.

University of Wisconsin Global Competence Task Force. (2008). *Global Competence Task Force report*. Madison: University of Wisconsin.

U.S. Census Bureau. (2007, June 25). "Lone wolves" boost nonemployer businesses past 20 million. Retrieved October 11, 2008, from http://www.census.gov/Press-Release/www/releases/archives/economic_census/010314.html

U.S. Census Bureau. (2008). Current population survey: Annual social and economic supplements. Table P-1. CPS population and per capita money income, all races: 1967 to 2006. Retrieved July 17, 2008, from http://www.census.gov/hhes/www/income/histinc/p01ar.html

U.S. Department of Education. (2002). *Closing the achievement gap in America's public schools.* Retrieved July 12, 2008, from http://www.ed.gov/nclb/overview/welcome/closing/index.html

U.S. Department of Education. (2006). *Answering the challenge of a changing world: Strengthening education for the 21st century.* Available: http://www.ed.gov/about/inits/ed/competitiveness/strengthening/strengthening.pdf

U.S. Department of Education. (2008a, February 4). *The federal role in education.* Retrieved March 13, 2009, from http://www.ed.gov/about/overview/fed/role.html

U.S. Department of Education. (2008b). *A nation accountable: Twenty-five years after A Nation at Risk.* Washington, DC: U.S. Department of Education.

Verton, D. (2003). *Black ice: The invisible threat of cyber-terrorism.* New York: McGraw-Hill Professional.

Vinovskis, M. A. (1999). *The road to Charlottesville: The 1989 education summit.* Washington, DC: National Education Goals Panel.

Volkmann, K. (2008, September 11). Log on to virtual St. Louis. Retrieved September 13, 2008, from http://www.bizjournals.com/stlouis/stories/2008/09/08/daily81.html

Wagner, M. (2007, April 10). 12 things to do in Second Life that aren't embarrassing if your priest or rabbi finds out. Retrieved September 16, 2008, from http://www.informationweek.com/blog/main/archives/2007/04/10_fun_things_t.html

Walker, J. (2003, June 6). Spirit vessels: The "Black Thing" gives birth to an art form. Retrieved October 4, 2008, from http://www.reason.com/news/show/33606.html

Wang, H. (2007, March 14). Beijing xuesheng shengti shuzhi zhibiao chixu xiajiang, Zhongkao jiangjia tiyu feng (Students' physical conditions continue to decline, PE grades will be added to admissions criteria for high schools). Retrieved August 30, 2008, from http://news.xinhuanet.com/sports/2007-03/14/content_5845276.htm

Wang, Z. (2004). *An antidote to modern test-oriented education: Toward a constructive postmodern education.* Paper presented at the Forum for Integrated Education and Educational Reform. Available: http://chiron.valdosta.edu/whuitt/CGIE/wang.pdf

Watson, J. L. (2004). Globalization in Asia: Anthropological perspectives. In M. M. Suarez-Orozco & D. B. Qin-Hillard (Eds.), *Globalization: Culture and education in the new millennium* (pp. 141–172). Berkeley: University of California Press.

Weimann, G. (2004, December). Cyberterrorism: How real is the threat? Retrieved September 19, 2008, from http://www.usip.org/pubs/specialreports/sr119.html

Wen, Z. (2008, May 5). Such as Beijing Hyundai: Only four wheels and one battery are made by China. Retrieved August 7, 2008, from http://news.xinhuanet.com/fortune/2008-05/04/content_8096718.htm

Wolf, B. (2002, August 20). Weird news: Unbelievable junk sold on eBay: The strangest items found on eBay. Retrieved October 4, 2008, from http://abcnews.go.com/Entertainment/WolfFiles/Story?id=91336&page=1

World Bank. (2006). *06 world development indicators.* Washington, DC: World Bank.

World Economic Forum. (2007). *The global competitiveness index report 2007–2008.* Geneva: World Economic Forum.

World Intellectual Property Organization (WIPO). (2007). *WIPO patent report: Statistics on worldwide patent activity (2007 Edition).* Geneva: World Intellectual Property Organization.

World Values Survey. (1999–2004). World Values Survey. Retrieved November 20, 2006, from http://www.worldvaluessurvey.org/

Xinhua News Agency. (2005, May 4). Bo Xilai: 800 million shirts for one A380. Retrieved August 7, 2008, from http://news.xinhuanet.com/fortune/2005-05/04/content_2913835.htm

Xinhua News Agency. (2008, March 12). 2003–2007: Significant improvement in universalization of compulsory education in rural areas. Retrieved August 9, 2008, from http://news. xinhuanet.com/video/2008-03/12/content_7776652.htm

Yang, D. (2006). *Bluebook of education: The development report of China's education (2005).* Beijing: Social Sciences Archives Press.

Yang, Z. (2008, April 23). Yigeyuenei sanming xuesheng zisha (Three students killed themselves in one month). Retrieved August 26, 2008, from http://www.ycwb.com/ycwb/2008-04/23/content_1871293.htm

Zhao, Q. (2008). Qingshaonian zisha de yuanyin diaocha (A survey of reasons for suicides among youth). Retrieved August 26, 2008, from http://www.sie.edu.cn/jpk/jpk2008/shehdcb/xtyxszy/22qingshao.htm

Zhao, X., & Wu, Q. (2005, December 20). End of year report: China to strengthen protection of intellectual properties and encourage domestic innovation. Retrieved August 7, 2008, from http://news.xinhuanet.com/politics/2005-12/20/content_3948433.htm

Zhao, Ying. (2007, August 7). First study of careers of *gaokao zhuangyuan* released. Retrieved August 20, 2008, from http://www.sciencetimes.com.cn/html news/20078785019772186334.html?id=186334

Zhao, Yong. (2007). China and the whole child. *Educational Leadership, 64*(8), 70–73.

Zhao, Yong, Lei, J., Yan, B., Lai, C., & Tan, S. (2005). What makes the difference: A practical analysis of research on the effectiveness of distance education. *Teachers College Record, 107*(8), 1836–1884.

Zhonggong Zhongyang (Central Committee of the Chinese Communist Party), & Guowuyuan (State Council). (1999). *Guanyu shenhua jiaoyu tizhi gaige quanmian tuijin suzhi jiaoyu de jueding (Decision to further educational systemic reform and promote quality-oriented education).* Retrieved September 5, 2008, from http://www.chinapop.gov.cn/flfg/xgflfg/t20040326_30741.html

Zhonggong Zhongyang Bangongting (Office of the Central Committee of the Chinese Communist Party), & Guowuyuan Bangongting (Office of the State Council). (2000). *Guanyu shiying xinxingshi jingyibu jiaqiang he gaijing zhongxiaoxue deyu gongzuo de jianyi (Suggestions for further enhancing and improving moral education in secondary and primary schools to meet the challenges of the new era)*. Beijing: Zhonggong Zhongyang Bangongting (Office of the Central Committee of the Chinese Communist Party).

Index

accountability, 5–6, 32, 184–185
achievement gap, domestic, 6–7, 13–16
achievement gap, international. *See also*
   globalization
     American competitiveness,
       persistence of, 41–46
     creativity gap, 91–95
     in engineering graduates, 70
     explanations for, 16–18
     goal of closing, 7–12
     in science literacy, 84–85
Adequate Yearly Progress (AYP), 2–3
African American culture, 15–16
Alexander, Lamar, 33–34
American Competitiveness Initiative
   (ACI), 3
American culture, and talent shows, 46–50
American dream, 57
anti-Americanism, 163–164
Asia. *See specific countries*
Asia Society, 69–70, 193–195
authoritarianism, 31–32, 38–39, 40

Back Dorm Boys, 126
baguwen, 76, 78

Baker, Keith, 16–17, 45
Bell, T. H., 26, 28–29, 32
Berliner, David, 13–14
biculturalism, 189, 190
bilingualism, 189, 190
Black Ice (Verton), 124
The Blank Slate (Pinker), 152
blogs, 127–128
Blue Ribbon schools, 1–2
Born Digital (Harvard Digital
   Citizenship), 197
Bo Xilai, 65–66
Boydkin, A. Wade, 15–16
British–North American Committee,
   125
Bush, George H. W., 34–35
Bush, George W., 1–6, 31
business leaders, 27–28, 37–38

Charlottesville summit (1989), 34–35
Chen Naiwei, 67
China
     cheap labor vs. technological
      innovation, 65–68
     creativity gap, 91–95

China *(continued)*
    damage from *gaokao* system, 85–90
    economic rise of, 11
    educational system, outside
        glorification of, 68–71
    English speakers in, 83–84
    gaokao system, 79–80, 82, 83, 96,
        182–183
    globalization and culture conflict,
        105
    "high scores but low ability"
        phenomenon, 80–85
    job losses to, 111
    keju system (Imperial Exam), 73–79
    outsourcing to, 104
    reforms in, 60–61, 95–97, 182–183
    road guides in, 133–134
    school-related measures vs. graduate
        performance, 71–73
    trade and investment with, 169
    Wen's education meeting, 64–65
Choi Yeon-sung, 122
Chong, Paul, 122
Chua, Amy, 52
citizenship, global, 112–113, 167, 175,
    188–192
climate change, global, 170
Clinton, Bill, 35, 37, 38
collectivist cultures, 92
competence, digital, 175–180
competence, global. *See* global competence
competition, international, 34–35
Compton, Robert, 9–10
computers. *See* virtual worlds and Internet
    technology
computer viruses, 124–125
conflicts, human, 105, 171–173
conformity, 92–93
Confucius Institute, 191
contest mobility model, 55–57, 58
creativity. *See* innovation and creativity
creativity gap, 91–95
cross-cultural communications, 111–112
cross-cultural competency, 173–174

cultural conflict from globalization, 105
culture, 46–50, 173–174
curriculum standardization, creativity and,
    94–95
cyber wars and cyber terrorism, 122–125
Cyberwars (Guisnel), 124

*Decision to Further Educational Systemic
    Reform* (China), 60–61
Dewey, John, 174, 202
dictatorial approach, 31–32, 38–39, 40
digital competence, 175–180, 195–198
digital natives, 196–197
distributed denial of services (DDoS), 123
diversity. *See* talent diversity
dropout rates, 7, 12, 13, 36
Duncan, Arne, 200, 201

eBay, 136–144
economy. *See also* knowledge in global and
    digital economy
    Chinese, 68
    global economics, 168–170
    U.S., 51, 53–54
Ed in '08 campaign, 12
Education for Global Citizenship (EGC),
    188–190
Education for Global Leadership, 161
Education in China, 69
Education Plan for the 21st Century
    (Japan), 62–63
Einstein, Albert, 47, 73
emigration, 108
emotional intelligence, 151
enGauge 21st Century Skills framework,
    146–147
English speakers in China, 83–84
entertainment, 137–139
entrepreneurship, 143–144
eSports, 121–122
Estonia, 122–124
European Union, 147–148
exit exams, 39
extracurricular activities, 50–51

Facebook, 130
"failing schools" label, 32
fear as political strategy, 22, 33
First International Mathematics Study
    (FIMS), 16–17
Florida, Richard, 51–52
foreign languages, 112, 118–119, 162, 164,
    174, 191
Frames of Mind (Gardner), 49
Framework for 21st Century Skills, 177
fraud and crime in testing, 89–90
Friedman, Thomas, 9, 10, 101, 168

Gardner, Howard, 49, 148–149
Gates, Bill, 11
genetic diversity, 51
geographic knowledge, 161–162
Gerstner, Louis, 37
global citizenship, 112–113, 167, 175,
    188–192
global competence
        costs of global incompetence,
            161–165
        cross-cultural competency, 173–174
        defining, 112, 165–166
        economics, understanding of, 168–170
        human conflicts and peace, 171–173
        inequalities, awareness of, 166–168
        problems, global, 170–171
        schools and, 192–195
Global Competitiveness Index, 41
global economics, 168–170
global enterprises, schools as, 188–192
global interdependence, 166–168
globalization. *See also* global competence;
    knowledge in global and digital
    economy
        death of distance, 99–102
        education challenges, 110–113
        free movement of goods, 104–106
        free movement of people, 106–110
        A Nation at Risk and, 27
        production, fragmentation of,
            102–104

global mindset, 158–159
global warming, 170
Goals 2000: Educate America Act,
    35–36
Going Global (Asia Society), 193–195
gold farming, 119–121
Goodall, Jane, 50
goods, global movement of, 104–106
Google, 130
governor reform initiatives (U.S.), 33–34
graduate performance in China, 71–73
graduation rates, 7, 12, 13
Graef, Ailin, 114–116
Guangxu, Emperor, 74, 78

Harding, Matt, 126, 142
Hargreaves, David H., 186–188
Harry Potter series (Rowling), 138–139
High School Reform Initiative, 4
high scores but low ability *(gaofen dineng)*
    phenomenon, 80–85
Hill, Lister, 23–24
Hitler, Adolf, 22
Huang Yixin, 126
Hu Jintao, 68
Hung, William, 125
Hurd, Paul, 27
hyperpowers, 52

immigration, 106–110
India
        economic rise of, 11
        engineering graduates in, 70
        international gap and, 71
        job losses to, 111
        outsourcing to, 104
individualist cultures, 92
individuals, 47, 62–63. *See also* talent
inequalities, economic and social,
    167–168
information technology (IT) and talent
    diversity, 53. *See also* virtual worlds and
    Internet technology
initiative, 48

innovation and creativity
    China and lack of, 66–68, 72, 77, 91
    creativity gap, 91–95
    as essential, 151
    global problems and, 171
    talent diversity and, 53
input-oriented accountability, 184–185
intelligences, multiple, 49, 148–149
interdependence, global, 166–168
interests, exploration of, 56–57
International English Language Testing
    System (IELTS), 82
international exchanges, 193
international skills. See global competence
international students, 192
Internet. See virtual worlds and Internet
    technology

Japan, reforms in, 62–63
Jaschan, Sven, 124–125
job creation through technology,
    142–144
job losses, 102–104, 168
Johnson, Dana, 102

Kang Youwei, 78
Kelly, Spencer, 135
Kennedy, John F., 20–21, 22
Khruschev, Nikita, 21
knowledge in global and digital economy.
    See also global competence
    changes in useful knowledge,
        135–136
    Chinese road guides and London taxi
        drivers, 133–135
    core assumptions, 150–151
    curriculum and individual strengths,
        154–156
    eBay illustration, 136–144
    European Union "key competences,"
        147–148
    feasibility issues, 151–154
    geographic, 161–162
    R-directed skills, 148–150, 152

knowledge in global and digital economy
    (continued)
        tolerance, diversification, and global
            mindset, 158–159
        21st century skills, 145–147
        unique talents in global market,
            156–158
        virtual world, nature of, 179

labor, cheap, 65–68, 111, 139–140
languages, 112, 118–119, 162, 164, 174, 191
late bloomers, 56
L-directed skills, 148–149, 152
The Learning Gap (Stevenson and Stigler),
    70–71
Lee Kuan Yew, 78
Lemmon, Michael, 164
The Lexus and the Olive Tree (Friedman),
    172
Lincoln, Abraham, 164
Linden Lab, 115
Lin Yifu, 77
The Long Tail (Anderson), 140–141
Lu Yonxiang, 67

market for technology strategy, 66
"massively multiplayer online role-playing
    games" (MMORPG), 119–121, 191
math, NCLB emphasis on, 3–4
Math and Science Education in a Global
    Age, 69
"Matthew effect," 153
McClure, Stewart E., 23–24
McDonald's, 105–106
McLuhan, Marshall, 100–101
McNamara, Robert, 21
metaverse, 115, 116–117. See also virtual
    worlds and Internet technology
Metiri Group, 146–147, 177
migration, 106–110
minority achievement gap, domestic, 6–7,
    13–16
missile gap, 19–21
mobility, social, 55–57

National Assessment of Educational
Progress (NAEP), 6–7
National Commission on Asia in the
School, 161
National Commission on Excellence in
Education, 26–31
*A National Conversation About Personalised
Learning* (U.K.), 185–186
National Defense Education Act (NDEA),
22–25
*National Educational Technology Standards
and Performance Indicators for Students*
(NETS.S), 177
National Education Goals Panel, 35
National Education Standards and
Improvement Council, 36
National Language Security Initiative, 4–5
national security, 163
A Nation at Risk, 26–31, 41–43
NCLB. *See* No Child Left Behind Act
(NCLB)
Needham, Joseph, 77
New Commission on the Skills of the
American Workforce, 111
Nixon, Richard, 20–21
No Child Left Behind Act (NCLB)
accountability system of, 5–6
achievement gap and, 6
damage inflicted by, vii–xi
as dictatorial, 31–32, 38–39, 40
globalization and, 113
Greely event (Chicago), 2
Obama and, 200
signing ceremony, 31

Obama, Barack, 200–201
offshoring, 102–104
online technologies. *See* virtual worlds and
Internet technology
outsourcing, 102–104, 149

Palin, Sarah, 160–161
parent expectations, 93–94
partnership education, 188

Partnership for 21st Century Skills, 146
personalized learning, 185–188
philosophical vs. technical aspects of
education, 45–46
physical condition, declining, 88–89
Pink, Daniel, 148–150, 151–152, 153
Play Money (Dibbell), 121
poverty, 14, 167
powersellers, 143
price in global markets, 139–140
production, fragmentation of, 102–104
Professional eBay Sellers Alliance (PeSA),
143
Programme for International Student
Assessment (PISA), 8
Progress in International Reading Literacy
Study (PIRLS), 8
public opinion on test scores, 32–33
Pu Songling, 76–77

Qian Xuesen, 64–65
Qi Ke, 80–81
quality, 2–5, 184–185

*The Race Between Education and
Technology* (Goldin and Katz), 150–151
"race to the bottom" problem, 200–201
Ravitch, Diane, 43
R-directed skills, 148–150, 152
reading, NCLB emphasis on, 3–4
Reading First program, 4
Reagan, Ronald, 28–29, 32
resources, global, 190–191
responsibility, 48
Riley, Richard, 34
Ringwood Secondary College, Melbourne,
Australia, 194–195
Rising Above the Gathering Storm, 8–9
Romer, Paul, 20
Romer, Roy, 43–44
Rypkema, Donovan, 51

Santayana, George, 26
science, NCLB emphasis on, 3–4

science literacy, 84–85
second chances, 54–57
Second Life, 114–119
selection through education, 74
self-employment, 143–144
Sim Wong Hoo, 158
Singapore, 62
Snow Crash (Stephenson), 116–117
soccer, 138
social mobility, 75, 79
social networking sites, 128, 130
Southern Regional Education Board, 34
South Korea, 61–62, 121–122
Soviet Union, 9–11, 19–21, 22–25
Spellings, Margaret, 1, 11–12, 43
Spencer, Herbert, 145
sponsored mobility model, 55
sports, 121–122, 137–138
Sputnik, 9–11, 19–21, 22–25
standardized testing under NCLB, 32
standards
    individuality vs., 46–48
    national development of, 35–37
    new calls to strengthen, 200–202
    as primary tool, 5–6
Starbucks, 105
Stephenson, Neal, 116–117
Sternberg Triarchic Abilities Test, 15
Stevenson, Harold, 70–71
Stigler, James, 70–71
Strengthening Education initiative, 4
strengths, 154–156
Strong American Schools, 43–44
student experiences, globalizing, 194–195
student voice, 187–188
Styranka, Mark, 142
success, 93–94, 182–185
suicide by students, 85–88
Synthetic Worlds (Castronova), 121

talent
    China and lack of, 72–73
    contest mobility and sponsored
        mobility models, 55–57, 58

talent *(continued)*
    homogenization of, x–xi
    local, 140
    long tail phenomenon and rare
        talents, 140–142
    nature and nurture in, 152–153
    strengths and specialization, 154–156
talent cleansing, 76–77
talent diversity
    contest mobility vs. sponsored
        mobility, 55–57
    economic systems and, 51–54
    global mindset and, 158–159
    personalized learning and, 185–188
    talent shows and, 48–50
    test-taking skill vs., 59
talent shows, 46–50
Tapping America's Potential, 10
Teacher Preparation for the Global Age, 194
teaching, NCLB as constraint on, 39
technology. *See also* virtual worlds and
    Internet technology
    globalization and, 100–101
    job creation through, 142–144
    migration and, 107
test bias, 14–15
testing, high-stakes. *See also* No Child Left
    Behind Act (NCLB)
    gaokao system (China), 79–80, 82,
        83, 85–90, 96, 182–183
    keju system (China), 73–79
test scores
    as indicators of quality, 2–5
    minority gap in, 13
    national success not correlated to,
        16–17
    NCLB and, 2
    public popularity of, 32–33
test-taking skill vs. talent diversity, 59
Thinking Schools, Learning Nation
    (Singapore), 62
Thompson, Tommy, 37
3e International Kindergarten (Beijing),
    188–189

time on task as performance predictor, 58
tolerance, 52
Trends in Mathematics and Science Study
    (TIMSS), 8
triarchic theory, 15
Turner, Ralph, 55
21st Century Partnership, 177
21st century skills, 145–147
Two Million Minutes (film), 9–10, 71

United Kingdom, personalized learning in,
    185–188
U.S. Department of Education, 4, 28
U.S.–China Center for Research on
    Educational Excellence, Michigan State
    University, 188–189

virtual worlds and Internet technology
        courses, online, 191
        cyber wars and cyber terrorism,
            122–125
        digital competence, 175–180,
            195–198
        education challenges, 128–132

virtual worlds and Internet technology
    (continued)
        eSports, 121–122
        gold farming and MMORPG,
            119–121
        grassroots Internet and You Tube,
            125–128
        Second Life, 114–119

wars and human conflicts, 171–173
Wei Wei, 126
Wen Jiabao, 64–65, 67–68
"What Knowledge Is of Most Worth?"
    (Spencer), 145
A Whole New Mind (Pink), 148–150
World Cyber Games, 122
World Values Survey, 57

Xu Haoyuan, 96

Your Child's Strengths (Fox), 156
YouTube, 126, 128, 131

Zhenzong, Emperor, 76
zhuangyuans (top performers), 82

About the Author

Yong Zhao is a University Distinguished Professor at the College of Education, Michigan State University, where he serves as the founding director of the U.S.–China Center for Research on Educational Excellence and the Center for Teaching and Technology, as well as the Executive Director of the Confucius Institute. Zhao was born and raised in China. Before he came to the United States in the early 1990s, Zhao taught English in China. He lives in Okemos, Michigan, with his wife and two children. He can be reached by e-mail: zhaoyo@ msu.edu or through his Web site: http://zhao.educ.msu.edu.